Cambridge Studies in Oral and Literate Culture 11

STORYTELLING RIGHTS

Cambridge Studies in Oral and Literate Culture

Edited by PETER BURKE and RUTH FINNEGAN

This series is designed to address the question of the significance of literacy in human societies; it will assess its importance for political, economic, social, and cultural development, and will examine how what we take to be the common functions of writing are carried out in oral cultures.

The series will be interdisciplinary, but with particular emphasis on social anthropology and social history, and will encourage cross-fertilization between these disciplines; it will also be of interest to readers in allied fields, such as sociology, folklore, and literature. Although it will include some monographs, the focus of the series will be on theoretical and comparative aspects rather than detailed description, and the books will be presented in a form accessible to non-specialist readers interested in the general subject of literacy and orality.

Books in the series

STORYTELLING RIGHTS

The uses of oral
and written texts
by urban adolescents

AMY SHUMAN

The Ohio State University

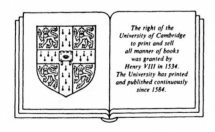

The right of the
University of Cambridge
to print and sell
all manner of books
was granted by
Henry VIII in 1534.
The University has printed
and published continuously
since 1584.

CAMBRIDGE UNIVERSITY PRESS

CAMBRIDGE
NEW YORK   PORT CHESTER
MELBOURNE   SYDNEY

Published by the Press Syndicate of the University of Cambridge
The Pitt Building, Trumpington Street, Cambridge, CB2 1RP
40 West 20th Street, New York, NY 10011, USA
10 Stamford Road, Oakleigh, Melbourne 3166, Australia

First published 1986
Reprinted 1990

Library of Congress Cataloging-in-Publication Data

Shuman, Amy, 1951–
Storytelling rights.
(Cambridge studies in oral and literate culture ; 11)
Bibliography: p.
1. Sociolinguistics.   2. Discourse analysis.
Narrative.   3. Urban youth – Language.   I. Title.
II. Series.
P40.S47   1986   401'.9   86–12968

British Library Cataloging-in-Publication Data

Shuman, Amy
Storytelling rights : the uses of oral and
written texts by urban adolescents. –
(Cambridge studies in oral and literate
culture ; 11)
1. Storytelling
I. Title
808.5'.43   LB1042

ISBN 0-521 32846-2 hardback

Transferred to digital printing 2004

For my parents and grandparents,
who make experiences into events
and events into stories.

CONTENTS

ACKNOWLEDGMENTS

The voices of the storytellers in this work are private and thus anonymous. The storytellers had not requested anonymity, for although the stories contain some secrets, confidences shared a few years ago are not necessarily secrets today. However, the stories belong to a particular place and time, and I have used pseudonyms to confine the information to its place and time. These are stories that might otherwise be forgotten by their many listeners, and as their tellers grow older, they may or may not want to be remembered by the incidents of everyday adolescent life.

It is no accident that Dan Ben-Amos, Barbara Kirshenblatt-Gimblett, William Labov, Erving Goffman, John Szwed, and Dell Hymes appear frequently in my citations. They have influenced my work as much through personal help as through their printed works, and their work on narrative and performance led me to consider the relationship between writing and speaking for this book. I cannot hope to have cited every written work that has influenced my own, let alone to have acknowledged those who contributed to the development of this work in conversations. Meetings with Simon Lichman, Rivanna Miller, and Shelley Posen gave me an audience for my ideas, and their ideas, from their own studies, have become so entwined with my own that I cannot possibly acknowledge their many contributions. Others have also helped to turn the writing process from a monologue into a dialogue. I greatly appreciate the conversations with Amanda Dargan, Henry Glassie, Shirley Brice Heath, Dan Rose, Dan Wagner, and Chava Weissler. Maxine Miska first talked with me about the notion of retellings. Without Rob Allekotte, none of my research would have been possible. Katharine Young helped me to refine my ideas, and I know she will be the first to discover other areas that need further work. Ana Cara Walker read the manuscript and helped me to see the whole picture. Susan Stewart helped me to see what was missing; Sabra Webber helped to identify the extraneous parts. Linda Sabo typed the final manuscript. Helen Greenberg found my bibliographic errors and Noreen Mulcahy resolved them. Michael Gnat provided editorial skills and Sue Allen-Mills oversaw the entire process. I am grateful to the Ohio State University College of Humanities for awarding me a publication grant. A final thanks to Craig Schaffer who listened to each new thought and helped me to sand the edges, and to Miss Hoober, Mrs. Stansky, or Cary (or whatever voice she uses next), who keeps me on my toes.

INTRODUCTION

Marci:	If Marie's the one who always gets into fights	1
	how come you're the one who's always in trouble with the teachers?	2
Stacie:	Cause Marie do the fightin' and I do the talkin'	3

Although relationships between talkers and fighters rarely work out so neatly, Stacie's explanation demonstrates the important and precarious relationship between narrative and event and, specifically, between the participants in an event and the reporters who claim the right to talk about what happened. This relationship, which can also be understood as the relationship between text and context, is an essential part of social conventions for communication and represents a missing piece of the puzzle of understanding the uses of oral and written communication in everyday life. The adolescent world presents a particularly transparent case of the relationship between an event (a fight) and a narrative (a fight story). The adolescents worked toward the possibility of replacing physical battles with verbal negotiations (and defined growing up in those terms). However, the relationship between the event and the narrative was not as simple as learning to talk about what happened, since narratives are never such direct references. The question of authorship of one's account, and the concomitant right to report what others had said, along with considerations of audience, presented as many problems for talkers, such as Stacie, as did fighting. Harvey Sacks provides an elaboration of Stacie's point:

> People in this world, in any event, are built to be the custodians of just about only their own experiences – which is consistent with a lot of other things that they are also built to be the custodians of; i.e. things that they can be made to care about keeping, taking care of, defending and the like – more or less whatever it is that can be conceived of by them, that the world has them conceive of as "their own" – where their experiences are but one class of such things.
> (Harvey Sacks, Lecture Notes, Fall 1971, 8:4–5)

The right of an author to own a story and control its uses is as essential to storytelling in everyday life as it is to writers who copyright manuscripts prepared for publication. However, as this study of oral and written narratives will demonstrate, storytelling rights are usually tacitly understood and require subtle negotiations and constant reassessments of entitlement. Oral storytelling rights differ among cultures and groups, and therefore are subject to constant misunderstanding among people who operate according to different systems. The study of storytelling rights shifts the focus away from the stories themselves toward their use. Such a focus calls attention to the issues central to these differences, such as authorship, face-to-face communication, and the relationship between text and context. Further, the study of rights provides a starting point for investigating the conventions for appropriate uses of texts.[1]

The stories to be examined here are themselves about rights. They can be categorized as junior high school fight stories, that is, narrative accounts of quarrels about who has the right to say what to whom.[2] Although storytelling rights are central to social interaction, they are perceptible only through infringements or violations and only among groups, such as junior high students, who call attention to the violations.

My purpose is to explore the multiple uses of texts among adolescents. Adolescents in this community have acquired the rudimentary mechanical and social skills of both oral and written communication to the extent that they can use these skills as tools for adolescent play. Furthermore, in this inner-city community, adolescents are the assigned managers of most written documents. Reading is considered to be too difficult for younger children and an inappropriate activity for older members of the community. Filling in forms is a regular part of an adolescent's life, at school, at play, and in doctors' and welfare offices, where the adolescents' assistance is sometimes required. The adolescents provide an excellent window for viewing the oral and written communications of the larger community.

My focus is on the differential knowledge and shared understandings involved in speaking and writing. "Differential knowledge" refers to the way skills are divided among the adolescents: What does everyone know and what do only some people know? "Shared understandings" refers to a process of defining expectations about intelligible communication. Shared understandings do not exist as given facts but rather grow out of continual reappraisals based on new experiences and on awareness of misunderstanding. Narrative involves differential knowledge, in terms of who tells stories and who listens ("entitlement"), and shared understandings, in terms of what bears telling ("tellability") and when it is appropriate for a certain person to tell a certain story ("storyability"). The rules were openly disputed and constantly renegotiated, and thus illustrate some of the complex relationships between speaking and writing and, more particularly, oral and written narrative.

Junior high interaction is accompanied by a running metacommentary on violations of appropriate speech or action. The conversations and playful exchanges of junior high students provide an excellent forum for examining the uses of oral and written texts, not only because adolescence is a period of mastery of both writing and speaking, but especially because it is a period of play with texts. The complexities of interpretation, central to any discussion of texts, hinge on play and the use of concealment, as well as on the transmission of informative messages.

The junior high fight stories, both oral narratives and written diary accounts, are themselves discourses on storytelling rights. The adolescents used both speaking and writing to categorize their experiences. In contrast to conventional models that assume the use of speaking for face-to-face communication and writing for absent-author communication, the adolescents often used oral narratives to convey messages to absent third parties (through he-said–she-said rumors) and used writing as part of face-to-face exchanges in which documents were collaboratively produced and read aloud or as solitary communication with oneself in diaries. (Of course, they also used speaking for face-to-face exchange and writing for communication with absent parties or to preserve documents for future use.) The adolescents transformed the conventional uses of writing and speaking for their own purposes. They had their own understanding of what could be written but not said, and vice versa. This description and analysis of their practices do not merely present anomalies to an otherwise accurate picture of writing and speaking uses. Rather, they demonstrate a need to reevaluate the current models used for categorizing writing and speaking.

0.1 The research community

This study is based upon two and one-half years of fieldwork (from January 1979 to June 1981) among the students of Paul Revere Junior High School, an inner-city school in the eastern United States.[3] The students attending this three-year junior high school were drawn in roughly equal numbers from adjacent black, white, and Puerto Rican neighborhoods.

Located in the white neighborhood, the school had once served an all-white population of working-class people. When it was opened at the beginning of the Depression, neighborhood residents were employed by the many factories located in the area. As the multistory factory buildings became obsolete and manufacturers moved to modern facilities in the suburbs or to nonunion shops in the South, and as some people left the neighborhood, to find either new work or a more suburban life-style, the white neighborhood diminished to a few blocks bounded by water and an elevated commuter rail line.

The neighborhood surrounding the school consisted primarily of two-story brick row houses with "postage stamp" backyards. There were many corner grocery stores, bars, dry cleaners, and other businesses. An elevated subway line divided the black and Hispanic neighborhoods from the white neighborhood, but the dividing line was not distinct. As black students quickly pointed out in discussions of racism, many white people lived among blacks and Hispanics. The black and Hispanic neighborhoods were not nearly as homogeneous as the white neighborhood surrounding the school, although some blocks were more Hispanic and others had more black families.

A few factories remained in the area, including a paper box factory and an envelope factory, and some of the students' parents worked there. Most of the parents either worked outside of the neighborhood or were unemployed and on welfare. Finding work was especially difficult for men under thirty. All of the young black men of this age whom I knew in the neighborhood were out of work. Some of the young Hispanic men commuted to agricultural fields during the growing season or to mushroom farms throughout the year. Some of the white men worked as roofers or in other building trades.

The multiracial composition of the school was seen as a problem by many people in the white neighborhood. They had attended the school when few, if any, minority families lived in the area, and they blamed the disciplinary problems on racial tension, if not on the minority students themselves. Few white parents were involved in parent–teacher groups at the junior high, although they continued to be involved in parent organizations at the elementary schools, attended primarily by white students. Black and Puerto Rican parents were often reluctant to go to the school, since they perceived the hostility in the surrounding all-white neighborhood. Although some parents from all groups did go to the school, whether to discuss their children's disciplinary problems, to register complaints, or to speak to teachers on the regularly scheduled parent nights, parents, teachers, and administrators all sensed a tenuous and necessary, rather than a collaborative and mutually interested, relationship between the school and the community.

Although few racial conflicts occurred at the school, many stories about racial tension were told by people in the school and in the community, and students entered seventh grade expecting to encounter tension. They perhaps saw little racial conflict during their three years at the school, but white students tended to keep to themselves, and identity began with the racial or ethnic group. The white students were predominantly Catholic and either Polish or Irish, but were aware of neither common religion nor different ancestry. Appearance and speech patterns were more significant in determining identity than was group affiliation. (I did not have the characteristic appearance of whites and passed more easily as Puerto Rican, but my California accent, familiar neither to whites nor to Puerto Ricans, and the additional clue of my accented Spanish made me simply an outsider.)

Most of the students arrived at school by buses that picked them up at their local elementary schools. Bus service was first provided in the 1960s following the drowning of a Puerto Rican boy in the river not far from the school. The white neighborhood surrounding the school has been characterized as explicitly prejudiced against outsiders and as racist. Many of the white students from the neighborhood specifically announced, when the subject came up, that they were not racist; others said that they were. All acknowledged that it was not safe for black and Hispanic students to walk through the white neighborhood, especially if they were alone. Bottles were sometimes thrown at the school buses carrying these students home, but such incidents were not an everyday occurrence. Since none of the students lived far from the school, the buses were not part of the school system's allotment. The junior high started earlier and ended earlier than other schools in order to be able to use the buses. Buses were provided from all of the elementary schools that were more than a few blocks from the junior high; many white students also took buses to school.

The means of transportation to school and the places and times for adolescent gatherings helped to encourage certain kinds of alliances. Students traveled to school with friends from their neighborhoods. Once they arrived, they tended to stay with these friends until school began. One of the major times for students to meet with each other was before school. They were not allowed above the first floor until school began at 7:50. They sometimes saw their neighborhood friends for brief moments in the hallways when they walked between classes, and almost always knew where to find relatives or neighbors when they wanted them. The lunchroom was the only place that brought students from the different neighborhoods together for a social, rather than a study, period. While they ate, jostled for a good place in the cafeteria line, negotiated over borrowing and returning money, and tried to find their neighborhood friends, they also fought and talked about fighting. Even fights that originated in the neighborhood were verbally intensified, if not actually fought out, in the lunchroom. There new alliances and enmities formed, and he-said–she-said rumors flourished. People who did not know each other very well talked about each other.

Although the neighborhoods would be seen as run-down by an outsider, since they contained abandoned houses and boarded-up stores, almost all of the adolescents would say that they felt safe in their own neighborhoods. They were sent out at night to purchase food at the corner stores, and they knew their own blocks well. They saw other people's neighborhoods as unsafe, and they rarely went to visit friends from school whom they perceived to live outside of the neighborhood. They did not always know where their school friends lived unless they took the same bus to school. Going to school meant learning their way around new territory.

The students arrived at school at about 7:30 in the morning. In good weather, some went to the playground across the street to play basketball; some of the girls brought jump ropes with them. They had about twenty minutes to meet with their friends before school started. After school, the buses left immediately; they were parked outside the school with their engines warming before the last bell rang. Students had just enough time to go to their lockers and get their coats before boarding the buses.

The school did not have a playground, but in nice weather the students were permitted to go to the fenced-in roof of the school for the second part of the lunch period. On the roof the boys played basketball and the girls jumped rope. Students were not assigned to areas of the roof, as they were to tables in the lunchroom, so this was one of the few times when they could meet with others outside of their assigned classrooms.

At the end of the school day, most students went immediately to their buses. The buses parked by the side of the school closest to the neighborhood to which they were headed so, unintentionally, the three sides of the school on which the buses were packed were unofficially assigned to either black, white, or Hispanic students. The students recognized the designation of the different school exits, and they rarely used doors not used by their group. One of the things that students knew about each other was which door someone was likely to use when leaving the school, and this was important information to consider when confronting or avoiding an antagonist in a fight.

Classrooms in the school opened onto a hallway that ran completely around the interior of the building on each floor. Of the approximately thirty students registered for each class, only twenty to twenty-five were in attendance at one time, and some of the teachers said that they did not have enough chairs to accommodate all of the students should they all attend at once. Approximately eighty teachers, representing all three racial and ethnic groups, were employed at the school in social studies, math, English, reading, art, "career education" (including sewing, cooking, wood working, printing, typing), physical education, and the bilingual program. Teachers frequently complained about those teachers who were often absent (since the school never had enough substitutes and teachers were constantly asked to fill in for absent colleagues in exchange for time off they could never use) or about administrators who stayed in their offices as if they were afraid to come out. Persons in both categories were called "bimbos." Some teachers also complained about what they perceived as problems that should be solved at home or in the community and that, in any case, were not a teacher's responsibility. They complained about the scarcity of teaching materials and the problem of using eighth-grade social studies and math books for students who read at a third-grade level.

Teachers said that students did not take responsibility for their schoolwork, that they did not care about what grades they received or about turning in homework. Some of the students said that they were given too little responsibility at school, that they weren't allowed to spend their free time, their lunch period, as they wished. At home, adolescents had major responsibilities, including meal preparation, laundry chores, care of younger brothers and sisters, and other household work, and the junior high restrictions seemed to them to be more severe than those they had known in elementary school.

Relationships between teachers and students were not as hostile as some of these comments about the general atmosphere might suggest. Some teachers organized trips on public transportation when school buses were not available, took students skiing or to amusement parks, and participated in community activities. In general, students and teachers perceived their worlds, including problems and goals, very differently.

In an atmosphere in which strangers were regarded suspiciously by the racial and ethnic groups and were considered as intruders by the teachers, beginning research was difficult. One of the teachers, whom I met as part of another research project, invited me to begin my research in his classroom. His class was part of a program in which students studied their four major subjects with two teachers in adjacent classrooms. Unlike other junior high students, who moved from one class to another with different students in each class throughout the school day, the students in the program stayed together for their major subjects and studied with the same teachers for two years.

The teacher introduced me to his class as a person who was interested in "What it's like to go to [this] junior high." In other classes and in subsequent semesters, I became known as someone who was writing a book about the school. In the school, I spent most of my time with students. I attended classes, went to lunch in the student lunchroom, participated in after-school activities and special interest clubs, and spent time in the hallways. Although I did not disguise my purposes, I attempted to fit in with student groups: For example, I dressed according to the norm of some of the female students. (To fit in with the students, it was as important to wear the same few clothes all of the time as it was to wear jeans and sneakers. Of course, some of the girls wore more fashionable skirts, low-heeled dress shoes, and current hair styles, but their attempts to look older made it easier for me to appear younger in my sneakers, jeans, and ponytail.) I was for the most part accepted by student groups.

I gradually became friendly with students of all races and was invited to their homes after school. The students' parents all treated me as though I was an adult from the school. However, in the community, I continued to spend most of my time with the adolescents, particularly with groups of girls. As alliances between groups of friends changed, my associations changed. I often had to avoid taking sides in quarrels and thus had to find new friends. By the time the original class graduated from the school, I had developed friendships with many girls who had long since separated from the groups in which I had met them. Stacie and Marie, two black girls whose names appear frequently throughout this book, maintained their friendship with each other and with me, and provided me with the deepest understandings of junior high life.

In my research, I utilized several methods. Most of my discussion is based upon participant observation. My aim was to investigate naturally occurring performances,[4] especially narrative performance in conversation. After a few months in the school, I began to bring a small cassette tape recorder. I recorded conversations in the hallways and lunchrooms and occasionally in the classrooms.

In addition to tape-recorded conversations, and still within the realm of participant observation, I undertook systematic investigations of particular aspects of behavior. My first investigation, intended in part as an illustration of my mode of inquiry for the teacher who had invited me into his classroom, was a study of interruptions at the school. I noted shifts in behavior and the signals that often precipitated them, and I observed how these shifts were managed. I made an inventory of such occurrences (which included school bells, entrances and exits of people, weather changes that could be seen through the windows, noises, and violations of rules), categorized the situations, and noted how similar signals were treated differently. The teacher found the study helpful for his own purposes, and it also served as a demonstration that my research was not intended to evaluate him. Other systematic investigations included studies of how food was purchased and shared and what students ate while at school, before school, and after school; studies of student excuses that were frequently demanded by authorities in specific places and at specific times of the school day; studies of social networks; and many other studies in the classroom.

I am making a distinction here between systematic investigations and specific foci of observations. An investigator can expect to find some behaviors, such as excuses or food exchange, in certain places or at certain times, and thus may make systematic studies of them. Other aspects of behavior – concerning, for example, the exchange of money, the communication of threats, and fights – are regular occurrences and can become foci of observation; but since the investigator cannot expect to find them in particular places at particular times, they can be noted only as often as they happen to be observed.

At the end of three years of observation, I conducted interviews and used some intervention techniques to gain information. Some of the students, when they learned that I was "writing a book about the school," designed a questionnaire that included all of the questions they thought I should ask, and they used the questionnaire to interview their friends. In addition, at the end of my research, I interviewed the students I had observed in the classroom. My interview concerned the social network, details about the student's household, and questions about where he or she acquired and spent money.

I used intervention only in classrooms other than the class to which I was originally invited and where I had formed friendships. One experiment concerned students' modes of reading aloud. In one intervention study, I taperecorded the students readings, tape-recorded stories told by them, transcribed the stories, tape-recorded the readings and stories so that the students could listen to them, and again taped the students reading aloud from the texts. The purpose of the study was to encourage the students to compare their readings and to suggest to them a relationship between spoken and written texts.

For a project related to this book, at the end of my research one of the ninth-grade Puerto Rican girls offered the following unsolicited account of her three years at the school. She described her first day of school in each grade and compared her lack of familiarity with the system in the seventh grade with her mastery of it by the ninth grade.[5] The account is presented here exactly as she wrote it, quotation marks and all, on lined notebook paper, except that pseudonyms replace the names of people and the school. As an introduction to the attitudes and atmosphere prevalent at the school, it provides a perspective usually unavailable to the outsider. Further, it presents one form of adolescent writing: in this case, a document intended for outside readers already familiar with the general situation but not with the details of personal experiences.

"7th Grade"

"When I first came to Paul Revere I was kind of scared but it was going to be my first year there but I was supposed too get used too going there. I started early in the Morning I was happy. Everybody talking about it sounded scarry, and nice. A couple of us caught the bus together. When we got there, since I was a seventh grader I was supposed to go to the audotorium – which I did. from there I appeared in the boys gym. I didn't knew until they announced where we were at. From there I appeared somewhere else. That was my home room. Which they called advisory. I copy something from the board called a Roster. After that a Bell rang. We waited for another Bell and left. I met with my friends and cought the bus back home. They explained how to used the rosters. Which I learned very quickly.

"The Classroom I was in like a regular elementary school which was only from one room to the other. I didn't understand that. Until our teacher explained that was called Mini School. Well we did a lot of things. Went on a lot of trips. And were all treated fairly by both teachers.

"I didn't hardly had any freinds until I started meeting a lot of them. I had a freind by the name of Luisa and Alicia. Those were the only two friends I had at the beginning of the year. Almost at the middle I met one girl by the name of Barbara. We were starting to get real closed to each other and were starting to trust each other. And as you know we still are very closed and trust each other.

Wilma

"8th Grade"

"This is how it all started. On the first day of school we went to our 7th grade classroom first. Our teacher will tell us where we will go. Barbara and I were hoping to be together. Mr. A. called both of our names together. And said "Yoos are in mini school again and have Mr. K. for your advisory. When we were on our way up there we decide not show up until the sencond day. We walked the halls.

The second day we show up together we noticed were we were at. We only knew a couple of people from our elementary school like Jimmy, Emma, Nancy, Courtney and Jeanine. We continue going everyday until we started meeting more and more it seem like it was going to be a super year. Everybody was getting along with one another. Which I liked that. There were no argument between races or color if you was white you were suppose to hate Puerto Rican it didn't worked like that everybody got along. We almost did the same thing in the 7th grade. But in the 8th we cutted a lot and did not obey the teacher. Since that was our sencond year and we know the school by heart we didn't bother. We were really bad made almost all the teachers had a hard time with us. Did everything we could of done to get in trouble. We had pink slip like we never seen before. I enjoy this year very much. had a nice time and enjoy every bit of it.

"9th Grade P.A.T.H."[6]

It all started when the first day of school came and we were happy especially Barbara and I though we were going to 9-2. So we went to K he called everybodys name and told them where they belong. Barbara and I were waiting he called Barbara's name first and said P.A.T.H. 9-7 Ms. S. We thought that was going to split us up since they kept saying they were going to split us up into one. He waited and called everybody's safed mines for last. When he called my name and said P.A.T.H. 9-7 Ms. S I jump with such of joy that I thought that was going to be the end of us.

"Well over P.A.T.H. is good if you could hang onto somebody strict. We stayed in one classroom all day. and only have two brakes at 9:30 and 1:15 and 50 mins. for lunch thats all. We have to be in before 8:00. or have our mother call before we come in thats if we are going to be late or absent.

"As soon the clock hits 8:00 you are not allow to sharpen pencil or nothing. We start writing until brake after brake we start writing again until lunch. The only thing I like about P.A.T.H. you learn a lot because she reviews what you had in the 7th and 8th grade.

"Like I say if you could hang until something thats very strict you do alright. But don't let her take over you at all. Stay quite when she talks to you in front of the class but when it by your self and her let everything out and you'll get everything your way.''

As Wilma's account reveals, life at the junior high school required understanding of its rules: the perplexities of the school program and learning how it worked from friends, making alliances, learning the system well enough to break its rules, the social rules of racial hostility, battles for control over making the rules between authorities and students. As a written statement, the account can also be examined for its use of reported speech to effect shifts in time, for its parallel structure in providing detailed descriptions of the first day of each school year, followed by more general characterizations of the year, and for its insider's voice. It might be characterized as a personal list of memories rather than as a guide to either outsiders or future students, except for the advice directed to other students concerning how to get along in the ninth-grade PATH program. This piece of specific advice about talking to the strict teacher is remarkable both for its explicit way of manipulating the situation and for its contrast with the author's lack of familiarity with the system at the beginning. The document provides detailed information on each grade level experience comparable to the author's increasing familiarity with the system.

Wilma's narrative is not the sort of text ordinarily discussed in studies of the relationship between oral and written communication. It is not standard grammatical writing; rather, it is ephemeral writing in the sense that it was written to communicate and then perhaps to discard. In this regard, it stands in contrast to standard grammatical printed texts.

Writing was an important activity in junior high life, both for school activities (notice that Wilma refers to her PATH schoolwork as writing) and for communication between friends or antagonists. Wilma's description of her school years contained the same kinds of observations girls made in their diaries, but as a separate document it was the only account of its kind I saw in my three years of research at the school. In its attention to the unwritten rules of the adolescents' conventions for written texts, it is perhaps typical.

My study of the uses of oral and written texts involved both systematic investigations and observations of spontaneous communication wherever it occurred, but since I was concerned not only with the texts themselves but also with their uses, I had to depend on what I saw and found in my daily observations. Self-reports of the uses of literacy would reveal only those uses within the boundaries of the categories as defined by the school. Whereas a study of the ability to use reading and writing could depend upon experimental measures, a study of the uses of texts requires ethnographic research.[7]

The taped conversations and stories in conversation provided the basis for my understanding of the adolescents' modes of talking about their experiences. The bulk of the conversations and stories described or discussed fights

and fight accounts and have come to represent what I know about the adolescents' orientation toward their world. Fights are commonplace occurrences in
the junior high school and are an important aspect of what every junior high
school student knows. They are fundamental to the adolescent worldview.
Fight accounts document the everyday, normal adolescent world.

In addition to recording oral narratives and collecting writings, I was able
to photocopy some of the girls' diaries. That the girls showed me their diaries
at all can only be attributed to serendipity. The book I chose for recording
field notes at the school had the words "Daily Diary" printed on the cover.
My policy was to show anyone who requested the notes I had written about
him or her, but nothing about others. Two of the girls said that since I had
shown them parts of my "diary," they would show me parts of theirs. Their
diaries, which recorded daily events, were actually not unlike my notes.
Occasionally, girls would bring me their diaries and allow me to photocopy
selected parts. These diary entries were extremely important to my collection
of oral and written narratives.

0.2   Storytelling rights: studying the uses of oral and written communication

The texts considered here – oral fight stories, written diary accounts, written
petitions, letters, and playful forms – are part of a single community's repertoire. They represent choices among channels and styles of communication,
and although they might be judged deficient when compared to standard
forms, they must be examined as appropriate (or inappropriate) within the
adolescent communication system. The examination of messages becomes an
issue of the appropriateness of revealing or concealing information rather than
of the adequacy of the message as informative. The question of form becomes
an issue of conventions rather than standards. Performance must be examined
closely to determine whether or not writing actually involves absent authorship and speech is actually face-to-face. The adolescents provide one
model for using orality and literacy in communication, and it must be understood as a coherent system that involves two potential sources of discontinuity: inappropriate use of a channel by insiders and lack of correspondence
with the larger adult system of communication.

The adolescent uses of oral and written narrative accounts raise issues
important to an understanding of the role of written texts in everyday communication. Since the adolescents were literate, the questions turn not as much
on abilities as on use – specifically, the uses of texts. Oral conversational
narratives are not bounded texts; it is only their transcription here that allows
us to treat them as bounded units. However, the adolescents did recognize the
difference between the flow of conversation and a story. Their understandings
of how to describe an event – how to begin, what to include in what sequence,

and how to end – reveal attention to stories as bounded units. We can ask whether the oral bounded units are the same as the written stories, whether the oral story forms are informed by notions of written texts, and whether the narrative devices used to create the boundaries are the same for the oral as for the written story.

The concept of storytelling rights, or entitlement, provides a way of discussing oral narratives in terms appropriate to the adolescents' communication and in correspondence with the issues usually assigned to written texts. Literacy scholarship depends upon certain concepts of written texts, including the ideas of authorship, standardization, and intertextuality. Identifiable authors who sign their works, standard forms of grammar and spelling that make writing accessible to anyone who knows the codes, and a known relationship between texts (written by the same author, available to an author who wrote a later text, historically related in some other way) are some of the recognized characteristics of writing. Verbal arts, in contrast, are characterized by face-to-face performance, anonymous authors, traditional forms, and varying versions.

Authorship is one kind of entitlement. The person called the author is entitled, to a certain extent, to control his or her compositions. In oral storytelling, the question of entitlement involves the rights of the people described in a story, people who claim to have seen an event, and narrators, as well as, occasionally, the person who claims to be a composer. Of course, the same issues may become significant for written texts when an account can be claimed (by anyone involved) to describe an actual event.

The relationship between storytelling rights and standardization is more theoretically complex and works on several levels. Most obviously, a group of people claim that a certain form is to be understood as standard, and thus they claim the entitlement to assert standards. In addition, within any group, certain conventions for communication can be said to be more appropriate than others; conventions of any kind create standards. Thus the adolescent writings belong to a variety called "nonstandard written English." I did not assume a set of standards or ideal forms of communication in my research but rather attempted to understand the conventions of use in a particular community. From the adolescent perspective, standard English was the equivalent of adult white communication; from their parents' perspective, it represented schoolwork; in either case, the perceived standard was inappropriate in the community. On yet another level, standards refer to fixed rather than innovative forms. However, standards can include improvisational forms. For example, the history of the novel and its relationship to the epic, as discussed by Bakhtin, suggests that the novel plays with its own standards and incorporates innovation by "laying bare" the literary conventions it uses (Bakhtin 1981:162). The use of innovative forms in the novel is one illustration of the fact that fixed and innovative forms do not correspond to written and oral channels of communication. The devices of improvisation and the uses of reported conversation in novels bear a greater resemblance to personal narratives (such as those told orally by the adolescents) than to other written forms. Especially in discussions of artistic texts, the issue of standardization raises more questions than it can answer.

The relationship between intertextuality and entitlement is particularly significant in the adolescents' fight stories. Oral narratives do not necessarily refer to other narratives, and when they do, in effect, they assign authorship to another narrator. The adolescent he-said–she-said stories (more often *she*-said–she-said) involve the entitlement to repeat someone else's words, a claim more precarious than the entitlement to report on what one has seen or experienced oneself. Another person's story is experienced as an event that can be reported. Thus, in oral storytelling, intertextuality, or the ways in which listeners or readers use knowledge gained from familiarity with similar kinds of texts to understand a particular text, is one kind of reference; the larger category is the relationship between narratives and the events to which they refer. In Chapter 1, which explores the relationship between narrative and event, I demonstrate that the relationship is not causal; events are not always prior to narratives.

The nonstandard uses of writing and speaking in everyday life provide an interesting ground for reconsidering the categories of oral and written communication. Conventions cannot be assumed but must instead become the subject of the investigation, and speaking and writing become relative rather than fixed categories. Authorship, standardization, and intertextuality can be considered as part of the category of entitlement rather than as attributes of writing. Performance, usually considered as part of the category of speaking, becomes part of the category of communication. Another way to perceive these category shifts is to ask what happens when the modes of inquiry usually used for written texts are applied to oral texts and, at the same time, the modes of inquiry used for investigating verbal arts are addressed to writings.

0.3 Face-to-face/absent-author communication

Speaking is generally characterized by face-to-face communication, and writing is characterized by an absent author. The performance situations for written and spoken texts can be phenomenally different, but the texts themselves may display no apparent contrasts.

This phenomenal difference in performance situations is the source of discussions concerning the impact of literacy on culture as well as the basis for discriminating between types of literature, but very little attention has been paid to comparisons of oral and written performances themselves. Educators have become increasingly aware that attitudes toward performance situations are crucial in classroom interaction between teachers and students.

As part of their research on the acquisition of reading skills, educators have begun to consider oral storytelling situations as significant in understanding attitudes toward orality in general.

An exploration of the relationship between text and context in specific speaking and reading/writing situations is necessary to understand the implications of the contrast between face-to-face and absent-author performances.

The words "reading/writing" and "speaking" themselves reveal the contrast. Reading and writing are usually understood as separate processes expressed by separate words. They can be and often are done separately, thus creating a distance between reading and authoring. "Literacy," the term that applies to both, is usually used to refer to the ability to create and use written texts.[8] Speaking, discourse, and oral communication, in contrast, imply both addressor and addressee, since both are necessary to any performance. The significant point here is that these terms reveal that oral and written communication are not perceived in parallel ways. Walter Ong's use of the terms "orality" and "literacy" (1982) suggests a parallelism that is useful for discussion but that belies the lack of symmetry between the processes.

Some of the differences between face-to-face and absent-author communication are obvious: The addressee cannot respond directly and immediately to an absent author or narrator; in face-to-face communication, the speaker cannot be anonymous, and familiarity with multiple versions is more likely when there are many absent authors rather than one present oral performer. For each of the assumed cases there are interesting exceptions, such as Catholic confessionals in which the speakers and, in some cases, the hearers are anonymous; the use of telephones for oral communication that is not literally face-to-face; or written messages handed directly by an author to the addressee. The assumed and generalized differences hide the more complex and interesting questions about the nature of face-to-face and absent authorship as forms of communication. Granted, the means of responding is different, but does this difference imply different kinds or qualities of response? Do multiple interpretations work differently in speaking than in writing?

Studies of oral discourse and written literature clearly approach the problem of interpretation differently. In studies of oral discourse, multiple interpretations are examined in terms of miscommunication, as the problem of speakers who do not share the same strategies or conventions for communication. The problem rests with the speaker and hearer rather than with the message or text.[9]

For the most part, examinations of literature focus on texts rather than on writers and readers. Even those schools of literary criticism that have endeavored to understand the intentions of the author or the style of a particular historical period have attempted to identify the meaning or meanings of the texts themselves.[10] Reader-response criticism, and in particular the early work of Stanley Fish (1976), offers an approach closer to that of discourse models, since the emphasis is on multiple meanings attributed by various readers rather than on texts. However, the multiple interpretations of written texts are still examined as a variety of solutions rather than as a problem attributed to miscommunication.

Writing and speaking are not the source of these differences, differences that stem from the uses of texts in scholarly research rather than from inherent properties of literacy and orality. The distinction between face-to-face and absent-author communication is most significant in studies of literature. Stated conversely, only when texts are examined in terms of absent authorship are they treated as literature. The category of literature depends upon absent authorship in part because it provides the possibility of multiple interpretations, rereadings, and copies of texts. However, multiple interpretations are not an exclusive property of writing.

Anonymity is no more essential to oral composers than is absent authorship to writers. Rather, anonymity and absent authorship are parts of larger social systems of communication. As Ruth Finnegan has demonstrated, authorship is a social phenomenon that differs tremendously between cultures.[11] Authorship is a statement of ownership, and cultures and groups have distinct, often unstated rules for claiming a text as one's own and for determining how and when another person's text may be used.[12] The issue of ownership and authorship is especially important for understanding adolescent fight stories and will be discussed at length as a problem of the "entitlement" to tell or to hear a story.

The cross-cultural comparisons, such as those provided by Finnegan, provide the best demonstration of a lack of correspondence between types of texts or types of performance situations and the relationship between writing and speaking. Although no one aspect of either writing or speaking constitutes the single significant factor of difference, there are groups of factors that tend to cluster around either writing or speaking.

A number of pieces of the communicative system seem to offer discriminations between writing and speaking. In addition to the absent-author/face-to-face distinction, devices of fictionalization, standard versus nonstandard forms of expression, and the relationship between text and context are significant for understanding the differences between written and spoken communication.

The differences become particularly interesting in terms of literature or the poetic uses of oral and written communication. What is the relationship between fictions and conventions in written texts? Does absent authorship lend itself to a particular kind of fiction? If we trace the idea of a privileged relationship between writing and artistic texts, and a corollary relationship between spoken forms and ordinary conversation, to the assumption that writing distances addressors from addressees more than speaking or that the act of fiction making is more developed in writing than in speaking, we find that the proximity of narrative to everyday discourse is neither a common characteristic of speaking nor a device unfamiliar to writing. For example, the novel, a historically recent form of fiction, presents a particular and idealized form of subjectivity that posits a different relationship between addressor and addressee than, for example, the epic.[13]

This study examines the multiple relationships between the ordinary and the artistic, the fictional and the true story, the standard and the nonstandard, absent authorship in various forms and face-to-face communication, in order to understand the significant differences between oral and written communication. One purpose of this work is to realign our categories of oral and written communication. Narrative, as one category of communication particularly significant for the adolescents, offers an arena for sorting out the enormous difference in entitlement assigned to either written or spoken, "ordinary" or "artistic" communication and for challenging the categories themselves.

This book begins with a criticism of some of the contrasts commonly assigned to writing and speaking and then explores alternative contrast sets – between ongoing and resolved narratives or mediate and immediate storytelling situations, between informative and meaningful messages, between ephemeral and collected texts, and between face-to-face and absent-author communication. Along the way, I define concepts, including entitlement and the distinctions between narrative, event, experience, and storyability and tellability. My purpose is to examine the contextual uses of writing and speaking, more specifically, written and oral narratives in everyday life. I contend that face-to-face and absent authorship are two of several available contexts in which speaking and writing are used.

Differences in the uses of oral and written communication in everyday life rest on conceptions of the relationship between text and context. The crudest and not always accurate distinction is that situations are contexts for oral communication and other texts are contexts for written communication. Thus situations provide the information necessary to make oral communication intelligible, and other writings inform readers of the conventions for reading. The problem with this distinction is that it assumes a difference between context-dependent oral communication and intertextuality. In what ways are they different, and do not both use conventions to create shared understandings? Of course, intelligibility is much more problematic than the provision of conventions or codes, and conventions actually explain more about miscommunication than they do about the communication of meaning. The relationship between text and context is not simply a matter of referential messages that require decoding.

The distinction between oral situational contexts and the intertextuality of written texts can be restated as a distinction between face-to-face communication and absent authorship. Any message can be examined in terms of the relationship between the addressee and the addressor. Whereas the distinction between situational contexts and intertextuality ultimately turns on the conventions, social or literary, for appropriate communication, the distinction between face-to-face and absent-author communication ultimately turns on the relationship between authors and their audiences. More specifically, the issue of absent authorship invites questions about point of view and the role of a narrator in asserting authority over a message.

Questions of social and textual conventions have been taken up by scholars interested in discourse, and studies of point of view and authorship have, for the most part, been the province of literary discussions.[14] One purpose of this book is to examine narratives from everyday life as a means of bringing the two orientations, the discourse and the literary, together.

In this book, narrative is considered one way of categorizing experience. Oral and written communications provide different ways of experiencing communication and entitle addressors and addressees to different roles. Entitlement is a way of talking about the relationship between authors and audiences at the same time as one considers the relationship between messages and their referents, texts and their contexts, narratives and events. Essentially, entitlement is a way of understanding communication with respect to ownership of experience – both the experience referred to in the message and the experience of the communication itself. Just as titles categorize texts (to a certain extent), the subject of entitlement raises questions about the processes of categorizing. The difference between a title and entitlement as it is discussed here, however, is that giving a text a title is usually understood as an author's right, whereas entitlement refers to the rights of both addressors and addressees as well as to the onlookers, witnesses, eavesdroppers, and third-party listeners to a message, as well as the characters in the message.

Chapter 1 lays the groundwork for analyzing one aspect of the text–context distinction by examining the relationship between narrative, event, and experience. Constructions of narrative become a problem of negotiating storytelling rights in Chapter 2, which elaborates the concepts of storyability and tellability. The negotiation of entitlement rights to written communication is discussed in Chapter 3. Concepts of the distribution of knowledge developed in discussions of oral fight narratives in the first two chapters are further elaborated in terms of playful, collaborative, and protest writings.

The first three chapters provide an ethnographic and theoretical framework for a discussion in Chapter 4 of oral and written retellings of an event. Chapter 5, a study of the adolescents' diaries, examines the textual conventions employed in oral fight narratives and written diaries.

Chapter 6 returns to the model for investigating literacy as a part of everyday communication and asserts that any text, whether authorized or stigmatized, is part of the process of entitlement or a negotiation of rights to write or speak and to report others' words. Although I rely upon a methodology for examining texts that has been developed for discourse and conversational narrative, I do not insist that all writing be considered in the context of speaking. Rather, I suggest that some of the tools for understanding the oral negotiation of rights to authorship and quotation are useful for demonstrating that the study of literacy is always a study of entitlement and that, in a society that has writing and reading, the use of written or spoken communication involves understanding, negotiating, and playing with the social constraints and privileges accorded to both channels of communication.[15]

1

FIGHT STORIES: WHAT COUNTS IS THE RECOUNTING

1.1 Relationships between narrative and experience

Stories categorize experience. The relationship between stories and experience is always problematic and can be stated in many ways. Most generally, it is a relationship between reality and the representation or appearance of reality, or between signifier and signified, or between language and action, or between art and life. The notion of a relationship between stories and experience should be understood as only one of many ways of stating the problem.

Stories, experiences, and events are different entities. Roughly, experiences are the stream of overlapping activities that make up everyday life. Events, unlike experiences, have potentially identifiable beginnings and endings. Events are a category of experience; stories are constructions of experience. Stories frame experiences as events. Stories are one of the forms that transform experiences into bounded units with beginnings, endings, and foci, and events are one kind of bounded unit. A story is the representation of an event segmented into sequentially arranged units.[1]

There has been a tendency in narrative scholarship to assign experience a sense of objectivity so that experience becomes invested with reality, in contrast to stories, which are supposedly understood subjectively.[2] This unfortunate tendency has led scholars to confuse events with experiences, as though one could experience an event. Events are ways of categorizing experience; in a sense, the category "event" makes experiences accessible to understanding by providing a language for talking about experience.[3]

The statement that stories categorize experience is an alternative to statements that stories replay, duplicate, or recapitulate experience.[4] Replays, duplications, and recapitulations imply a sequential relationship between stories and experiences. They imply a direct correspondence between the incidents described in a story and actual incidents in everyday life. Although this correspondence is possible, it is not necessary. Further, experiences are not necessarily ordered as they are perceived to be ordered in stories. Those stories that purport to refer to actual events only appear to duplicate the perceived order of experience. If anything, stories give the appearance of order to experience rather than vice versa.

The purpose of this chapter is to examine the relationship between the experiences and narratives of a group of adolescents. The adolescents' narratives demonstrate the possibility that stories that purport to report actual experiences represent a negotiable reality. Reports of past events may appear to convey information, but at the same time, they also demonstrate relationships between tellers, hearers, characters, and others. Barbara Herrnstein Smith writes,

> The factuality of the subject does not compromise the fictiveness of the tale, for it is not the events told that are fictive but the *telling* of them. That telling is set apart from reports of past events and from such allusions to them as may occur in natural discourse. (1978:128)

In the case of the adolescent narratives, an example of natural discourse, the supposed factuality of the subject is used to create the illusion of a report. As we will see, reports in natural discourse are also fictive tellings, and both oral and written accounts of events may rely upon the supposed actuality of the events they recount to convey the illusion of a report. A report is always a fictive construction.

One of the problems with assuming a direct correspondence between narratives and events is the sometimes erroneous presumption that good or competent narratives recapitulate the sequence in which incidents actually happened.[5] The recapitulation of sequence is expected of oral rather than written narratives, and this arbitrary distinction disregards the possibility that narrators may play with sequence in oral tellings as well as in written works. One purpose of preserving the sequence of incidents in a narrative is intelligibility. The listener must know certain things in order to understand what follows. Also, changes in sequence can change the meaning of a story. However, narrators may not always intend to provide the utmost clarity for their listeners, and they may knowingly change the meaning of a story. Intentions aside, the sequential order of incidents is never a fixed truth, and narratives impose order and causality upon reality.

Listening to a narrative requires the listener to unpack the relationship between the incidents described and the interpretation of what actually happened. The narrative text provides only one of several resources for understanding the incidents described. Storytelling involves several contexts: the context described in the story; the listeners' and the teller's prior knowledge of contextual information not described; the inferred as opposed to the stated context of the incidents described; other relevant situations in which the participants of the storytelling situation interact, either with each other or with people mentioned in the story; and the storytelling situation, itself composed of the conversation, other stories told before and after or at other times, and the frame provided by either the listeners or the teller. Not all of these contexts are equally available as resources; not all of the participants in the storytelling situation have equal access to contextual resources. Further, individuals[6] have different "horizons" of understanding. The phenomenologist Hans-Georg Gadamer has used Alfred Schutz's term "horizon" to refer to situatedness or perspective. The advantage of this term is its focus on the *limits* of observation. The disadvantage is that it fails to account for the stance of the observer, the ideological position of persuasion, point of view, or worldview.[7] A horizon implies a changing perspective. Situatedness is not a static fact; it involves constant realignments. Situatedness is not a property of individuals, but rather refers to understandings between individuals in terms of their perspectives. Erving Goffman's term "evidential boundaries"[8] similarly considers a point of view as a relationship between people, and in addition suggests that people become aware of each other's perspectives as "boundaries" or limits.

Several factors, including horizons of understanding, the uses of contextual information, and the expected sequential presentation of events, contribute to the intelligibility of narratives. However, intelligibility can also be inhibited by either the listeners' or teller's horizons of understanding, and is neither guaranteed nor prevented by certain kinds of sequences or temporal relationships between events.

1.2   The storytelling situation

Personal stories slip in and out of conversations, often without notice or ceremony, and are often told to people already familiar with the characters or types of events recounted. Their meaning and interpretation is a matter not only of the content of the story, but also of the patterns of social interaction involved in story exchanges. Not all accounts of experience are stories, and not all stories recount personal experiences; personal experience stories elaborate events without stretching them beyond the limits of credibility.

Adolescents' personal stories offer a particularly transparent example of how personal stories work in social interaction. The adolescents played with the relationship between stories and events by reversing their status and by requiring justification for the storytelling occasion rather than for the events described. Since many stories concerned quarrels or potential fights, the stories were at the same time about their social interactions and part of the interactions.

The adolescents told stories as part of their daily interactions. The stories were told on the way to school and at school, either during class, during brief meetings in the halls between classes, during classes that allowed talking, during lunch, on the way home from school, in the neighborhood, and on the telephone. The adolescent environment provided regular meetings and separations of friends and relatives, and stories were told whenever allied people met after a brief separation. Some friendships existed only at school, others only in the neighborhood. In the neighborhood, the adolescents did not stray far from their own blocks, and unless a nearby community center was available, they met on the sidewalks in front of their houses. The school provided a meeting ground for the adolescents, but the meetings were limited by the structure of the class schedule and by the yearly regrouping of students into different classrooms. When the students first came to the school in the seventh grade, they were somewhat arbitrarily assigned to classrooms. Although many of the seventh graders recognized some of the students in their classes from their previous schools or neighborhoods, very few found themselves in classes with already established friends. The school structure allowed little opportunity for students to interact with friends in other classrooms.

Two staircases separated up and down traffic between classes and, for the most part, students followed each other in a stream of one-way traffic and did not meet each other head on. In the lunchroom, tables were assigned according to classrooms, so the same students who studied together ate together. In each subsequent year, students were regrouped, and they frequently commented at the beginning of each year that they never saw their friends from the previous year. Although they rarely saw either friends from previous years or current neighborhood friends, they did hear about them. In their new classes, they met the neighborhood friends of their classroom friends from the previous year, and although face-to-face contact become difficult, the networks for talking about and hearing about their alliances continued and grew.

The climate in which narratives were shared at the school was dominated by the fact that people who rarely saw each other at school talked about each other. Much of this communication concerned relationships formed in the neighborhood. Neighborhood friends and enemies carried their grievances to school and often settled their accounts on the school grounds. Situations in which adolescents talked about each other were a function both of the school structure, which placed friends in the same institution without giving them much opportunity for face-to-face meetings, and of the intersection of neighborhood and school alliances in the school.

As Erving Goffman has pointed out, interactions involving people who are not present to the occasion involve particular problems.

> We must also be careful to keep in mind the truism that persons who are present are treated very differently from persons who are absent. Persons who treat each other with consideration while in each other's immediate presence regularly show not the slightest consideration for each other in situations where acts of deprivation cannot be immediately and incontestably identified as to source by the person who is deprived by these acts. (1953:41)

In the junior high school, talking about others occurred daily, as a function of the limited opportunity for face-to-face interaction, but at the same time, talking about others was considered an offense. The situation was similar to the one Marjorie Goodwin reports from her fieldwork among black girls:

The speaker, as author of her own actions, has a right to monitor descriptions others make of her. The accusation is a challenge to the hearer about whether the hearer in fact made such a statement about the speaker. The structure of the utterance further locates the statement about the speaker as having been made in the speaker's absence. The act of the hearer at issue thus constitutes what the participants describe as "talking behind my back" and this act is considered an offense. (1978:435)

For the adolescents, the advantage of talking behind others' backs, instead of meeting them face-to-face, was that arguments could be dissipated in the process of sending accusations through the network. People learned of each other's grievances without actually speaking to the offending person, and concern about the grievance lost prominence in the face of concern about the networks of information. Quarrels about particular offenses turned into quarrels about who talked about whom behind whose back.

Talking behind people's backs was not limited to the school setting. He-said–she-said talk also flourished in the neighborhood. Since the school setting did not permit lengthy conversations between all of the members of a group, in the junior high conversations one person told others what two or more people who were not present had said about each other. The teller was often a witness rather than a participant in a dispute.[9] The limited number of listeners and the absence of one or both of the disputants permitted elaborated narratives in which the point of view and the horizon of understanding of witnesses prevailed.

The configuration of tellers and listeners and their relationship to the disputants and witnesses were essential parts of the storytelling situation, since they took into account not only the familiarity of the listeners with the events of the past but also the potential alliances and hostilities between participants in the future. Thus the relationship between text and context operated on three temporal levels: the description of the past situation, the immediate storytelling situation, and the ongoing situation.

Participants in the conversations in which narratives about others were told at the junior high also often included characters mentioned in the story, but the degree of involvement in the story was often disputable. The question of whether or not listeners were entitled to hear the story, whether or not it was "any of their business," was a source of constant controversy.

Entitlement is not only a matter of the storyteller's right to tell but also concerns categories of listeners, especially unratified and ratified hearers. Goffman distinguishes between three kinds of listeners: those who overhear, whether or not inadvertently, those who are ratified hearers but not specifically addressed, and those who are ratified and not addressed (1981:9). Overhearings were prevented, as much as possible, in the junior high conversations by physically excluding others or by speaking directly and quietly into someone's ear. Where overhearings were intended, as in conversations that girls wanted boys to overhear, the speaker often directed her gaze at the boy who was supposed to overhear while turning her mouth toward the ear of the listener.[10] Speaking into someone's ear also afforded the opportunity to avoid looking at the listener; thus the speaker could use her eyes to monitor overhearings. Listeners, too, were responsible for monitoring overhearings. The differences between ratified hearers who were and were not addressed was constantly negotiated in the junior high conversations. If a ratified person offered an interjection, the speaker could challenge her entitlement and designate her as unaddressed by saying, "I wasn't talking to you."

Entitlement is usually considered an issue concerning speakers rather than hearers because hearers cannot easily be held responsible for listening to something that was not their business. However, listeners can be held accountable for withholding information, and the corollary to entitlement to tell narratives is the expectation that an ally who hears relevant information has an obligation to pass it on to others who figured in the conversation.

In the junior high, the issue constantly shifted from the question of who was entitled to talk about something to the question of who was entitled to hear it. Girls challenged each other for "talking about me behind my back," which meant that the speaker was not entitled to speak, and they also challenged each other for offering statements when they had not been addressed, saying, "This is none of your business."

The adolescent concern with entitlement shifted the focus of attention from the content of the message to the identities of the participants listening to and telling the account. Further, the identities of the participants in the conversation had a direct relationship to the identities of the characters mentioned in the narrative.[11] The events described in the narrative and the current lives of the people listening to it were totally intertwined. The subject of the narratives was people and their relationship. The same people mentioned in the narrative listened to it, and that storytelling occasion was also about the relationship.

1.3 The relationship between the fight and the fight story

The sequential aspect of narratives is more easily understood than the referential aspect. Narratives can be defined as extended turns at talk in which utterances are sequentially organized (Sacks 1972:325–45), as the recapitulation of past experiences in the order in which they are believed to have occurred (Labov 1972:359–60), or as proposing a world other than that inhabited by the listeners (Jason 1972; Young 1983). The sequential aspect of narrative is complicated by the possibility that the sequence can be explicitly presented or recovered through a narrative device. The referential relationship between narrative and events is especially complicated in personal narratives in which the world of the storytelling situation and the world in which the story takes place are so close together that one can forget that they are different worlds in which knowledge is differently distributed.[12]

The adolescents' stories were, on one level, about fights. The stories often began with fighting as the designated topic:

> "Did you hear about Jo Jo fight . . ."
> "Me and Rose had a fight . . ."

The stories did not report the entire fight sequence, but rather began with the fact that there was a fight and then accounted for how the fight started and sometimes projected what would happen next. The narratives rarely described the physical actions of the fight.

The following narrative was told by one white girl to another on a school trip. The teller, Joan, offered to tell what had happened to disrupt her friendship with Mary and clearly hoped that the listener, Linda, would become an ally against Mary.[13]

1

J:	It was me and Mary	1
	we had a fight and right	2
	yesterday	3
	my sister went over to her	4
	and she grabbed her	5
	and she pulled her	6
	and she says that "You want to fight my sister?"	7
	she said, "Go do it"	8
L:	By your place?	9
J:	So I went over to her	10
	and then she wants to fight me	11
	so then I walked away	12
	so then when I was goin' up to lunch	13
	it was about third period	14
	and I was goin' up to lunch	15
	and she grabbed me	16
	three girls	17
	right?	18
	colored girls	19
	they grabbed me and started beating me up	20
	so I went down to the office	21
	and she said, "Go ahead"	22
	and I called my mom at work	23
	and she said that uh	24
	just to stay home	25
	and then she called the principal and told him	26
	and then	27
L:	You didn't do nothin' else?	28

J:	And then I lay down	29
	so I lay down until I got home	30
	and then we had to come back again	31
	and then um she started	32
	and then she didn't come to school because she was afraid	33
	that I would get into a fight with her	34
	so I told my mom	35
L:	Uh oh	36
J:	I shouldn't of said anything because it made her mad	37
	my sister said that if she touched me	38
	she would kick her butt	39
L:	That was the fight with Mary?	40
J:	That was the fight	41
	yah	42
	that's when I was walkin' to the next room	43
	and she hit her elbow in my stomach, right?	44
	but I didn't say – but I just walked away	45
	and then when I got up to lunch	46
	that's when the girls jumped me	47
L:	Mary jumped you?	48
J:	No	49
L:	Oh, other girls	50
J:	she got some friends of hers	51
	her girlfriends jumped me, colored girls	52
L:	Mary's friends	53
J:	Yah, but if you ask Mary who did it, she won't say nothing	54

Joan's story could be seen (by an outsider) as either a jumble of incidents presented without attention to sequence or as a carefully constructed account that cleverly describes a fight that never actually came to blows. Both are structural problems best understood in terms of the relationship between narrative and event and the accompanying relationship between listeners and teller and the people mentioned in the story.

The incidents in the story include, in order:

> a confrontation between Joan's sister and Mary,
> a confrontation between Joan and Mary in which Joan walked away,
> a confrontation between some alleged ''colored'' friends of Mary and Joan on the way to lunch,
> and Joan's interactions with her mother and the school principal.

The sequence ended with the report of Joan staying out of school to avoid a confrontation with Mary. The opening lines referring to the fight are not necessarily the beginning of the story, but rather constitute an atemporal orientation.[14] ''Yesterday'' refers not to the fight but to the quarrel between Joan's sister and Mary. There are only two references to the fight between Joan and Mary:

(1)

J: so I went over to her	10
and then she wants to fight me	11
so then I walked away	12

and the repeat in the replay:

(1)

that's when I was walkin' to the next room	43
and she hit her elbow in my stomach, right?	44
but I didn't say – but I just walked away	45

Fight stories about fights that have not (yet) come to blows raise questions concerning the reliability of the narrator and the purpose of the telling. Joan and her sister told their stories to many people both in the school and in the neighborhood, and each retelling included some revisions to strengthen the antagonism or to make the account more plausible. Joan's account of being jumped by "colored girls" was questioned by all of her listeners. Joan could not identify the girls and said that they were "outsiders" who did not attend the school and had come in "from the outside." Since both Joan and Mary were white, the listeners did not believe that black outsiders would aid Mary. After a few days, Joan dropped the incident from her story and relayed instead the following story concerning her confrontation with Mary at school.

2

J: I was gonna fight Mary against my locker, man	1
I started pushin' her, I said how often you [. . .] at the school	2
I says, "Come on I'll fight you right now"	3
I wasn't afraid	4
I started pushin' her and shovin' her	5
That's when she started fightin' back	6
That's when she got in trouble	7

Oral narrative 1 was not about the details of the fight; it was an accusation of an offense and a challenge for a confrontation. Joan's narrative was about her allies, and one purpose of telling it was to gain more allies for a future fight with Mary.

Joan's sister's role as an instigator was particularly important. Mary had been Joan's best friend until Joan's sister created antagonism by telling Joan that Mary had called her an "H" (whore). The instigator often played an important role in the fight sequence and was the chief source of challenges to entitlement. Fights between friends were often instigated by a third person who told one of the friends something her friend had said about her. When friends instigated a fight between other friends, the instigators were often the first to report on the events; they protected their own interests by presenting the situation from their own perspectives.[15] The instigators could be, and often were, accused of not minding their own business. Joan's sister was justified in reporting something she claimed to have heard about her own sister, but she was still charged with meddling and with wanting to cause trouble between Joan and Mary. At times during the following weeks, the focus shifted from a dispute between Mary and Joan to a dispute between Joan and her sister.

Joan's story is primarily a listing of people who were talking about each other. As Joan reported in oral narrative 1, she told her mother that she fought with Mary and that Mary's alleged black friends had attacked her. Joan's mother spoke with the principal; Joan told something else to her mother, Joan's sister stated a threat against Mary, and Mary wouldn't "say nothing."

Whereas oral narrative 1 was an accusation that Mary caused trouble, oral narrative 2 was Joan's self-testimony of her willingness to fight. Oral narrative 1 involved a complex association of characters: Joan, her sister, some outside black girls who were supposedly Mary's friends, Joan's mother, and the school principal. Mary hardly figured in the story. Oral narrative 2 was about the relationship between Joan and Mary. Joan asserted that she was a heroine and implied that Mary had gotten her just desserts, both from Joan and from whomever she "got in trouble" with. Joan's two stories were not necessarily contradictory, although they did supply different pieces of information. Oral narrative 2 could be seen as the content of the supposed fight mentioned in oral narrative 1. Each of the stories was inextricably related to its placement within the month-long quarrel. Oral narrative 1, told at the beginning of the quarrel, reported Joan's efforts to appear victimized in the eyes of her mother and the school principal. The story, told to a friend, was typical of stories told at the warning or challenge stage of a quarrel. It established many potential moves in retaliation for further offenses, including the assertion that the sister would "kick [her opponent's] butt," that the mother would defend her, and that the principal would come to her aid through the mother. Oral narrative 2 did not suggest future moves; rather, it explained the state of the current situation in which Mary and Joan did not speak to each other.

1.4 Entitlement and information states

Erving Goffman uses the term "information state," borrowed from John von Neumann, to describe varying parameters of knowledge among participants in a speech event.

> By an "information state" I mean the knowledge an individual has of why events have happened as they have, what the current forces are, what the properties and intents of the relevant persons are, and what the outcome is likely to be. (1974:133–4)

Goffman uses the examples of the con man and the dupe as people with different information states, and the example of players in a play as people who share the same information state and know the entire play but who, for the purposes of the play, act as if they have different information states.[16] Information states are important on two levels for the adolescent narratives. First, as previously discussed, the adolescents had limited knowledge of each other's family lives, and both the prohibitions concerning storytelling entitlement and the challenges to violations of privacy maintained the limited state of knowledge. Second, the adolescents did not assume that everyone had equal access to knowledge about specific events.

Access to knowledge followed rules of entitlement; in other words, in a system that valued both access to knowledge and the privilege of privacy, information was restricted to a few people rather than accessible to many. However, the adolescents often knew more than they were entitled to know and often saw more than they were entitled to speak about. Further, they operated with pieces of knowledge rather than entire pictures, and they had few ways of completing their pictures or knowing that these pictures were incomplete.

This relationship between entitlement and information states, one in which information oversteps the boundaries of entitlement and entitlement does not guarantee information, is particularly important to fight stories. When fights actually happened, the fighters claimed that they did not see what happened; they depended upon onlookers to explain the events. Thus onlookers were placed in the sometimes awkward, but in this case necessary, position of telling someone else's story. The witnesses who recounted the incident to the fighters were usually the same people who instigated the fight. They were also the people who urged the fighters on and who tried to stop the fight if it got out of hand. The instigators, interveners, and mediators, in their multiple roles, often knew more about the fight than the fighters themselves.

The stories did not provide a way for the adolescents to learn more about each other; if anything, the possibility of speaking about someone improperly suppressed the flow of information. Often the narratives reinforced the lack of shared knowledge of family background. The adolescents behaved as strangers, wary of stories that invaded privacy and victimized by the principle that speaking about each other constituted an invasion. Whereas in other communities people may similarly disdain rumors and gossip as invasions of privacy, they often attempt to discover more facts in order to arrive at a closer approximation of what really happened.[17] In their quest for knowledge, some people uncover a plethora of perhaps irrelevant facts. The adolescents, on the other hand, omitted details and reduced their stories to the statement that he (she) said something about her (him).

In the adolescents' stories, the focus often shifted from improper deeds or offenses to improper talk as the offense. The improper deeds themselves ceased to appear in the stories, and talking about them became itself an improper action. Talking about other people was considered a challenge to fight. As long as the verbal exchange was prolonged, a fight was averted, but at the same time, when a story circulated for a long time, the claims escalated.

The shift in focus from deeds as offenses to talk as offenses was often accompanied by a shift in the protagonists of the dispute. The person who talked about someone else's offense often became the target of accusations. However, the only person who could make such a claim was one of the people involved in the original dispute. In the fight between Joan and Mary, for example, either Joan or Mary could have accused Joan's sister of having meddled. The only people who were entitled to make such accusations were the people who were improperly discussed. However, since the talking went on behind their backs, the offended persons rarely had enough information to know whom to blame. In some cases, third parties made the accusations in the name of a friend.

The obvious relationship between entitlement and information states is one of necessity rather than propriety: One must have information in order to talk about something. However, the people with the information are not necessarily entitled to tell what they know.

The adolescents' narratives were inextricably connected to the situations in which they were told. The narratives were connected not only to the immediate storytelling occasion but also to the larger situation of ongoing relationships between the people involved in the incident. The storytelling occasion often implicated the tellers and listeners in the larger ongoing relationship. They were implicated in the situation by being told the narrative. Thus, oral narrative 1, actually a retelling of several previous stories, revealed that a number of people had been implicated in the dispute between Mary and Joan. The sister, mother, and principal were some of them, implicated by the process of storytelling. Entitlement to either tell or hear a story implied involvement in the situation. Since Joan told a story in which she was a main character, she was entitled to tell it. The mother was entitled to hear the story since it concerned an alleged assault on her daughter and since Joan needed her mother's permission to go home from school. The principal was entitled to hear about what happened since it happened at his school. Not all of these people would necessarily become involved in any fight. The value of telling her mother about each incident was clearly questionable, as Joan said in her story to Linda:

(1)

J:	so I told my mom	35
	I shouldn't of said anything because it made her mad	37

The principal limited his own involvement in the situation. At one point in the month-long dispute, he called Joan and Mary into his office and asked them to agree not to bother each other anymore. He closed his remarks with the statement, "Now, I don't want to hear anymore about this." His statement suggested that if *he* did not hear anything, there would be nothing to hear. Actually, the principal and Joan's mother were entitled to hear only one episode of the dispute, the claim of victimization. Joan's stories of retribution or of victimizing Mary and getting her "into trouble" would not appropriately be told by Joan to either her mother or the principal.

The relationship between information states and entitlement is further complicated by the distinction between accusations and narratives. Accusations and narratives are two very different ways of communicating information. Both can be third-party communications. Marjorie Goodwin has pointed out that accusations and storytelling involve different turn-taking structures. "Arguments characteristically involve the principle current speaker selects next (generally prior speaker). However, turns at talk with stories are governed by the principle of self selections" (1978:413). The following conversation becomes a monologue when the absence of the addressee of the threats turns listeners into potential antagonists who are careful not to respond as addressees. The participants included Wilma, who wrote the description of the school (in the Introduction), Teresa and two other students, all Puerto Ricans, and myself, and took place in a classroom during the lunch period.

3

W:	Linda keep	1
	You know Linda act like she bad and she write all of them things	2
T:	Who?	3
	Linda	4
W:	Yah	5
	I'm gonna break her face	6
	She scared of me	7
	I'm just gonna fight her before I get out o' this school	8
	I'm just gonna grab her	9
	You watch	10
	I don't care where	11
	She scared	12
	She gonna learn how to fight . . .	13
	She'll learn to cry	14
	That's all	15
	[. . .] come to her face	16
	Bet you I'll come to her face . . .	17
T:	I never had a fight	18
W:	You wanta fight now?	19
	]	
T:	[laughter]	20

Conversations shifted easily from a volley of accusations between two disputants to a dispute over the accuracy of competing narrative versions of an event. Goodwin suggests that stories have the advantage of permitting all participants to engage in the discussion instead of only those who were parties to the dispute. The participants not immediately involved in the dispute could then support one version or the other. The implication of Goodwin's suggestion is that anyone can participate in a storytelling discussion, but only the disputants can make accusations. A significant distinction between accusations and stories is that accusations involve confrontations, whereas stories do not.[18] Goodwin discusses accusations as part of an utterance pair that includes questions and denials.

> The first pair part is viewed as "asking about something" in order to "get something straight." There is not, however, a particular term for this action. For purposes of discussion first pair parts which are followed by denials I will call "accusations"; . . . The accuser's action may be formulated in two different ways, as a request for information or as a declarative statement. The request for information references only the act of talking about the speaker, an activity known about by the hearer and unknown directly to the speaker. By way of contrast the declarative statement *informs* the defendant of something he does not know: that at a prior stage an intermediate party told the speaker about an act committed against her. (1978:434)

The adolescents' accusations, threats, and fight stories all used he-said–she-said forms, with different consequences. He-said–she-said accusations made references to narratives. They reported that one person told a story about another. The significant difference between he-said–she-said accusations and he-said–she-said stories was not in their form but in their use. The accusations were followed by counteraccusations or denials. Threats rarely got a response unless someone joined in the complaint or challenged the speaker in defense of the accused. The stories were followed by questions requesting elaboration or by second stories. All three could refer to absent speakers or addressees.[19] He-said–she-said accusations and threats often contained reports of he-said–she-said stories. In the story, one person told another about a third person. Alternatively, one person told another what a third person had said about him or her. In the accusation, the offended person confronted the accused person with a report of the offense.

In the adolescent communications, he-said–she-said accusations and narratives were also differentiated by their sources and presentation of information. He-said–she-said accusations revealed a statement and its source. Their purpose was to antagonize a relationship between two people. He-said–she-said narratives, in contrast, purported to be neutral. Nonneutrality would call their tellers into question. Narrators did not necessarily reveal their sources or specify what happened. Often they made the hostile relationship between listeners and tellers more explicit than the supposed original cause for the hostility. This was the case in Joan's narratives about her disputes with Mary.

Accusations, threats, and stories could be made either face-to-face or behind someone's back. Face-to-face accusations, in which one person charged another with an offense against him/herself, and face-to-face stories, or personal experience stories, in which a person told a story about him/herself, displayed relatively unquestionable entitlement.[20] Accusations, threats, and stories made the speaker vulnerable to challenges. Threats depended on a he-said–she-said report to the challenged person. Challenges made to he-said–she-said accusers most often concerned the accuracy of the accusation or the source of the speaker's information. The challenge concerned the substance of the accusation, not the speaker's right to make it. It was assumed that the accuser spoke in her or his own best interest, but in reporting an offense to the offended person, the mediator could have either the accused person's or the offended person's interest at heart. Any storytellers who told about events that they had witnessed or heard reported but that did not concern themselves were vulnerable to challenges of their entitlement to tell the story.

An additional distinction between stories, threats, and accusations concerns neither the substance of the account nor the identity of the speaker as a witness to or protagonist of the story, but the identity of the listeners. Accusers or conveyers of accusations were not challenged by the offender as long as they conveyed accusations directly to the offender. Storytellers were challenged for telling stories to people not directly involved. People who reported threats could easily be challenged for meddling and instigating, and instigators sometimes became participants in a fight. Accusations were justifiable because they conveyed information to people for whom the information was directly relevant. Storytellers were vulnerable because they conveyed information to people for whom the information was "none of their business."

The rules concerning who was entitled to tell and to hear episodes of a quarrel corresponded to the rules of privacy. The adolescents rigidly enforced the right to privacy, and although they often revealed details of family life in offhand stories, they never asked each other questions about such areas. Knowledge about private family affairs could easily be used as a weapon, and statements about someone's family, whether true or not, derogatory or not, were often perceived as insults or as invasions of privacy.

Details about family life were rarely shared by adolescents from different families. Friends rarely knew each other's religion; they rarely knew the relationships between people in each other's households; they did not know what someone else's parents did for a living; and they did not know each other's family plans for things such as travel or moving away from the neighborhood. Only the closest friends knew each other's phone numbers, and giving out a phone number without permission was cause for a fight. For example, one Puerto Rican girl told me that she was moving and asked me not to tell anyone. I asked her why it was a secret, and she said, "It's none of their business."

Although the adolescents constantly spread rumors about each other, details of family life were not the subject of rumor. The statement that someone was pregnant or that a boy and a girl were "messing around with each other" was an accusation made as a challenge for a fight, not a fact of interest to be shared. Rumors that girls were pregnant were spread constantly, but when a girl actually became pregnant, great care was taken to slow the spread of news.

For example, one eighth-grade Puerto Rican girl was absent from school for a long time. Her close friends talked about her having cut school without permission. None of them had seen her in the neighborhood or at the school, and they thought she must be going to an older sister's house every day without her parents' knowledge. One day when I was walking through the neighborhood with some of the girls' friends, we met the absent girl on the street. Her friends asked her where she had been and said, "Oh, you're gonna be in trouble when your mother finds out you haven't been in school. Mr. A [the teacher] was askin' about you." The girl told us that she had married her boyfriend and that she was going to have a baby. She said that the husband was nineteen years old and had a job, and he made her stay home all day. He wouldn't let her go to school anymore because he did not want to "hear about her messin' around." A few days later, some of the same girls from the classroom and two other girls were sitting in the school lunchroom. One of them mentioned that Luisa, the married girl, was lucky to be home having a baby. The next day, a rumor spread that an old friend of Luisa's was going to fight Leona, the girl who had "talked about Luisa." Leona was not entitled to talk about Luisa.

A white girl, Karen, who had been absent for a long time came back to school, and her friends asked her where she had been. (Absences from school often warranted stories.) She told her two closest friends (the others were not entitled to know) that she had been taken away from her father because he had locked her and a younger sister in his office in town every night, and they had no way to escape a fire. As an adult friend of Karen's, I was involved in the custody trial and learned many more details about the situation. One of the stories Karen never told concerned the way the authorities found out about her situation. It was a dramatic story and involved a transfer of information between various school authorities at her younger sister's school. The story was told among teachers at the school, but not among the adolescents. I asked Karen if she had told anyone about how the police found out where she was or if the story was a secret, and she said, "It's not a secret; it's not important."

For the adolescents, storytelling was not a means of gaining unlimited information about each other. When false accusations were made, they were simply denied, and little if any attention was given to substantiating the details reported in a narrative. The adolescents had very little knowledge of anything other than what they could see, and they based their narratives, accusations, and insults on what they witnessed and/or heard. They often stretched the limits of entitlement to include anything they saw or heard, and they accepted the challenge to fight as the consequence of having spoken about someone else's business or behind someone's back. Often problems of entitlement concerned a speaker's inadequate knowledge of the events she described.

Not all stories reporting complaints and accusations were subject to challenges of entitlement. The relationship between the form of talk and the storytelling situation, not the content or form of the talk alone, determined the appropriateness of a challenge. The following stories were told before school began in a special daily reading class with students who shared no school time outside of this class. The first storyteller was a white girl who was responding to another white girl's complaint about the police in her neighborhood. The second storyteller was the only black girl in the class. The teacher, a ratified listener but not explicitly an addressee, took part in the conversation, and her participation could be considered a further indication of the students' lack of concern about entitlement for these stories.

4

S:	If you're married they think it's a family problem	1
	It happened to me	2
	My mom and dad got in a fight	3
	The police came, they said they couldn't take him because	4
	He's coming in drunk all the time	5
	And the cops came	6
	They can't do nothing because it's a family problem	7
	But if she ain't married to him – but if they're not married – like my mom's living with somebody now?	8
	If he punches her or something or hurts her in any way	9
	She can get him put in jail	10
J:	Yeah	11
S:	They're not married, it's not a family problem	12
J:	Assault and battery	13
	He's six foot something	14
	Like if he makes her bleed, they would have to lock him up	15
	because he would hurt her bad	16

5

T:	Well, I'm going to tell about my sister and her boyfriend	1
	Really she was married but she had to divorce him	2
	Well, every Friday and Saturday, right, he'd get drunk	3
	and he come in there and start fighting her	4
	and she'd call my mother and tell my mother about it	5
	Like, last Friday	6
	she ain't staying at her house now	7
	She's staying with a friend of hers, cause her boyfriend she was staying with	8
	well, he got drunk, he be taking chairs and throwing them all around, you know	9

and they be fighting, you know, and he'd take chairs and thrown them down in the cellar	10
Friday, just passed, he took and turned off the lights, you know	11
so she can't come back in there and he turned the heat off	12
and everything so she ain't staying in her house	13
She's staying with somebody else	14
My sister's thirty some years old and she came from Georgia somewhere	15
And my mother cry and beg her not to move out with him	16
cause they had to stay with my mother for a while until they got their house	17
And you know he was beating her while he was staying with my mother?	18
My mother say he used to come in all hours of the night drunk	19
He used to crawl up the steps to get to bed	20

Tchr: What could your sister do?   21

T: She fighted him back, you know	22
but when she do that she doesn't even stay home	23
She be staying over one of her friend's now	24
She got three kids and got to put up with him	25
She said she went to City Hall but my mother said she don't think they can do anything	26
because she don't got no marriage papers	27
something	28
they ain't married	29
You should see her house, the way he tore it up	30
My sister didn't get her house together	31
She just moved up to Livingston	32
and her house is right at the corner	33
She got a nice house for him to be messing up everything	34
I mean she got leather furniture and couch and stuff	35
It's big and she got a whole lot of furniture in there	36
for him to be doing that	37
Even her son	38
he just turned nineteen or eighteen	39
he help pay rent and stuff	40
because he working	41
He plays on a basketball team	42
He help get them money to pay rent and stuff	43
Her little daughter just eight years old and	44
she be so nervous because every night	45
they get into a [. . .]	46
My mother she said she going to try to get somebody to go up there	47
and try to straighten him out	48
cause she said that's her daughter	49
and she told him whatever he do	50
try not to hurt her because that's my mother's child	51

So something about he be lying to the people	52
so he can get checks	53
and stuff like that	54
My mother said she should go up there	55
and tell them about something	56
so they can take him off his job	57
and my mother said she be glad when he get his car out of the shop	58
so she can get somebody to go over there and steal it	59

The preceding stories include many accusations of the kind that fostered fights when told about people familiar to the listeners. Since neither Shelley's father, whom she accused of hurting her mother, nor the police, whom Shelley accused of "doing nothing," nor Tanya's sister's boyfriend, whom Tanya accused of destroying furniture, turning off the utilities, and lying, were familiar to the students or teacher who heard the stories, there was little chance that either Shelley or Tanya would be accused of having told stories they were not entitled to tell. In this case, the tellers, listeners, and accused did not have a day-to-day association.

The telling of the stories in the classroom creates two problems. First, these are just the kinds of stories that fostered fights when adolescents told them to each other about each other. Second, the substance of the stories, family problems, were the cause of insults when one adolescent spoke about another's family. The stories told by Shelley and Tanya were invasions of privacy, except that they were provided by the family members themselves. In the absence of a relationship between either of the girl's families and the members of the class and myself, who heard the stories, the narratives could be considered first-person accounts about one's family, rather than stories told behind someone's back and therefore susceptible to challenges of entitlement. The listeners, tellers, and accused were not part of the same social network, and the story did not serve to bring them any closer together. The stories did not demand any reply by the listeners of any retaliation or efforts to clear one's name by the accused.

1.5 Fight sequences

The supposed fights, consisting of verbal disputes that alluded to, but did not necessarily include, physical disputes, may be seen as a ritual exchange involving conventional behavior. The first part of the sequence, the offenses, are examples of what Emmanuel Schegloff and Harvey Sacks call "adjacency pairs," sets of acts that accompany each other, the first evoking the second.

> Briefly, the adjacency pairs consist of sequences which properly have the following features: (1) two-utterance length, (2) adjacent positioning of component utterances, (3) different speakers producing each utterance, (4) relative ordering of parts, i.e., first pair parts

precede second pair parts and (5) discriminative relations (i.e., the pair type of which a first pair part is a member is relevant to the selection among second pair parts). (Schegloff and Sacks 1973:295)

An offense, for instance, was properly followed by an apology. The adolescents played on this expectation. They interpreted accidental offenses as intentional and then demanded apologies, or they intentionally committed minor offenses and then refused to apologize. Aggressive demands for apologies (which the adults in the school considered to be as rude as the offense) were justified by the offense, according to the adolescent system. The adolescents turned the system for making amends into a system of retaliation.

Offenses were more often imputed than intended. For example, in another version of her fight with Mary, Joan insisted that Mary had intentionally started a fight.

6

J:	Well it was like me and her, right	1
	were just walkin'	2
	and she shoved me	3
	and I started pushin' her	4
	I says you play too much	5
	and then she started getting real rough with me after I turned around	6
	and I punched her in the teeth	7

The beginnings of fights were most often constructed and contrived retrospectively, and much of the discussions about fights concerned how they began. Part of the offense stage of a fight usually involved talk about offenses. Further, fights rarely began spontaneously, but rather followed a period of time in which a warning was issued or forces were rallied. Some of the warnings included "stop messing with me," "I'm going to beat you up," "I'm going to beat you up after school," or "I told him if he do it again, I'm gonna punch him in the face." Rallying forces usually meant finding an ally, often a relative, who was better suited for a fight in terms of either age or gender. When girls and boys fought with each other, girls often threatened to get a brother to fight the boy. For example: "Carlos was messing with Marla and Marla went to tell her brother." "I told him if he keeps it up I was going to get my cousin on him." The following boy's story describes the more exaggerated rallying of forces in gang fights:

7

M:	Danny threw a rock at the car passing?	1
	The rock missed the car and hit a boy on the head	2
	We thought it was a young boy but it was a rat	3
	one of the gangs called the rats	4
	So he got his gang and we got ours	5
	So there was the biggest fight I ever saw . . .	6

The offense stage of the fight involved different kinds of claims than any other stage of the fight. The offense was the rationale for the fight. Among girls, the offense claim was always that someone was victimized, that someone was messing with her, or that she did not want to fight but had no choice but to retaliate. The reasons for people to be messing with each other in the first place were rarely mentioned, but in talking about fights in general or about people who got into a lot of fights, the adolescents said that some people "showed off," so other people "messed with them." Showing off was the main complaint that led to messing with someone, but the adolescents rarely confronted each other with this charge. A common justification for a fight, among both girls and boys, was that someone said something about one's family or specifically about one's mother. Often "your mother" was sufficient comment to start a fight. Here again, this was the justification for feeling victimized, and does not explain why the two people were in conflict in the first place. Comments about one's mother did not imply that someone knew something about one's family; the comments were not invasions of privacy that would reveal a source of knowledge. The statement that someone said something about someone else's mother was always made by the person claiming to be a victim; in the fights between people who knew each other, both claimed to be the victim. In actuality, the beginning of a fight was difficult to determine, for the fine line between playing around and messing with someone was not drawn.

Offenses demanded apologies. Stories about offenses often foretold retaliations. Since offenses were not always clear, but were constituted retrospectively in discussions, the chance to apologize rarely occurred. Usually what happened was that a person heard from another person that he or she had committed an offense. The accused claimed to be innocent or to be justified in retaliating for an earlier offense. People then fought over the disagreements about the offense rather than about the offense itself. The accused person claimed that she had been unjustly accused, and this was the basis for her claim that she was the victim rather than the aggressor.

The structure involved a three-way relationship between narrative and event. "Events" here refer to the offenses, confrontations, and fights. The reporting of events is itself an event, and a purpose of the Figure 1.1 is to show how the situation of reporting is itself reported as an offense (one kind of event). Reports of events are essential to the system. Another purpose of the figure is to illustrate how it is possible to have a fight story without a fight. The reports are listed in the order in which they occur, but not all parts occur in actual interactions, and rather than proceed sequentially, more often the reports return to the beginning or to an earlier stage several times before a resolution occurs. Thus a third purpose of the figure is to illustrate the linearity and circularity of the system. The adolescents acted as if there were no alternatives to their acts. (In the figure, more than one arrow leading from a

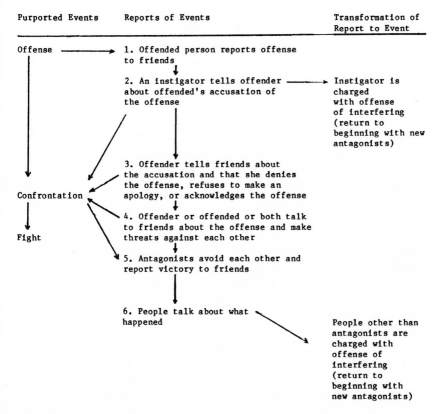

Purported Events	Reports of Events	Transformation of Report to Event

Offense ⟶ 1. Offended person reports offense to friends

2. An instigator tells offender ⟶ Instigator is about offended's accusation of charged the offense with offense of interfering (return to beginning with new antagonists)

3. Offender tells friends about the accusation and that she denies the offense, refuses to make an Confrontation apology, or acknowledges the offense

Fight 4. Offender or offended or both talk to friends about the offense and make threats against each other

5. Antagonists avoid each other and report victory to friends

6. People talk about what happened People other than antagonists are charged with offense of interfering (return to beginning with new antagonists)

Figure 1.1 Fight sequence.

point in the sequence indicates multiple alternatives.) Although the adolescents did not draw strategies from a list of alternative responses, but instead considered offenses, accusations, and threats to have inevitable consequences, they did attempt to manipulate situations.

The linear sequence was most disrupted, the confrontation most easily derailed, by the transformation from report to event. When someone other than an antagonist reported an event to another person, the reporter, here termed "instigator," could be challenged for offending one of the antagonists by meddling. In this case, the sequence returned to the beginning, to a new offense between new antagonists.

The virtue of Figure 1.1 is that it preserves the distinction between reports and events while admitting that reports, too, are events and can have the same consequences as other kinds of events. Further, the figure reveals the linear sequence of fights as presented in the stories and does not presume to identify the linear sequence of the experience of fighting. (The figure focuses on how experience is rendered as a linear structure in stories.) Since the fight stories did not present every part of a sequence of events, but rather relied on the listeners to infer the missing pieces from their understanding of the system, the last purpose of the figure is to provide a complete linear sequence as a contextual framework for any narrative.

The physical fight rarely occurred. It was often threatened and was often discussed as though it had happened. In some cases, it was fabricated and described later. But the kind of information described allowed the dissemination of stories about fights that never came to blows.

The adolescent stories were told at different stages of the dispute. Most studies of oral narratives, especially those that rely upon oral history, discuss stories told sometime after the event purportedly took place. Although narrative necessarily refers to a time other than the present, the distance between the current situation and the narrated one can vary from the immediate to the remote past. Further, stories may refer to episodes of ongoing experiences that are current and resolved. Stories that refer to completed events offer a relatively uncomplicated relationship between story and experiences, in contrast to those that refer to ongoing events with both past and future episodes.

Much of what we know about stories concerns those about resolved past events.[21] The structure of the story, the explanations of unfamiliar people or places needed to make it intelligible, and the justifications for telling it are all dependent on the relationship between the story and the completed past events. The examination of stories told at different points in an ongoing experience reveals different patterns of explanation, different justifications of entitlement, and different assessments of the value of the story.

1.6   Stories told at the beginning of a dispute

The following story is embedded in a conversation about a fight. The brief story, which recounts a dispute over potato chips, was told minutes after the incident occurred. It was told within earshot of someone who could potentially get involved in an elaborated dispute (the accused's alleged girl friend), but was addressed to someone who had no particular interest in the incident. The story was told not for its intrinsic interest but as an explanation of the claim that there would be a fight.

8

R:	Me and her boyfriend gonna fight	1
	Cause I was sittin' over on the table	2
	Eatin' my potato chips	3
RS:	I don't go w' him	4
R:	And he asked for some, right	5
	I'm givin' him some	6

	I took 'em outa the bag	7
	and he walked past and smacked 'em outa my hand	8
	and I told him if he do it again	9
	I'm gonna punch him in the face	10
E:	And that's how it happened?	11
R:	And then he said	12
	if I punch him in his face	13
	he was gonna stab me, right	14
	and I told him if he do that	15
	he'd better never come to school	16
	then he just walked away	17

This story was told in the school lunchroom. Robert, the narrator, told it to Elena, an acquaintance, within earshot of Rose, a girl who spent a lot of time with both Robert and Allen, Rose's alleged boyfriend. Rose disavowed her relationship with Allen at the beginning of the story, and she turned away from Robert and offered no further comments. Robert's audience, however, continued potentially to include Rose, who, as Allen's alleged girlfriend, might report Robert's story to Allen. In his story, Robert described himself as a victim of Allen's offenses. Robert had both the right and the responsibility to retaliate for Allen's offenses. He did not necessarily have to retaliate, but he had to demonstrate his willingness to stand up for himself. "If he do it again, I'm gonna punch him in the face" was both a defensive and an offensive statement. If Rose had reported the story to Allen, a larger dispute might have developed. Rose, however, ignored Robert's remarks and said nothing to Allen, and the two boys resumed their friendship. Similar stories were told everyday about minor offenses that could have developed into disputes. The stories were an important part of this development. Although Robert's narrative reports a dialogue, it is not strictly a he-said–she-said story. Robert quoted his own speech, but he referred to Allen's request for potato chips without quoting Allen's words, and he used the third person to report Allen's threat to stab him. If Rose had reported Robert's story to Allen, her story would have been a he-said–she-said story.

Joan's oral narrative 1 was similarly told following an initial offense but before a dispute occurred. Joan's story was an assertion of her intention to continue the dispute. One of her friends told me that Joan was using her fight with Mary as an excuse to cut school. The friend said that Joan liked to leave school after lunch and that if she told her mother that Mary was bothering her, her mother would let her stay home. She had been going home after lunch for a while before her mother found out, but then her mother had asked the principal to call her at work and tell her whether Joan was in school. It is unlikely that Joan's dispute was so premeditated, but it is possible that she fabricated her account of being jumped by black girls in order to create a legitimate excuse to stay home. At this stage of the ongoing experience, after a minor offense, stories were often used to set the stage for an elaborated dispute.

Stories told at the beginning of a dispute were characterized by currency, first-person narration rather than a retelling of someone else's account, presentation of the heroine as a victim, and allusion to unfinished business, usually in the form of retaliation for minor offenses. Currency, the temporal proximity of the narrative to the incident described, was essential for the purposes of the story. Stories about minor offenses were told to set the stage for an elaborated dispute or to make it clear that a victim of a minor offense would not stand for repeated offenses. The story had to be told soon after the offense and in the company of people who knew both the victim and the offender. The stories concerned unretaliated offenses, and the stories were the first and sometimes the only step toward retaliation. The story was not relevant if the offense was not current. The stories were told by the person who made claims to retaliate. Although this person was not necessarily the victim, the narrator had to be the person who was speaking for the victim and who threatened retaliation.

Stories told by third parties or witnesses involved different sorts of claims. The person who threatened to retaliate claimed that an offense had been committed and that retaliation was in order. Third parties often reported only the retaliation, not the offense. The third-party narrators did not necessarily present the avenger as a victim; persons threatening retaliation always did.

The point of the stories told at the beginning of a potential dispute was to assert the possibility of the dispute; the offense was presented as a piece of unfinished business, and the point of the story was to announce a threat. Often this announcement sufficed to resolve the differences between the victim and the offender. If the offender avoided the victim, the victim could claim that the threat had been heeded.

The offenses described in the stories were often minor insults. The storytellers made little attempt to exaggerate the extent of the offense, but at this stage of the potential dispute they did not present the offense as trivial or trifling.

1.7 He-said–she-said: stories told at the height of a dispute

He-said–she-said stories occurred at the height of a dispute. In fact, the height of a dispute could be defined in terms of the amount of talk about the dispute by people who were not direct combatants. Goodwin reports:

> The he-said–she-said phenomena constitute procedures for making a relevant scene available to coparticipants. (1978:72)

He-said–she-said stories enlarged the audience for the story and, at the same time, enlarged the audience for the dispute. They turned attention away from the offense and toward the fight challenge. They raised expectations about a potential fight. Often they raised the expectations of the disputants as well as those of the witnesses and listeners. The he-said–she-said stories turned listeners, those who heard the account, into witnesses of the potential fight. Often in this period of the ongoing dispute, listeners chose sides and aligned themselves with one of the disputants.

It is important to point out that neither the account of the offense nor the he-said–she-said accusations were necessarily in narrative form. They might consist of single-phrase remarks. However, most often they were reported in narrative form. The narrative form had particular importance for the ongoing dispute since it posited a sequence of events, not merely the events themselves isolated from the chronology. The chronology was an essential part of the dispute, and tellers were careful to insist upon their version of what happened first. The beginning of the dispute was almost always undefined or difficult to identify, and the witnesses' justifications for aligning with one side rather than another usually rested on a particular version of how the dispute started.

Whereas reports of offenses told at the beginning of a dispute were part of a threatened retaliation, those told during ongoing disputes became negotiated realities. The roles of victim and aggressor shifted, depending on which offenses were recounted. In the ongoing dispute, new supposed offenses could become the motivation for new ways of constructing events.

The adolescents recognized that the he-said–she-said stories often intensified the dispute, and they often blamed the storytellers, rather than the initial offender claimed by the victim, for creating the dispute. The stories told at the beginning of a dispute by the victim about a minor offense were not a necessary part of the fight, but very few fights continued without he-said–she-said stories. Of course, some physical fights began spontaneously without the instigation of third parties, but when such fights were recounted as stories, they were considered the initial offense, and he-said–she-said stories were told about who started them.

The difficulty with the he-said–she-said narrative stage of the dispute is that the relationship between the event and the story is ambiguous. It is uncertain whether the offenses were actually committed as reported, and often conflicting versions of the story or inconsistencies in a person's narrative challenged its accuracy. The stories were rarely if ever challenged for their factuality, and they were told whether or not a past offense had been committed or a future fight was at all certain. Such stories existed independently of the events they described and forecasted, but they depended upon the likelihood of both the initial offenses and the future fights.

The uncertainty concerning the actuality of the events gives the stories the status of rumors. Stories that are rumors have special qualities of entitlement and effect. Most obviously, rumors can be challenged for their accuracy. However, among the adolescents, challenges of stories as rumors usually concerned the right of the storyteller to tell the story. Challenges to entitlement turned the telling of a story about someone else's offense into an offense itself. This was the pivotal moment in the use of narratives in ongoing disputes, for at this point the initial offense and the initial disputants could be forgotten, and attention could turn instead to the people discussed in the stories as victims (who might be the original offenders) and to the storyteller as the offender. The adolescents recognized he-said–she-said stories as instigators of fights. Such stories were sometimes perceived as statements of alliance and at other times as instigations for unwanted disputes. In neither case was the accuracy of the story disputed; rather, judgment was based on the potential effect of the telling.

Following is an account of a rumor that instigated a fight. The story was told by Rose, one of the fighters, after the fight but referred to the rumors that preceded it.

9

R:	Ginger and Allen were talking	1
	And Ginger said, "I better not be around you	2
	or Rose will get in my face"	3
	Mary said, "If Rose is bothering you	4
	I'll kick her ass"	5
	So people started saying that Mary wanted to fight me	6
	So I went up to her	7
	and said,	8
	"I hear you want to fight me"	9
	And she said she didn't say that	10
	and that if she wanted to fight me she'd tell me personally	11
	That's when she slugged me	12

Rose's story refers to a discussion between Ginger and Allen as the basis for a later fight. According to Rose, who was not present at the discussion, Ginger admitted that she should not be talking to Allen, who was Rose's boyfriend. Among the adolescents, "talking to" a person of the opposite sex meant flirting.[22] The statement "Rose will get in my face" meant that Rose would start a fight to retaliate for Ginger's having talked with Allen. The potential fight between Ginger and Rose never materialized, and instead rumors spread that Mary said she wanted to fight Rose. Finally, when confronted, Mary denied that she would talk behind Rose's back about wanting to fight her.

Rose's account reports a typical dispute sequence. The first offense was caused by Ginger, who talked to Allen. Ginger allegedly admitted her offense and Mary, who either was present during the talk or heard about it later, said that she would retaliate if Rose bothered Ginger. The potential dispute between Rose and Ginger was never substantiated, and the possibility that Ginger flirted with Allen became unimportant, except as a basis for the dispute between Rose and Mary. Mary's involvement began as an alliance with Ginger against Rose, but Ginger dropped out of the dispute (if she was ever in it), which focused on Mary and Rose.

Mary understood Rose's statement, "I hear you want to fight me," as a challenge, regardless of its accuracy. Mary had to back up what people said about her on two counts. First, and most obviously, she had to back up her alleged willingness to fight Rose, whether or not she had said she wanted to fight. This was not a matter of being held to one's word but of being willing to fight in general.[23]

Mary also had to counter the charge that she had meddled in Rose and Ginger's business. Talking about people behind their backs was grounds for fighting, and Mary had not only talked about Rose, she had supposedly threatened her behind her back. Stories told at the height of a dispute often shifted the focus from the offense to other participants, including intermediaries such as Mary. In particular, he-said–she-said accounts could themselves be considered offenses and their tellers could be accused of meddling. Talk about offenses was itself an offense and was understood as a challenge to fight. The narrative mode was particularly important to this shift, since narrative attaches significance to chronology and suggests that the order in which things happened is important.[24]

The use of reported speech in he-said–she-said narratives is an important factor in the potential designation of the narrative as an offense. Narratives that repeat a challenge in the challenger's words are substantially different from those that describe an offense. Stories told by an offended person at the beginning of a dispute emphasize specific offenses; stories told at the height of a dispute focus on the participants and their aggression rather than on the original offenses. In both stages, the narrative form is important for asserting a sequence of actions that require further actions. The narrative form relies upon an if–then sequence in which one action is interpreted in terms of a previous action and in which an action sets the stage for further actions. The entire dispute framework of the adolescent world is predicated upon if–then sequences that are articulated in narrative. People fought because previous actions required a fight. In both the offense stage and the he-said–she-said stage, the subject of stories was current, and the people who listened or were within earshot of the teller were potential participants in the dispute, either as disputants, as instigators, or as mediators. The stories were told either to clear a reputation or to defend oneself in the face of an offense. In many cases, simply telling the story was sufficient to earn the desired reputation; in others, the threats stated in the account had to be carried out.

1.8   Stories told after a dispute was resolved

Stories told after a dispute was resolved had different purposes, rationales, explanatory devices, and justifications of entitlement. William Labov's statements concerning the evaluative point of a story refer to such stories. As Labov states,

> That is what we term the *evaluation* of the narrative: the means used by the narrator to indicate the point of the narrative, its raison d'etre: why it was told, and what the narrator is getting at. There are many ways to tell the same story, to make very different points, or to make no point at all. Pointless stories are met (in English) with the withering rejoinder, "So what?" Every good narrator is continually warding off this question; when his narrative is over, it should be unthinkable for a bystander to say "So what?" Instead the appropriate remark would be, "He did?" or similar means of registering the reportable character of the events of the narrative. (1972:366)

The point of stories told after a dispute was resolved was to document an important event or to establish the importance of a person. Such stories were not necessarily told to people familiar with the incident. In any case, whether or not the people were familiar with the incident, the significance of stories told after a dispute was resolved was not a matter of currency or immediate relevance to the listeners, but, as Labov suggests, had to be demonstrated in the telling. The stories told at the beginning of a dispute often reported a minor offense, and the storyteller rarely made any attempt to exaggerate the extent of the offense or make it seem more important. Similarly, when the offense was reported in stories told at the end of a dispute, it could be reported without exaggeration, but often the triviality of the offense was specifically mentioned. The following account of Mary and Rose's fight, told by Stacie, focused not on the quarrel but on the basis for it.

10

S:	Mary wanted to fight Rose so bad –	1
	she wanted to fight her so bad	2
	Mary was jealous of her	3
	that's what I think	4
K:	Do they like the same boy	5
S:	They both like Allen	6
	but Mary likes him for a friend	7
	Rose likes him for a boyfriend, um	8
	Mary she tells um Lewis things about him	9
	Cause that's Rose's boyfriend	10
	She tells things that Mary – Rose – do with Allen	11
	She tell her boyfriend –	12
	Mary tell Rose' boyfriend	13

If I was Allen I wouldn't go with neither one them 14
Cause they act dumb – 15
They act dumb . . . 16

Stacie's account (oral narrative 10) was not strictly a narrative. It described a situation rather than a chronology, using the present tense to describe general activities: "Mary she tells um Lewis things about him . . . Mary tell Rose' boyfriend." Stacie dissolved the offense–retaliation sequence into a general malaise. She described the situation preceding the fight not in terms of a particular offense followed by an expected retaliation but in terms of the attitudes of both parties to the dispute. "They both act dumb." According to Stacie, Mary wanted to fight Rose, and she used whatever offense she could find as an excuse. Stacie's statements could have been challenged as an offense on several grounds. She could have been challenged for implying that she was better than other people, that she wouldn't act so "dumb." She could also have been challenged for specifically insulting Rose and Mary or for interfering in their business. However, Stacie was not challenged, although she made her remarks publicly among a group of students who ate their lunch in an open classroom. Since Stacie did not speak about specific incidents, she could not be challenged for saying things that were not accurate, except that she said that Mary wanted to fight Rose. However, even this statement was general and did not refer to a specific statement made by Mary. In fact, Stacie's account did not quote anyone. Although her opinionated comments might have made her the target of a dispute, the form of the comments, as a general statement told about a resolved situation rather than a narrative of he-said–she-said threats, protected her somewhat from liability.

Labov does not make the distinction between stories told following a dispute and those told during a dispute, but in collecting the stories, he and his field workers specifically requested stories about prior experiences.

> "What was the most important fight that you remember, one that sticks in your mind . . ." (1972:358)
> "You ever been in a situation where you thought you were gonna get killed?" (1972:361)
> "Were you ever in a situation where you were in serious danger of being killed?" (1972:363)

Labov states that evaluative clauses articulate the point of the story and that one can discriminate between reportable stories or those with a point, and pointless stories of vicarious rather than firsthand experience, by the presence or absence of evaluation (1972:366–7). The implication of Labov's statements is that the tellability or reportability of a story about experience (he is not discussing fairy tales or intentionally fictional stories) is determined, at least in part, by whether or not it is told as a firsthand experience and by whether or not it includes evaluation. Two questions arise: First, what is the bearing of Labov's model on stories told during a dispute rather than following its resolution? Second, is the implied relationship between vicarious experience stories and nonreportability necessary or merely illustrative in Labov's discussion? Both questions concern the relationship between stories and the experiences they describe.

Stories told during an ongoing dispute often reported a sequence of what happened without evaluative phrases. (Consider oral narrative 8 about the dispute over potato chips.) Yet the stories clearly identified the teller as a victim of some offense. The stories offered evaluation in the form of implied social imperatives.

Stacie's discussion of Mary and Rose's fight (oral narrative 10) provided only explicit evaluation and omitted details about the fight itself.

(10)

S	that's what I think	4
	they act dumb	16

In telling a story told after the fight was resolved, Stacie was less interested in describing what happened than in presenting her opinion of the participants and their behavior. Her remarks could easily have fostered a new quarrel, and she was not really entitled to make them.

Stories told following the resolution of a conflict were often recounted to people removed from the situation described. When the situations had no direct consequences for the listeners, entitlement was less likely to be challenged. In contrast, stories told during an ongoing dispute often had immediate consequences for both the listeners and the tellers. These consequences included a possible fight, a challenge to the listeners to align themselves with a particular disputant, or a challenge to the teller for meddling in someone else's business or instigating a quarrel. The consequences of nonreportability in stories without evaluation, as Labov states, is the statement "So what?" Labov suggests that one type of story that evokes the "So what?" response is the vicarious experience story. Labov's example is the account of a television program, but vicarious experience stories can include any story about someone else's experience. They can include the stories adolescents tell about each other's fights; in other words, they can include rumors. Rumor, especially when it involves trivial incidents, can be challenged by the "So what?" response. After all, this response is essentially a comment on the triviality of the story. However, the adolescents' accounts of trivial offenses were rarely met with the "So what?" response by other adolescents (though they were frequently so received by adults). Instead, these stories were the basis for elaborated interaction between tellers and listeners, and the basis or excuse for major conflicts. Stories that might be considered trivial if told long after a dispute was resolved (that is, stories about someone else's minor offenses) met the most opposition when told during ongoing disputes. Instead of the response "So what?", such stories told during a dispute were often met with "Who says?", which was a challenge not to the interest or importance of the story, but to the entitlement of the teller to recount it.

The issue in Labov's model of evaluation in narrative is the balance between the importance attributed to the intrinsically interesting content as structured by the story and the importance attributed to the telling of a story in particular circumstances. As Jonathon Culler said in a discussion of Labov's model,

> The question of whether any given story is being told primarily in order to report a sequence of events or in order to tell a tellable story is of course difficult to decide, but the ethical and referential lure of stories makes listeners want to decide (is that the way it really happened or is he just trying to impress us?). Labov avoids this question, either because he thinks it makes no difference to his analysis or because he thinks that the two projects can and should coincide, evaluative clauses being added to narrative clauses to produce a good story. (1980:36)

In stories told during an ongoing dispute, the question of the report's accuracy was ever-present, yet direct challenges were rare. The point of the story was not necessarily the incident described (the minor offenses), and in retellings, as a dispute was elaborated, the focus often shifted from the offenses to the participants (i.e., from an account of an offense to a he-said–she-said account). The significance of the telling often took precedence over that of the events described. As Culler says, "For any report of an action there is always the possibility that it should be thought of as evaluative, as determined by requirements of significance, rather than as a representation of a given event" (1980:36).

In the stories told about resolved past disputes, the evaluation was often articulated and trivial offenses were often identified as such. In stories told during ongoing disputes, the evaluations were often provided by listeners. Whereas "So what?" statements indicate a lack of sufficient justification of tellability in the accounts of resolved disputes, "Who says?" statements can be considered as evaluative statements that are part of the story. In the investigation of stories told during ongoing disputes, it is especially important to consider the listeners' responses essential to the storytelling. Some of the listeners' responses included statements such as "That's cold-blooded" or "Ooh, she ba-ad." In stories told about resolved past disputes, the question "And then what?" could indicate that either the story or the resolution was unsatisfying. In stories told during ongoing disputes, questions such as "And then what?" or "What happened then?" or "What you gonna do?" referred to expected responses to actions. In stories about past resolved fights, the beginning and end were supplied by the story; in stories told during ongoing disputes, the story was often one piece of the sequence of events; the story itself was an event that followed certain actions and precipitated others. This may be seen as a special case of a phenomenon of all storytelling: The telling is itself a part of the ongoing behavior. Stories about ongoing disputes are a special case insofar as the participants and concerns of the story and of the storytelling occasion may be indistinguishable. In such cases, explicit narrative evaluation is not essential, since tellers and listeners presumably share recognizable interests, and no one can ask, "So what?" Implied in the preceding discussion of the relationship between disputes and stories is the notion that in ongoing disputes, fights and narratives have a deterministic relationship. The fight sequence, including narratives about the fight, can be said to be determined in the sense that utterance pairs or adjacency pairs are determined. The order is predetermined, but the response to a behavior is a matter of social expectations rather than social imperatives. Although Labov may be accurate in suggesting that storytellers attempt to avoid the "So what?" response to their stories, few listeners actually say "So what?" to a pointless story, except to offer a bigger claim, such as "So what? My dad gets a new car *every* year." Listeners have various ways of assessing stories, and in the case of stories about ongoing experience, "So what?" is rarely a viable option. (However, Labov's point does not focus on the accuracy of "So what?" as a listener response; his larger concern is the reportability or tellability of stories.)

1.9 Summary: the transformation of experience and narrative

The conventions for narrating experience in the adolescent community relied upon shared understandings and prior expectations concerning the category of experience that was narrated (fighting) and upon shared understandings concerning the entitlement to talk about a particular experience. The adolescents were so familiar with fighting as a category of both experience and narrative that they often omitted details that they took for granted. Also, what was considered relevant in a telling changed as concern shifted from the account to the entitlement. Acceptance of an account rested on conformity to conventions for recounting events. The adolescent narrators were constantly monitored by their listeners. When a story was challenged as a lie, the challenge was directed not only at the content of the events described but also at the right of the narrator to the information it contained and to the propriety of the telling. In the adolescent world, the exchange of stories was part of a larger continual battle of wits. The stories were about quarrels, and storytelling itself involved quarreling. The events described were often illusory; the stories were about what almost happened; they were often told to make mountains out of molehills.

The stories were told as part of conversations; the responses of listeners were interjected conversationally as expected interruptions; and the stories themselves were filled with dialogue or reported conversations that replayed the event. However, the adolescent conversational stories, close as they were to actual experience, are a reminder that stories are not duplications of events, since the participants constantly reminded each other that talking about events involves more than knowing what happened. If, as Harvey Sacks said, people are the custodians of only their own experiences, then storytelling demonstrates the proprieties for maintaining and exchanging custody. The adolescents had custody over very little except their bodies and their words; storytelling offered them a way to fight without exchanging blows. They fought over who said what to whom, and these quarrels were elaborated into blow-by-blow accounts of fights in which blows were rarely exchanged. Their tales of ongoing rather than resolved disputes display more process than product. As Chapters 3 and 4 will demonstrate, the adolescents' writings were similarly concerned with the ongoing process of negotiating both the authority and entitlement of addressors and addressees and the interpretation of events.

2
STORYABILITY AND TELLABILITY

Whereas storyability (what gets told as a story) concerns seemingly unlimited possibilities for the content of stories, tellability (who has the right to tell a story) concerns limitations or prohibitions on telling. Tellability is potentially limited by concerns for discretion, sanctions against invasion of privacy, promises of secrecy, and discouragement of immodesty. The adolescents were particularly concerned with these limitations and focused more concern on whether a person had violated the unstated prohibitions in telling a story than on whether the story was good. Their evaluations focused on entitlement more than on the amplification of the incidents described. This focus was safer from challenges of exaggeration or inaccuracy and, in addition, redirected attention from the incidents to the current storytelling situation.

Storyability is most often evaluated retrospectively, although categories of storyable events may exist prior to individual instances of them. Further, people may engage in certain behaviors with a prior awareness that their behaviors belong to a certain category. People sometimes play out behaviors as though in a script, and they may announce, while in the midst of an activity, their intention to report the experience to others. The statement ''Just wait till I tell my friends about this'' acknowledges that the experience is storyable. In contrast, some events may not be appropriately told as stories.

Storyability and tellability are concepts that most often arise in discussions of oral narrative since they both concern relationships between text and context, a concern central to oral communication and not always considered in the examination of written texts. However, storyability and tellability can be restated as ways of understanding the distance between teller and audience and the related distance between the characters in a story and the participants (readers, listeners, tellers, narrators, authors) in a storytelling situation. This distance is as central to written narratives as it is to oral ones. Speaking and writing do not necessarily share the same assessments of what makes a subject storyable, but both channels have means for asserting that a story is worth hearing or reading and for distinguishing between different storyable functions, such as the newsworthy or the exotic. Writing often escapes assessments of tellability, since the reader has the prerogative to put down the book, but writers nevertheless make claims of authority, just as speakers assert that they have a privileged relationship to the experiences they recount.

On the surface, the concept of storyability seems to be a simple matter of noteworthiness.[1] However, not all storyable experiences are tellable, and this discrepancy raises some important issues for the relationship between stories and events. These include the following:

1. the difference between mediate and immediate stories;
2. the difference between newsworthy information and tellable experiences, a distinction I have termed the difference between the reportable and the repeatable; and
3. the consequences of the differences between mediacy and immediacy, storyable and tellable, reportable and repeatable, for understanding differences between writing and speaking.

2.1 Mediate and immediate storytelling

The terms "mediate" and "immediate" are borrowed from Alfred Schutz's discussion of multiple realities.[2] According to Schutz, immediacy is "the fundamental characteristic of all actual experience, of experiencing, immediacy is spatial and temporal; here and now" (1970:318). However, "We interpret both our own behavior and that of others within contexts of meaning that far transcend the immediate here and now" (1970:220). Schutz applies the mediate–immediate contrast to how people come to know each other, whether through "indirect social experiences," including the experience of cultural objects, institutions, and conventions, or through "the direct mode of apprehension" (1970:224).

If the distinction between mediate and immediate is applied to storytelling, and in particular to the relationship between the events described in a story and the events going on at the time of the storytelling occasion, then a mediate relationship presents stories as stored over a long period of time, as part of a storyteller's repertoire. The stories and the occasions on which they are told may have several possible mediated relationships. The topic of the story, the identity of the storyteller and his or her relationship to the listeners, and the concerns of the occasion are all part of the connection between the story and the occasion. In contrast, in an immediate relationship, a story and the occasion on which it is told are explicitly connected such that the story is *about* the current occasion. In immediate relationships, stories are presented as unresolved, and the situations in which they are told are made part of the ongoing unresolved situation. Such situations may lead either to further conflict or to resolution, and the interactions of the storytelling situation determine, in part, the direction of the resolution or conflict. In mediate relationships, stories are often presented as past resolved events, or, in any case, the storytelling occasion is not the same as the resolution of the events. In immediate relationships, the stories are current and contemporary with the ongoing situations in which they are told.

The distinction between mediate and immediate relationships (between stories and storytelling situations) involves issues similar to those raised in Schutz's discussion of mediate and immediate relationships between people. The central issue is how people come to know and share understandings and how they use their knowledge in particular situations. Schutz discusses this as a matter of direct versus indirect means of establishing connections between people. In a sense, it is a matter of networks. For Schutz, mediate networks involve an intermediary; immediate connections do not. Similarly, in terms of stories, shared understandings depend on the accessibility of the "realities" described, and ultimately, this is a matter of the proximity of the reality described to the current reality of the storytelling situation. Proximity may be temporally and spatially immediate or it may be a mediated connection. The relationship between mediacy and immediacy, whether applied to social connections between people or to storytelling situations, focuses attention on the problem of the verification of communication.

Veracity is a complicated issue in narrative scholarship because the "truthfulness" of a story depends upon whether people challenge or accept it, as well as on the grounds on which they base their challenges. Among the adolescents, the veracity of stories was frequently challenged, and tellers often asked for the support of one of their listeners while they told a story. For example:

11

D:	And JW here was there	1
	He saw what happened	2
J:	You never fight	3
L:	I was in a fight, right	4
	Wasn't I in a fight, Diane	5

In the absence of a witness as a listener, tellers often reported the identities of witnesses. For example:

12

S:	The whole class heard it

Challenges to veracity did not necessarily occur as interruptions or comments immediately following a story. Often they were asserted in later conversations between the teller and someone who had heard the story from a listener.

13

J:	I heard about you tellin' lies	1
M:	I don't tell no lies	2
J:	You tell lies about you fight with my sister	3

Such challenges can be seen as metastatements that have relevance both for the story and for the current situation. The statement "You tellin' lies" refers both to specific statements in a story, as indicated by the placement or juncture of the challenge, and to the current right of the storyteller to hold the floor. Similarly, statements such as "And JW here was there" comment on both the current and past occasions. Among the adolescents, these metastatements signaled a shift in concern from the matters discussed in the story to the current relationships between tellers and listeners. They were a means of indicating that the matters discussed were current and ongoing rather than past and resolved.[3] Further, the storytelling situation became part of the ongoing concern described in the story. The adolescents told several kinds of mediate stories including stories read in the newspaper; stories about their families (mediate in the sense that the characters in the stories, members of the family, were unfamiliar to and thus socially distant from the listeners at school); stories about past relationships between peers; stories that were fictional, such as dreams or made-up stories; and stories about the soap operas that the adolescents watched daily after school. In addition, the adolescents were familiar with mediate stories presented in school in reading and social studies classes. A common characteristic of all of these stories was that the tellers were rarely challenged as liars, although in many cases the stories were not accepted as true. Even when the stories or the tellers were challenged, the challenge was not regarded as a fight challenge, as in the case of immediate stories. The mediate stories all involved the mediation of a distant reality with the current one, as well as some unfamiliarity on the part of the listeners.

In one case, a newspaper story was challenged for its veracity. The local city newspaper reported a stabbing that had occurred at the school. (Stories of the stabbing are discussed in detail in Chapter 4.) One of the students, a witness rather than a participant in the fight, wrote a letter to the editor challenging the veracity of the account. She wrote, "You projected our school as if it's a very bad and brutle school. You should have gotten the bare facts before you assumed what you thought may have happened." However, as this challenge revealed, the student considered that the newspaper story had direct consequences for the reputation of the school. She treated the newspaper account as an immediate story in the sense that a misrepresentation could damage a current reputation. According to the newspaper, the facts concerned a single violent incident at the school. According to the student, knowledge of the facts required an understanding of the prior relationship between the fight participants and included the broader issue of the school's reputation. In her view the matter was still unresolved, and the newspaper article unfairly influenced the course of events.

The adolescents often watched the soap operas when they returned home from school each day. They called the soap operas "the stories" and often reported the incidents of a particular episode on the telephone after the program or on the following day at school. Many students considered the soap operas to be true or at least based on truth. For example, when they found out that I came from California, they asked me if I had ever been to "General

Hospital," the site of one of the programs. I asked, "Is that a real place?", and one member of the group responded, "Yah, it's in L.A., California." The soap operas were an unusual form of mediate stories in that they were totally removed from the lives of the adolescents and yet were discussed frequently or even daily as part of ongoing experience. The adolescents offered recommendations for actions on the part of certain characters and hypothesized about future events. They disputed whether or not the characters spoke authoritatively, but they did not dispute their existence.

Another form of mediate stories was stories presented in the classroom. At one point, I brought tapes of storytellers to school. The tapes included tall tales and ghost stories told by Southern black and white women. The students asked if the stories were true, and the teacher responded, "What do *you* think?" The students argued about the likelihood of certain incidents, such as whether or not a headless man could talk, but did not dispute the general conditions described in the story. As one student said, "I don't think it happen like that; she wouldn't go back in the house," asserting that the general scene was true but denying that it happened exactly as it was told.

The success of tall tales and ghost stories in convincing listeners of their veracity often rests upon a believable general situation in which unlikely things happen. These stories were challenged for their incongruence with the familiar reality of the adolescents' world. Since they were told by an adult, a potential authority, they could have been accepted as part of the unfamiliar and supposedly truthful accounts of the teacher. The social studies teacher, who had traveled all over the world, made a point of reporting what he considered unusual, and his descriptions of unfamiliar practices in other cultures were frequently challenged as fabrications.

In telling stories among themselves, the adolescents clearly distinguished between fantasies describing an unfamiliar world and stories purporting to be true that described the familiar everyday world. They rarely, if ever, told each other fantasy stories. They did, however, make up stories about the everyday world. The following story, an exaggerated account of a confrontation, was told by a black girl to a group of black girls in the lunchroom.

14

C:	I was eating some ice cream	1
	and she jumped up in my face and said	2
	"Give me some of that ice cream"	3
	and I said, "No!"	4
	So she smacked me in my face	5
	And I got up	6
	I got up and tore her up	7
	I made her –	8
	I made her cry so bad	9
	when she went home her mother didn't even know her	10

D: No, she lyin'   11
C: When we went down to 105 [the discipline room at the school]   12
G: Didn't I get in a real fight?   13

The story is not entirely untrue, but it was challenged by a listener as a lie. The untruth is the exaggeration that the narrator "tore her up" and made the girl "cry so bad when she went home her mother didn't even know her." Such hyperbolic statements were common in the group's talk, but they were usually used as threats or challenges, such as "I'll make you cry so bad your mother won't even know you." Their use in an account of a past fight marked the story as a lie. The listener's challenge did not discount the possibility that one girl demanded ice cream from another, for such things happened all the time; rather, it questioned whether or not the incident happened as recounted by the narrator.

The categorization of mediate or immediate with regard to storytelling is based not on the text of a story but rather on the relationship between the events described and the current situation in which the story is told. In mediate storytelling situations, the boundary between these is clear and requires some mediation between the world described in the story and world inhabited by the listeners. All narratives are mediate in the sense that language itself involves a mediation of reality or thought. However, not all storytelling situations are mediate. Mediate storytelling situations are characterized by the willingness of the participants to accept a story as presenting a reality other than that of the everyday reality of the listeners. This does not demand that mediate stories be fictions but rather requires the recognition that the incidents are not occurring at the moment they are being described, at the place where they are being told, or to the people who are listening. Mediate stories have the potential for immediacy, and the transition is accomplished by the shift in focus from a story that presents another reality to a story that somehow happens to the listeners. The shift can be accomplished in several ways.

The shift from mediacy to immediacy can be seen as involving a metanarrative frame, as discussed by Barbara Babcock:

> Metacommunication in narrative performance may be described as any element of communication which calls attention to the speech events as a performance and to the relationship which obtains between the narrator and his audience vis-à-vis the narrative message. (1976:66)

On one level, any metacommunication in narrative potentially signals a shift from mediacy to immediacy, since, as Babcock points out, metacommunication signals attention to the speech events themselves. However, I must emphasize that some metacommunications do this by asserting that the narrative involves unfinished business and that the current speech event is part of the ongoing business described in immediate narrative situations.[4] The self-reflexivity often attributed to writing is exemplified by metanarration, but, I suggest, is a characteristic to be attributed not to writing but to mediacy.

Immediacy often involves an intrusion of one reality upon another. Consider, for example, a letter from John Hinkley, Jr., President Ronald Reagan's attempted assassin, to a film actress, Jody Foster, indicating that he would kill the president to force her to notice him (Hinkley). Here Hinkley claimed that a mediate relationship depicted on film (a scene in which Foster's film lover promised to kill the president to prove his love for her) had immediate relevance to him and consequences for his life and his possible relationship with Foster. He confused the character played by Foster with Foster herself. This is one of the most obvious forms of the shift from mediacy to immediacy. The confusion concerns a fictional film that involves nonfictional pieces of everyday life. The character played by Foster in the film was fictional, but the president discussed in the film is a real person or has a real counterpart. Similarly, the film *The Amityville Horror* brought thrill seekers and tourists to the scene of a supposedly haunted house in Amityville, New York, and the horrors depicted on the film screen became the basis for daily interruptions from people seeking out the thrills they saw in the film.

> The real Amityville horror does not lurk beneath the cellar steps in the elegant, sunny, three-story house with its half-moon windows and heated backyard swimming pool. The real horror knocks on the front door and demands house tours, shines flashlights into the living room windows at 2 A.M., digs up pieces of the front lawn for souvenirs and goes through the current tenant's garbage searching for who knows what.[5]

Both of the preceding examples illustrate a shift from mediacy to immediacy. In these cases, there is a shift from the context of film to the context of current everyday life. Immediate relationships involve the storytelling situation in the unresolved incidents described in the story. In mediate storytelling relationships, the stories refer to incidents in another space or time but can concern situations much like those in or applicable to the present. One way in which the shift from mediacy to immediacy is accomplished is through metastatements, by either the teller or listeners, concerning the veracity of the incidents described. In order to shift to immediacy, these metastatements must suggest that the matter discussed in the story is still unresolved. The lack of veracity may itself be a statement that the incident is unresolved. The dispute over veracity shifts the focus to the storytelling situation. Implied in disputes over veracity is the possibility that the listeners have prior knowledge of the incidents recounted. Listeners may assert either specific knowledge of the incidents or general knowledge of the kinds of incidents described.

The shift from mediacy to immediacy in storytelling depends upon how the knowledge is used. In immediate storytelling relationships, the knowledge of a discrepancy, or the accusation of a supposed discrepancy, between the teller's version and that asserted by the listeners is used not only to discredit the storyteller (as either a storyteller or as a reputable person) but also to propose a fight. The difference between the ways of using prior knowledge of incidents (by either the teller or the listener) is a matter of tactics. The knowledge may be used either to assert authority or to challenge entitlement.

Authority and entitlement are related concepts, the first referring to the right of the storyteller to tell a story in a certain way and the second referring to the negotiable right of any person to tell a certain story. In the first case, it is the mode of telling that is in question; in the second case, it is the relationship between the teller and the events described. The two concepts invoke each other, and when one is called into question, so is the other by implication. Challenges to authority suggest that the teller did not tell the story correctly, and this implies the question, ''What right have you to tell the story in that way?'', an issue of entitlement. Challenges to entitlement suggest that the teller has inappropriately revealed some information that he or she had no right to convey; in other words, such challenges suggest that the teller did not have the proper authority over the information. Authority places the blame on poor narrative skill; entitlement places the blame on indiscretion. Mediate storytelling may be challenged for errors of authority; challenges to entitlement or to the discretion of the teller mark the transition to immediate storytelling.

Not all hostilities created during storytelling may be categorized as immediate relationships. Challenges to the floor or accusations of impropriety are not necessarily immediate unless the dispute involves a continuation of unfinished business described in the story.

Barbara Kirshenblatt-Gimblett provides an example of immediacy, or what she terms ''the immediate context of use'' (1975:107), in her discussion of the use of a parable in context. Kirshenblatt-Gimblett uses the term ''immediate'' to distinguish between (quoting Malinowski) ''the situation in which the utterance is being made and the situation to which it refers'' (1975:106). I have used the term ''immediate'' to refer to a much smaller part of the relationship between the storytelling situation and the situation to which the story refers. In my model, immediacy refers only to those relationships in which the two situations are interwoven, interdependently referential, or in some cases confused. However, Kirshenblatt-Gimblett's chosen example fits these criteria.

In her example, the ongoing dispute was the scene for storytelling, rather than vice versa. The storyteller, Dvora, came upon a dispute between her brother and sister-in-law. After the brother told his version of the unresolved situation, Dvora told a parable that illustrated his error. Dvora's parable was metaphorically concerned with the same matters as the current dispute. In this sense, it was a metastatement about the ongoing dispute and was immediately implicated in it. One may infer that the storyteller was potentially subject to the counterchallenge of interference by her listeners. She had entered into a dispute between husband and wife and could have been charged with meddling. Instead, her parable was accepted as a peacemaking gesture. This result may be attributed to the indirect form of the parable, and the storyteller herself suggests that this is the function of parables. She describes her use of parables as "putting things in such a way that no one is hurt" (1975:108). Among the adolescents, who did not use parables, but rather stories that concerned the participants directly, the storyteller was often charged with interfering. Whereas Dvora's story led to the resolution of a conflict, the adolescents' stories often led to further conflict.

In Kirshenblatt-Gimblett's example, the storytelling situation and the situation to which the parable refers are particularly well integrated. Further, the situation involves a conflict and the parable helps to resolve it. This sequence is the opposite of the usual sequence of the adolescents' stories, discussed previously, but the storytelling nonetheless involves a shift to immediacy.

In the adolescents' storytelling, a story about a fight that was still unresolved was told to listeners who were familiar with the disputants. The shift to immediacy implicated the storytelling situation in the ongoing dispute. This was often accomplished either by a listener's challenge to the veracity of the story or by an assertion of its veracity backed up by a listener. The social alignments or rifts created during the storytelling became the basis for the continuation of the dispute.

The parable discussed by Kirshenblatt-Gimblett meets an additional criterion for immediacy: the shared knowledge of the participants. In both mediate and immediate storytelling relationships, the listeners *may* have prior knowledge of the incidents described, but this is *essential* for immediate relationships. Listeners base their challenges and tellers base their assertions of veracity or entitlement on the assumption of this prior knowledge. In the case of the parable, the prior knowledge does not involve the parable itself, which could have been either unfamiliar or familiar to the listeners, but the situation of conflict. In an interview concerning the use of the parable, Dvora said that no one needed to tell her what was going on when she entered the situation. Her brother spoke to her first, and her sister-in-law "wasn't even talking. She was just too upset and too disgusted and she didn't have to tell me what preceded. She knows I know what the situation is at home all the time" (1975:115). She based her interference on her assumed prior knowledge of the situation. "He was going to do the same thing next Saturday, so that I thought that this was just the situation that needed this kind of an example" (1975:115).

The shift from mediacy to immediacy can be accomplished by the recognition that someone mentioned in the story has been victimized by the story, by the assertion that a listener was wrongly influenced by the story, or by otherwise persuading the listeners to act as a result of listening to the story. In all cases, someone is presented as victimized by the story; in the last case, the victim requires the assistance of the listener. However, in the first case, the telling of the story is itself the impropriety. In the last case, the story merely reports the insult. This distinction is important in regard to the adolescent stories, in which the storytelling was itself often challenged as an impropriety. Although the stories contained information about victimization, the focus of blame shifted easily from the person mentioned in the story to the storyteller. Here the potentially mediate stories lost the status of mediacy and became immediate confrontations.

The relationship between mediacy and immediacy dramatizes the concern for veracity and credibility (depending on whether the focus is placed on the story or on the storyteller). Immediacy concerns the relevance of the story for the situation in which it is told. Since all stories have some relevance for the situations in which they are told, and since all stories have some consequences that extend beyond the storytelling situation, the distinction here between immediacy and mediacy is subtle. In immediate storytelling situations, the doubts about the veracity of the story or the credibility of the storyteller may be used to challenge the storyteller to a fight, to incite a fight between other parties involved either as listeners or as characters in the story, or to resolve a conflict. Immediacy involves a shift in focus from the story itself – which may never be investigated further or proven true or false, but rather may be subordinated to the struggle between the participants – to the situation in which the story is told. Immediate storytelling situations are so characterized because they have the potential to erupt into disputes or to resolve ongoing disputes. In immediate storytelling situations, the boundary between the story and the actions described is constantly negotiated and constantly changing, and the relationship between tellers and listeners is at stake. The classification of storytelling situations as immediate does not depend on the assessment of the listeners' prior knowledge of the events described. In both mediate and immediate storytelling situations, the listeners may have prior knowledge of the incidents. In both types of situations, the listeners may use their prior knowledge to challenge the teller, and both types of situations may involve disputes over the right to speak or to hold the floor for an extended turn at speaking.

The significant difference between mediate and immediate storytelling situations is the relationship between the teller and the story. Storytellers are always held accountable for their stories, but this accountability is a matter of degree. Further, the story and the teller may be assessed separately. In immediate storytelling situations, the assessment includes the propriety of the telling as well as the veracity of the story; more importantly, a judgment of impropriety may invalidate the claims made in the telling. In mediate storytelling situations, the propriety of the teller and the veracity of the events recounted are accepted as distinct; in immediate storytelling situations, one implicates the other. Adolescents played with this system and charged each other with either lying or improperly telling a story in order to discredit the speaker.

2.2   The reportable and the repeatable

The relationship between mediacy and immediacy, and especially the concern with veracity, is further played out in the classification of news. In narrative scholarship, there has been a tendency to discriminate between narrative and news.[6] The first is categorized as an artful form displaying ordered, elaborated description; the second is categorized as a more practical form designed to convey information. (There is a tendency among journalism scholars to make a similar distinction between objective reporting and sensationalist description.[7]) Such distinctions confuse the content of a story with its form of presentation.

The confusion between narrative and news is apparent in discussions of murder reports, a subject that has interested both folklore scholars with a bias against newspaper reports and journalism scholars with a bias against sensationalist reporting. Ann Cohen addresses the problem in her study of a ballad about a murdered girl, ''Poor Pearl, Poor Girl.'' Cohen points out that the earliest newspaper accounts of the murder of Pearl Bryant suggested that Pearl, who was found dead in a field, was a prostitute from the nearby city. The accounts pictured her as a ''loose woman'' whose fate was an inevitable result of her profession. A few days later, when the reporters learned that Pearl lived in a small town rather than in the city, and that her accused murderers were her boyfriend and his roommate, she was depicted as an innocent victim of city evils. Cohen suggests that the later newspaper accounts followed the formula for discussing the murder of young women. She demonstrates that a number of formulas appeared in both the newspaper and ballad versions of such events, including stock plots, stock scenes, stock characters, stock sequences of words, and stock dramatic devices. According to Cohen, the newspaper reporters never investigated Pearl's character, as either loose woman or innocent victim, but rather utilized the available stereotypes to fill in the picture of ''what happened.''[8] Although we might justify the interpretive license taken by the ballad writer, we cannot as easily condone the journalist's reliance on stock sequences. This distinction between art and information is not as clear-cut as the categories appear to be.

When the narrative mode is used to convey news, the narrative form as well as the code provides information. In the absence of information about what happened to Pearl, the reporters filled in blank spaces in the sequence with the expected explanations and consequences. The relationship between form and content is essentially a matter of the ways in which contextual expectations are relied upon to provide information. The newspaper accounts told people what they supposedly expected to read in the form in which they expected to read it. Scientific writing, as Roland Barthes points out, attempts to present content without calling attention to context or form.

> As far as science is concerned language is simply an instrument, which it profits it to make as transparent and neutral as possible: it is subordinate to the matter of science (workings, hypotheses, results) which, so it is said, exists outside language and precedes it. On the one hand and *first* there is the context of the scientific message, which is everything: on the other hand and *next*, the verbal form responsible for expressing that content, which is nothing. (1970:411)

In contrast, Barthes states that literature is concerned primarily with form:

> For literature, on the other hand, or at any rate that literature which has freed itself from classicism and humanism, language can no longer be the convenient instrument or the superfluous backcloth of a social, emotional or poetic "reality" which pre-exists it, and which it is language's subsidiary responsibility to express, by means of submitting itself to a number of stylistic rules. Language is literature's Being, its very world. (1970:411)

Barthes suggests that the distinction is rooted in the assertion that literature is written rather than spoken:

> The whole of literature is contained in the act of writing, and no longer in those of "thinking," "portraying," "telling" or "feeling." . . . Science is spoken, literature written, the one is led by the voice, the other follows the hand. (1970:411–12)

Barthes's purpose is to examine the focus of structuralism as the "science of discourse" and to suggest that structuralism should turn to an examination of science itself as a kind of language.

> The logical continuation of structuralism can only be to rejoin literature, no longer as an "object" of analysis but as the activity of writing, to do away with the distinction derived from logic which turns the work itself into a language-object and science into a meta-language, and thus to forgo that illusory privilege which science attaches to the possession of a captive language. (1970:413)

The question for the present discussion is, what are the implications of Barthes's statements for oral narrative or for the distinction between oral narrative as art or as information? The assumption in Barthes's discussion is that written literature avoids the naive scientific focus on content alone. He suggests what he calls "integral writing," in which the form is congruent with the content (1970:416). However, the challenge to veracity is not a problem faced by written literature, and to write, rather than to speak, is to shift the problem away from the arena in which it occurs to an arena in which it is difficult to locate and in which the problem appears unimportant. The problem is rooted in the relationship between stories and the incidents they describe, and the issue is the precedence of either text or context in determining the standards for assessing the story.

Although Barthes is accurate in his criticisms of scientific language and in his suggestion that structuralism examine its own use of this language, the casualty of his discussion is oral narrative, which is placed in contrast to literature and is left straddling the categories of news and art (which unnecessarily exclude each other).

Not all oral narratives are implicated in this discussion. Narratives that do not purport to be about everyday experiences, and legends that, although about the everyday world, can record exceptional and therefore potentially otherworldly experiences, can be categorized as art rather than as news. Stories that are current – which does not necessarily mean that they are told only once or that they are not passed orally from one group to another – are more likely to be categorized as news. Walter Benjamin makes a definite distinction between storytelling and a report of news, which he says is "incompatible with the spirit of storytelling" (1976:282). He says that reported news has as its primary requirement "that it appear 'understandable in itself.'" In contrast, "It is half the art of storytelling to keep a story free from explanation as one reproduces it." By "explanation," Benjamin means explicitly psychological connections (of the type used by the reporters of the Pearl Bryant murder) that are "forced on the reader." According to Benjamin, in storytelling the reader may "interpret things the way he understands them, and thus the narrative achieves an amplitude that information lacks" (1976:282–3). Further, Benjamin claims,

> The value of information does not survive the moment in which it is new. It lives only at that moment; it has to surrender to it completely and explain itself to it without losing any time. A story is different. It does not expend itself. It preserves and concentrates its strength and is capable of releasing it even after a long time. (1976:183)

The adolescents' stories are an example of the kinds of stories that could be labeled news. They concerned current incidents that could be challenged for their veracity. However, the adolescents rarely if ever investigated the authenticity of claims made in stories; their challenges were more often formulaic responses and were rarely based on actual information. Further, the stories did not contain much information. As discussed earlier, the stories did not provide a forum for the adolescents to learn anything about each other. The adolescents relied upon already known bits of information or conjecture and most often counted on the possibility that any adolescent would have had certain kinds of experiences. The claims referred to these general categories of experience rather than to unusual specific or idiosyncratic behaviors. The adolescents' stories that could be potentially classified as news were of three kinds: stories about one's family, stories about changes in relationships between peers, and stories actually taken from a newspaper.

The adolescents' stories about their families have been presented earlier in this book, in discussions of mediate stories, in discussions of privacy, and in discussions of what the adolescents knew about each other. The stories were never requested by the listeners and rarely received a response. The following story was told by Elena, a Puerto Rican girl, to another Puerto Rican girl on the bus during a school field trip. (Bracketed ellipses indicate words said in a whisper and difficult to hear over the sound of traffic.) Elena began her story as the bus passed a residential institution.

15

E:	My grandfather should be in there	1
	I hate to say this but my grandfather	2
	El viva en lo [. . .]	3
	He's crazy like any other crazy person	4
	They're messing him up	5
	[. . .]	6
	He threatened to kill my mother	7
	My father	8
	Oh, and we were tiny	9
	And I remember when he had a knife	10
	and he'd be all [. . .]	11
	He wouldn't open the door to my mother	12
	and like that	13
	My mother was crying	14
	And the last time my mother brought him home [. . .]	15
	He started to come over	16
	He doesn't want to go back to that place because he doesn't like it	17
	My mother brings him to the house to *visit*	18
	Y el dice when it's time for him to come back – go back	19
	el dice "Tu no me quieres"	20
	[. . .]	21
	He said a lot of bad things to my mother	22
	and my mother starts crying	23
	Y el dice [. . .]	24
	I don't know he's doing	25
	[Interruption]	
	He goes to my mother que le dice – que – that my mother's crying for nothing	26
	because he doesn't really care	27

Monica, the girl who listened to Elena's story, said nothing, and it was unclear whether or not Elena had her attention. (The fact that Elena intended her story for Monica is clear in Elena's use of Spanish; Monica was the only Hispanic person within earshot.) This situation was not unique. When "second stories" were offered, they were told after long pauses, as though prompted by an environmental cue, such as a city cited in Elena's story, rather than by the topic of the story.[9] The stories were not necessarily presented as news and were not treated as news.

A second, and frequent, kind of potential news story consisted of accounts of changing relationships between people. Although these stories often purported to be news, they rarely were. They often began with the statement that two people had fought, but most often revealed that they had yet to fight. The following accounts were told after school. The listener had been absent from school, and the teller was filling her in on what had happened during the day. The listener reported what she ate and what she and her grandmother discussed. The following accounts were the only pieces of news offered by the girl who had attended school.

16

M:	Elizabeth's gonna get in trouble, Stacie	1
S:	Why?	2
	Tell me now	3
M:	Cause she went to the gym room	4
	and she wasn't supposed to	5
	She always do that	6
S:	I know	7
	Everytime	8
M:	Cause she didn't like	9
	Missin' out on the test	10
S:	Oh, y'all took the test	11
	didn't y'all	12
S:	I studied for that test while I was home with my grandmother	13
M:	Keep studyin', Stacie	14
S:	I am	15

[five minutes later]

17

M:	Ooh, Stacie guess what	1
S:	What	2
M:	Cornie and Sylvie was gonna fight	3
S:	Who?	4
M:	That girl Sylvie Fox	5
S:	They use to live around our way?	6
	I mean they used to go to our school?	7

M:	She still do go to our school	8
	Sylvie	9
	not Pearl, Sylvie	10
S:	Who – who the hell is that?	11
	I don't know	12
M:	She used to be with Sonya and them	13
S:	Oh yah	14
M:	Her	15
	She was gonna fight with Corny	16
S:	Corny	17
	That boy is –	18
M:	Corny kept on messin' with her	19
S:	He is too grown for –	20
	I mean too big for her	21
	He could beat her up anyday	22
M:	He kept on messin' w' her	23
	[interruption]	

In oral narrative 17, the information conveyed concerned the identities of the participants in a possible fight. The story told nothing about what had happened, but rather reported on an existing state of affairs. Stacie did not learn the details of any incidents from the account, but only that two people were going to fight, that one was messing with the other, and that both of them still attended the school. The subject of oral narrative 16, Elizabeth, was a rival of Marie, the storyteller. Again, the story did not report any incidents of central importance. This story provided one detail central to the cause of trouble: Elizabeth's prohibited visit to the gym. However, Stacie responded that Elizabeth "always do that"; in other words, it was nothing new to Stacie. The purported news in both stories was expected trouble involving certain people.

The third type of potential news story was taken from the newspaper. The adolescents often discussed what they had learned from television, radio, or newspaper accounts of incidents. The following series of stories was told during lunch. The storyteller began by reading a summary of a newspaper clipping that she had turned in to the teacher for a current events homework assignment. The newspaper story concerned a cesarean birth. Oral narrative 18 followed immediately as part of a lengthy (by the standards of lunchtime talk) monologue.

18

S:	Oh, I want to tell y'all about something else	1
	This lady, her baby	2
	She had um – she had a little girl	3
	She dressed her little girl up	4

	Oh, it was Eastertime	5
	She dressed her little girl up in pretty clothes	6
	So the father could come and take her out	7
	Because the parents were separated	8
	And do you know what she did?	9
	She put the – she beat the girl up and started stabbing the little baby and everything	10
	And then she put it in the oven?	11
M:	Oh!	12
S:	And then this other lady, she	13
	She – her son just got finished taking a bath	14
	She dried him up and put him in the oven	15
	This lady she drowned her little daughter	16
	She drowned her little daughter because her little daughter was putting water all over the floor	17
	You know how little kids like to play?	18
M:	Hm	19
S:	In the tub and stuff? Well she kept on telling her daughter to stop	20
	She went in there and drowned her little daughter	21
	and hung her neck all up on a hanger	22
	she put her head in the hanger	23
M:	Ooh, that is so gross, ooh my	24
S:	That is terrible	25
	This lady, she also had a daughter, she	26
	you know what	27
	she whupped her daughter terrible	28
	and she beat her daughter up and killed her	29
	and threw her down the basement,	30
	and took these other kids to the, um, party	31
	and her daughter was retarded	32
	that's why she didn't take her to the party because she was embarrassed	33
	She killed her daughter	34
	went down to the basement	35
	then took the other kids	36
	because she was – she was embarrassed about her daughter being retarded	37
M:	Um, tell me, where do you get such . . . stories	38
S:	From the newspaper	39
L:	[. . .] was up on the third floor and they was going to a [. . .]	40
S:	I wasn't talking	41
L:	And the lady was [. . .]	42
S:	You don't [. . .]	43
M:	You know about that fire where the lady threw the baby out the window?	44
S:	Yeah	45
L:	Yeah	46

S: That was a shame	47
Somebody – somebody should o' caught the baby with sheets	48
That's what my mother always say, get sheets, when there's a fire and stuff	49
put a lot of sheets on, when people jump out the window	50
a lot of people be around	51
And all those people who were around where I live, where Milo live	52
[	
M: Yeah	53
S: All those people that were around, nobody helped	54
M: That's what they said, a lady called somebody	55
So that way they could catch the baby	56
S: And nobody didn't do nothing	57
M: And [. . .] that shattered	58
and the fire [. . .] made the glass break	59
and the glass fell	60
soon as – same time the baby got tossed out the window	61
S: That was pitiful	62
Babies is dying, keep dying	63
and ladies is going crazy	64
I think they be going crazy because their husband leave 'em	65
or whatever happened to 'em	66
Now this girl	67
she was having a baby	68
but she was – she wasn't having a baby yet	69
but she was pregnant still	70
And she was young . . .	71

The preceding story sequence, derived from newspaper stories, concerns what Labov has categorized as stories about vicarious experience. Labov suggests that such stories typically lack evaluation and orienting devices (1972:367). However, the use of evaluation and other devices may be related more to the distinction between completed ongoing storytelling than to personal or vicarious experience. Among the adolescents, accounts of completed rather than ongoing events often contained evaluation. The preceding story sequence is interesting for its elaborate use of evaluation, especially:

(18)

That was pitiful	62
Babies is dying, keep dying	63
and ladies is going crazy	64
I think they be going crazy because their husband leave 'em	65

This comment describes the storyteller's position as an outsider in relation to the events she recounted. The stories she told were about people who lived near her or whom she might know, but they were not about herself. They were about the adult world, and as such, they presented an adolescent view of that world, a view that is particularly important to an understanding of the stories the adolescents told about themselves.

Some vicarious experience stories, such as those provided in Labov's discussions (from the television program "The Man from U.N.C.L.E."), involve more ellipses than the stories about oneself. One of the problems with the vicarious experience stories is that the teller has limited access to information; the information is restricted to that presented in the television program or the newspaper account.[10] The problem is further compounded, especially in the case of television programs, when the information is presented out of sequence. The teller then has to reconstruct a sequence that may never have been complete.

The adolescents' vicarious experience stories, such as oral narrative 18, provided more evaluation and more information than many of the adolescents' stories about themselves. The adolescents' news stories could be the kind of vicarious experience story considered to be potentially uninteresting or pointless by Labov and to belong to the category of news, rather than story, deplored by Benjamin. Benjamin favors what might be called "repeatable" rather than "reportable" stories.[11] News stories are reportable. However, the adolescents' news stories did not convey news, and they were not valued for their potential currency.

The distinction between reportability and repeatability concerns the justification for telling a story. Reportability and repeatability may be distinguished by the referential systems used to justify a story or to assert its tellability. The referents for a reportable story are the recent past incidents that are presumably unknown to the current listeners. The central point of reportable stories is "what happened," and the justification for telling the story is that the events are presumably of interest or relevance to the listeners. Thus reportability is determined by the recency of the incidents, by the listeners' lack of knowledge about them, and by their relevance to the listeners.[12] These criteria are, however, not often clearly identifiable. Recency is subject to the relative triviality or weight of the information to be recounted.[13] Relatives who have not seen each other for a long time, for example, may have comparatively old news of comparatively great importance to tell each other. The listeners' knowledge of the situation involves the possibility that they know that information is forthcoming, although they may not know the specific details. Anticipated news is qualitatively different from unexpected news. Further, the information conveyed may be expected or unexpected. These factors contribute to the value of a story.

In stories about their own activities, the adolescents often revealed the assumption that others saw the world as they did. In describing incidents to adults, they rarely provided enough information for the adults to understand what happened. When the adolescents described incidents to each other, many of the details were so familiar that the tellers omitted those that were assumed to be understood. The constant condensation of information and abbreviation of orienting details required an insider's understanding and sometimes involved the naive expectation that anyone would know what every adolescent in the community knew. (Alternatively the elliptical accounts could be intentionally elusive to exclude outsiders and to keep authorities from interfering. It is just as likely that some incidents were so familiar that the abbreviations were made out of awareness.)

H. P. Grice's rules for politeness require information to be conveyed rather than withheld (1975). Grice does not suggest that such rules are consistently followed, but rather that they are significant only insofar as we can understand departures from them as marked. [14] In the case of news stories, which perhaps come closer than other stories to following or accommodating to Grice's rules, the value of discretion must always be considered as a rule that may supersede the rules of quality, quantity, relevance, and manner. [15]

Rules of discretion subject news stories to considerations of entitlement. Listeners or readers can evaluate the news bringer's statements not only in terms of their accuracy but, equally important, in terms of the teller's entitlement and the value or purpose of spreading the information. The categories of news and gossip are distinguished as much by entitlement as by other factors, such as the content or accuracy of the information.

Benjamin's contrast between news and art states that news is "understandable in itself" and thus does not give the listener/reader the opportunity to interpret the material. However, the assertion that "this is news" is itself subject to interpretation. Benjamin bases his distinction between storytelling and news on the notion that stories are repeated and may be told over a longer period of time, in contrast to news, which has a limited circulation in time. Benjamin is concerned with the difference between newsworthiness and tellability. However, these qualities are difficult to distinguish, and neither the number of times a story is told nor the time period over which it is told is sufficient for distinguishing between stories and news. Benjamin bases his distinction on texts, but the distinction applies only in the most general ways and only to the most typical examples of stories and news. Accounts that have elements of both news and story may be distinguished not as texts but as performances. The distinction rests on the relationship between the listeners, the tellers, and the texts.

Benjamin suggests that the significance of stories is in their preservation over time, in contrast to news, which "does not survive the moment in which it is new." However, news is always new to someone, and other stories do not always claim to be old. Many forms other than news (jokes, for example, and sometimes stories that listeners hear for the first time) make the claim of novelty. The justification for telling something because it is a first hearing is separate from the claim that something is worth telling because it refers to recent events. The first favors rules of entitlement, the second, rules of information. First hearings can include long-preserved stories that the teller presents to appropriate first-time listeners. The reverse is also possible; recent incidents may be discussed in a form that presents them as repeated texts rather than news.[16] Where the contrast between news and story may not be viable, the contrast between formal and informal or public and private communication,[17] or between the story form and other conversational forms, may provide distinctions relevant to the issues of storyability and tellability and to the underlying concern of Benjamin's position.

One could argue, with John A. Robinson, that the presentation of the commonplace as remarkable makes personal narratives storyable. Robinson suggests that personal narratives concern commonplace activities and constitute "a linguistic resource for making life interesting" (1981:63). He suggests that the commonplace is a reputable storyable category insofar as it is made remarkable either in terms of the relationship between the storytelling participants or to the extent that "a storyteller may exploit expressive and stylistic devices to heighten audience interest, or [to] contextualize the episode in ways which impute a degree of remarkableness or novelty to the narrated events" (1981:62). Robinson implies a correspondence between personal narratives and actual experiences. His implied recommendation that "making life interesting" be understood as a process for transforming the commonplace into the remarkable is essentially a statement that the fact that "something happened" can be seen as remarkable or storyable. Newsworthiness is only one possible justification for tellability. The most important determinant of tellability is the listeners' prior knowledge of the incidents recounted and the teller's related awareness of the listeners' knowledge. Tellability takes into account the listeners' prior knowledge and also considers how the listeners might use their knowledge in the future. Assessments of entitlement are one possible way in which the listeners and tellers make use of their awareness of what each other knows.

One possible way to examine tellability is to consider it as a matter of *discours* rather than *histoire*,[18] or as a concern belonging to the storytelling situation rather than to the content of the events recounted. By making such a distinction, it is possible to examine metanarrative questions in a story, such as "Have you heard this?" or "Did you know what happened?", as framing justifications for tellability. However, although the *discours–histoire* distinction clarifies the problem of mistaking the content for the form of presentation, it does not account entirely for tellability. Tellability does not reside in a text alone, but neither does it reside in the metanarrative remarks.

Benjamin and Labov were both concerned with the quality of stories. Labov's aim was to distinguish evaluated personal stories from nonevaluated vicarious ones. Benjamin's purpose was to deplore the predominance of information and news and the absence of storytelling as an art form. Both scholars were essentially concerned with tellability, with the form that transforms experience into an artful or evaluated story. However, they based their criteria for classifying potential stories on storyability, or the relationship of the tellers and listeners to the content of the story. Benjamin insisted on the distance between the tellers and listeners and the material, as in traditional tales; Labov insisted on the familiarity of the teller with the material as a personal experience.

This confusion of storyability and tellability has particular importance for a study of stories such as those I collected from the adolescents, which included various combinations of what could be considered news, both personally and vicariously experienced. Among the adolescents, news about personal experiences did not necessarily provide information, and whether or not the stories concerned actual recent incidents, they need not necessarily be considered news. In contrast to the personal stories, which included little evaluation unless provided by the listener, the vicarious stories, such as those taken from newspaper accounts of mothers killing their babies, were explicitly evaluated. Explicit evaluation was one way for tellers to insert a point of view into a story about strangers. Stories told about familiar people and experiences conveyed a point of view implicit in the characterizations of victim and aggressor.[19] The personal stories were told by adolescents to other adolescents who were familiar with each other's personal experiences. They were told as part of daily conversations. Labov's stories were told primarily to people who were unfamiliar with the incidents recounted and who requested the stories in open-ended interviews. The use of evaluation and the necessity for it with tellable stories might be reconsidered in terms of the relationship between the tellers, the listeners, and the knowledge of the incidents recounted. Stories involving greater distance – either because the listeners are unfamiliar with the incidents recounted, or because the category of experience described is unfamiliar, or because the social distance between listeners and tellers is greater – might require more evaluation to qualify as tellable.

Roland Barthes writes, "Historical discourse does not follow reality, it only signifies it; it asserts at every moment: this happened, but the meaning conveyed is only that someone is making that assertion" (1970:154). In personal narratives, it may be easy to overlook the possibility that the form, and not the experiences, dictates the conventions for storyability and tellability. Barthes's comments expose historical discourse as a discourse with conventions for representing "reality," and they insist that the devices of historical discourse are no less conventional than the conventions for representing fiction. Personal narratives are often told in conversation and report experiences that the listeners may recognize as having actually occurred, but the incidental form of discourse does not erase the fact that they are narratives. The histories discussed by Barthes more explicitly assert their claims than do personal narratives; nevertheless, personal narratives, like histories, use conventions to convey the assertion that something happened. In making an assertion of storyability, a narrator can use the close alignment of experiences described in a story and the everyday experiences of the listeners to demonstrate what Barthes calls "the reality effect." As Barthes states:

> The prestige of *this happened* is of truly historical importance and magnitude. Our whole civilization is drawn to the reality effect, as witness the development of genres like the realist novel, the diary, the documentary, the *fait divers*, the historical museum, the exhibition of ancient objects and above all the massive development of photography, which differs from drawing only in conveying the additional meaning that the event portrayed really happened. (1970:154)

3

COLLABORATIVE USES OF LITERACY IN THE
ADOLESCENT COMMUNITY[1]

3.1 Text and context

Literacy research concerns at least three levels of context. In the most general sense, context is considered as equivalent to culture, or the general social structure of a community and its bearing on the uses of and attitudes toward literacy. The term "cultural context" will be used to refer to this level. On a more particular level, context has been used to refer to the relationship between participants engaged in communication in a situation involving oral or written communication. The terms "situational context" or "context" indicate this level. A third level concerns whether or not speaking and writing constitute different relationships between text and context. (Here the term "context" refers to either or both of these levels, and the term "text" has various definitions.) I use the term "text" both for oral communication transcribed into writing and for written communication, and the terms "strategies," "conventions," and "devices" to describe text–context relationships.

The first level, writing in the context of social structure and culture, concerns the consequences and implications of literacy for technological change, worldview, education, communication, and most generally, culture. The increasing amount of scholarly material in this area provides strong backing for a theoretical model of multiple literacies, a variety of ways in which oral and written communication can be categorized.

The second level, a communicative approach to writing and speaking, has long been important for analyses of oral discourse, in which the situational context has been recognized as important for understanding the use and meaning of utterances (Hymes 1974; Finnegan 1977; Gumperz 1982) but has received little attention in the study of writing. Reader-response criticism might be seen as a move in the direction of understanding the relationship between addressor and addressee in written texts, since it insists on examining the role of the reader in literature and provides a consumer, rather than a producer, orientation toward texts. However, for the most part, reader responses have been represented by ideal and imagined rather than actual communication.

Contrasts between writing and speaking on the third textual level can be stated in different ways depending on whether messages, forms, or performances are considered centrally. When messages are the focus, the contrast concerns how much and what kind of information is presented. Writing is seen to contain "decontextualized" messages as opposed to the contextualized information presented in speech. When forms are the central concern, the contrast is between genres or structures of communication, and writing is often seen as a vehicle for standardizing forms of communication and establishing canons. When performance is identified as significant, speaking is characterized as face-to-face, in contrast to the absent authorship of writing.

In this study, message, form, and performance are considered to be interrelated. The kind of information presented in a message is considered part of social rules about when, how, and what information is appropriately related to whom, and writing and speaking are two channels for communicating appropriately or inappropriately. The appropriate use of forms is always a matter of how forms are categorized into a society's recognized canons, but the issue here is not the canons themselves but the discontinuities in the status ascribed to standard and nonstandard forms. Performance is an essential piece of this puzzle since it provides understanding of the social relationships between author or speaker and audience.

On the level of texts, the distinction between orality and literacy has been difficult to make. In the examination of oral texts, Ruth Finnegan has convincingly argued that written and oral literature cannot be definitively distinguished by either "narrative, composition, style, social context, or function" (1977:272). She suggests that only performance distinguishes the oral from the written. "In one respect it [oral literature] is different: a piece of oral literature, to reach its full actualisation, *must be performed*" (1977:28). Thus the second kind of context, the situation, provides the clearest basis for understanding the difference between writing and speaking.

A number of generalizations about differences in writing and speaking, reading and listening, have formed the grounds for categorizing writing and speaking as distinct modes of communication. As Finnegan states, oral literature is performed. In general, orality has been characterized as face-to-face, in contrast to the private acts of writing and reading, in which authors and narrators are distanced from their readers. The author–narrator differentiation is not exclusive to writing, since, for example, a narrator of oral poetry may perform another's works. Authors and narrators are entitled to perform differently in writing and speaking. For example, in writing, an author who repeats another's words may be accused of plagiarism, and at the same time, borrowed texts repeated in a different historical context do not necessarily represent the same text. As J. L. Borges (1962) suggests in "Pierre Menard, Author of the Quixote," repetition can distort the relationship between author and narrator. In speaking, as the adolescent narratives discussed here demonstrate, authors are entitled to report their own experiences, but they often use reported speech to narrate what they have heard about others' experiences. In both writing and speaking, narrators report texts authored by others, but whereas writers often use narrators to create distance from their audiences, speakers can use the speech of others to minimize distance.

3.2 Differential skills and uses

In the community where I conducted my research, the uses of literacy varied widely.[2] Some of the adults who knew how to read and write rarely used their skills. Adolescent uses of literacy differed greatly from adult uses, and in some situations writing was considered something appropriate for school-age children but not for adults. Many of the Puerto Rican adults, for example, read and wrote Spanish rather than English. Their children read and wrote English but not Spanish.

In my investigation of the differential uses of literacy, I focused on three interrelated areas: proficiency, repertoire, and the delegation of experience. The study of proficiency has been a matter of dispute in literacy discussions,[3] and the quest for a definition of "functional literacy" in particular has baffled investigators. For my purposes, I distinguished only between people who could not read or write at all in certain languages and those who could read or could write something. My investigations concentrated on repertoire, on what people read or wrote, rather than on their abilities.

The repertoire approach involves the recognition that literacy skills may be attached to particular kinds of texts and that a person may be proficient in reading or writing certain kinds of texts but not others. An advantage of the repertoire approach is that it demands a broad definition of texts, including, for example, telephone messages, grocery lists, and numerical graphs. Each of these may involve different skills, which are not necessarily equivalent and not necessarily measured by proficiency tests. One problem is that the repertoire study cannot hope to be exhaustive in inventorying even a single person's reading and writing habits. Direct questions about what people read and write reveal only what they consider writing or reading, not what they actually do. However, although inexhaustive, observation reveals that people do use reading and writing for more purposes than they account for in answering direct questions. In addition, these uses are varied and involve not only a particular skill but also a somewhat consistent pattern of use.

The third area, the study of literacy as the delegation of expertise, focuses on how people manage differential literacy skills and how texts are made accessible or inaccessible to different people in a community. It focuses on literacy as a problem of the distribution of skills and attempts to differentiate between what everyone does, what is delegated to experts, and what is done collaboratively.

All of the adolescents in the classrooms I observed knew how to read and write to some degree. Some of the students read awkwardly, and some refused to read aloud in front of the class; some wrote slowly. Awkward reading was indicated not only by stumbling over words or "sounding words out" rather than reading fluently, but was most evident in the uses of pauses. Even students who read quickly paused in the middle of phrases:

19

She was a	1
shamed of her	2
poor house	3
with its dark walls	4

A student who claimed to be a good reader because he read quickly and who sometimes complained about slow readers used the following phrasing:

20

Why my dear	1
I thought you would be	2
glad to	3
receive it.	4
What am I to	5
do with that?	6
We never go	7
out in the evening	8
and this would be a great	9
opportunity	10
for us	11

Curiously, the students did not recognize the similarity in the phrasing of slow and fast reading. The teacher said that the students read in a monotone (which was not quite accurate) and asked them to read more expressively. He gave the students copies of the play *West Side Story* and said, "It doesn't sound right to read lines such as 'I'm dying' without expression." The students accepted his point and began to correct each other's readings. They mocked readers who read dramatic statements without a change in voice. Ostensibly, the purpose of these reading sessions was to help students gain facility in reading. However, all of the students reported that they read better silently than aloud, and the ability to read aloud may not be indicative of the ability to read silently. In particular, the ability to read aloud expressively may not be a factor in reading silently. The reading sessions demonstrated that the students did not read aloud as they spoke. However, standards for reading aloud may not duplicate those for speaking, and the black, white, and Puerto Rican students who used different phrasing in speaking nevertheless shared a standard for reading aloud.

Many of the students knew people, especially old people and children, who could not read or write. Children were said to be "too young to read," and old people, the students explained, either did not know how to read or write, or knew how to read but not write, or had difficulty seeing well enough to read. The students believed nonreading children and old people to be "normal," just as they believed non-English-reading, Spanish-speaking adults to be "normal," but they said that people of their own age who could not read and write at all were "stupid."

The adolescents did more reading and writing at home than people of other ages in the community. Many of them entered contests through the mail or participated in mail-order sales programs in which they bought quantities of stationery or greeting cards and received cash or points toward prizes for selling the products. The mail-order sales programs offered one of the only opportunities for employment. (Other jobs included babysitting, doing neighborhood errands, and selling pretzels and flowers on street corners.) Sometimes several members of a family participated in mail-order sales programs, but the adolescents usually took responsibility for corresponding with the companies.

At school, the students engaged in various writing activities outside of the writing required for class.[4] They often forged notes to show to hall monitors when they were out of class during class periods. These notes involved a complex set of understandings on the part of both students and hall monitors. A detailed description of how forged hall passes were used reveals an important aspect of the uses of written texts in face-to-face interaction. Rather than verify the authenticity of the written text, authorities questioned the behavior of the student. When students were not in class during class periods, it was the responsibility of the hall monitors to find out the students' business and to send them where they belonged. The monitors could ask either "Where are you going?" or "Can I see your pass?" If the student showed a pass, the monitor asked no further questions. The passes were rectangular pieces of colored paper covered with clear plastic and had the name of a teacher printed in large letters on both sides. Each teacher had one pass. When a teacher found that his or her pass was missing, an announcement was printed in the daily staff bulletin, and that pass became invalid. Some teachers did not allow more than one student at a time to leave a class and made one student wait until another student had returned with the pass.

In some cases, students had notes, rather than passes. Notes were used when more than one student needed to be absent from the class at a time, when a student would not be returning to the class and could not return the pass, or when a student gained permission from someone other than a teacher (usually an administrator) who did not have a pass to give. The notes were sometimes explanations or requests from one person in authority to another. More often they simply allowed a student to move from one place to another and stated the student's destination. The students' forgeries always took this form and stated, for example, "To lunch," including the date and the signature of an authority. Notes were easy to forge but were, in a sense, unnecessary. When students were asked "Do you have a pass?" or "Where are you going?", only the official pass enabled them to move on without announcing a specific destination. Whether or not a student had a note, the monitor was concerned only that the announced or written destination corresponded to the student's direction. Thus notes were unnecessary if a student actually intended to go to an acceptable destination. However, students used the notes to delay the interference of hall monitors. They forged notes that said "to class," showed the notes to the hall monitors, walked in the general direction of the classroom, and avoided actually going to class until they were seen going in the wrong direction or were intercepted by the same hall monitor more than once. The authenticity of the notes was never challenged.

In another exchange between the monitors and students, the written document was also regarded as a formality. Students who arrived late at school were required to sign in at a special desk. If they did not sign in, they were marked absent rather than late, since they had missed the attendance count at the beginning of the day. When they signed in late, they were required to fill in an excuse form. They wrote their names, the date, their advisory classroom (where attendance was taken), and the reason for lateness. Dozens of students were late each day, and almost all of them, with one or two exceptions, gave as an excuse either "missed the bus" or "I overslept." The monitor who accepted the forms reported that some of the students who used the bus as an excuse did not take a bus to school. In addition, although the bus often did not show up and some students were justified in being late, the monitor always checked on which buses had arrived. The reasons for lateness were not given any attention, beyond the amusement of the monitors, unless a particular parent asked to be notified if her child had arrived on time. Even the "inexcusable" reasons for lateness were accepted; one student who was frequently late always wrote, "I walk to [sic] slow," and others wrote, "Playin basketball" and "Playin ball."

With the exception of students who stated that they were playing ball, students never wrote what would be considered acknowledgments of deliberate lateness, just as they never forged notes that acknowledged their true destination. In addition, they did not often attempt to write legitimate excuses for lateness, except when a bus did not show up and a whole group of students arrived late together after walking or taking a trolley. They did not concoct excuses for lateness, and they did not attempt to forge notes that justified unusual destinations. They did not use these forms of writing to subvert the system.

The students' use of the notes required for certain kinds of communication with authorities reveal a difference between the students' and authorities' perceptions of the notes. At the same time, students and authorities complied with the system as though there were no alternatives. Students forged signatures but did not change the content of the notes to suit their purposes.

Notes always said "to class" or "to the lunchroom," not "Please allow Nancy to ask her sister if she can loan her 50¢ for lunch." Signing a teacher's name to a note the teacher had written many times was somehow more acceptable than inventing the message. The system perpetuated an understanding of written messages as preformulated texts with added signatures.

3.3 Writing as play

The students rarely used writing for deception. In one exceptional case, a class was given an assignment to write letters to anyone for National Letter-Writing Week. The teacher said that he would mail the letters from the school, since the school had offered to pay the postage, and that he would distribute school envelopes (which included the school's return address), and students could seal their letters before giving them to him if they wished privacy. One girl wrote a letter from a school authority, whom she named "Miss Hoober," addressed to her grandmother. The letter said that the girl's older sister had been absent from school too often and that she would have to have a special meeting with the authorities. The younger sister asked another member of the class to rewrite the letter so that it would not be in her handwriting, and she placed it in the school's envelope and sealed it. The entire interaction, including the writing of the letter and the report of how it was received by her grandmother and sister, provide insights into some of the uses of literacy as play among the adolescents. The writing session and the report a few weeks later of the receipt of the letter were discussed in the lunchtime conversations between the author, Stacie, and her classmates, Lorna, Monica, Carla, and Linda. Stacie is black; the other girls are Puerto Rican. In writing the letter, Stacie read her various attempts aloud to the other girls. The following exchange demonstrates a central feature of adolescent writing: the use of adult forms of writing, in this case a business letter, for adolescent purposes. Stacie's letter from Miss Hoober to Joanie was a form of play with writing.

21

S:	"Dear Miss Joan Caldwell,	1
	Would you please come to Saint Joseph Hospital.	2
	We would like to run some test on you. If you	3
	need a refill of medication"	4
	Then I stopped.	5
	then I put, "No good at all."	6
	Then I put:	7
	"Dear Miss Joan Caldwell,	8
	You will be assigned to a girls' detention	9
	center on September 9, 1980."	10
	[laughter]	

Then I stopped that one	11
Now I'm writin' this one:	12
"Dear Miss Joan Caldwell,	13
You haven't been attending school properly	14
Please contact the . . ."	15

C:	Is that true?	16
S:	It's true that she don't go to school all the time	17
C:	That's a shame	18
S:	What else am I gonna put?	19
	"We will send a –	20
	If you are not in school by Monday –	21
	We are –	22
	If you are not –	23
	Attending –	24

[interruption]

	Attending school properly"	25
	What's that lady that they send to the um	26
M:	Truant officer	27
S:	How do you spell "truant"?	28

A few weeks later, one of the classmates asked Stacie what happened to the letter. Stacie responded:

22

S:	See my sister used to never go to school	1
	I sent the letter	2
	It came to my house, too	3
	And um, my grandmom had got the letter	4
	My sister was readin' it, right?	5
	When I walked in the room	6
	then I went back out the door	7
	I had to shut the door back	8
	and then –	9
	I came in the house	10
	My grandmom told me to write down these letters	11
	Cause my sister's in this Olympic Sales Club	12
	and you sell somethin' and you get prizes	13
	She told me to write these names down	14
	So I said,	15
	"Okay, give me the names	16
	Start givin' me the names"	17
	I started writin' names	18
	All the names she give me started with a "J"	19
	So she give me her name	20
	She give me Joseph	21
	She give me James	22
	all these names	23

Then	24
And I asked my grandmom,	25
"What are the names?"	26
Cause I didn't know "John Short"	27
And I asked my grandmom	28
Then my grandmom say, this um –	29
Then she say, "Okay Miss Hoober"	30

[laughter]

She calls me "Miss Hoober"	31
She knows me cause I make funny kind of "J"'s	32
She gave me all these "J" words	33

M: There was "J"'s in your letter?   34
S: I wrote the front of the letter to "Miss Joan Caldwell" cause that's   35
my sister name

Then my grandmom found out I wrote that letter	36
She say, "Miss Hoober"	37
Then I didn't want to laugh	38
So I picked up a pillow and put it over my face	39
Then I looked at my grandmom	40
Like I didn't know what she was talkin' about?	41
She say, "Stacie, Joanie received a letter today	42
and I think that somebody wrote it that lives in this household"	43
I say, "Now who could of done that?"	44
then she say,	45
"Well it's from Miss Hoober and Joanie went there today"	46
And my sister say, "And the lady – there wasn't no Miss Hoober there	47
And so me and you gonna go and we're gonna find out who write this letter"	48
I say, "Joanie I got a lot o'things to do	49
I can't help you with that today"	50
then she say, "No, you have to go. Grandmom gonna take	51
care of everything you have to do	52
She gonna be waitin' for you when you get home"	53
She say, "Come on, Stacie,"	54
And we started runnin' to the corner to catch the bus,	55
and I say, "Joanie, I got somethin' to tell you before we get on this bus"	56
She say, "What. Tell me, Stacie 'cause here come my bus"	57
I say, "Joanie –	58
let's go"	59
And I was so scared	60
I didn't want to say nothin'	61
I say, "Joanie, I wrote that letter"	62
She say, "You did what?"	63
I say, "I wrote the letter"	64

She say, "Well, we gotta go back home and tell grandmom that you   65
    wrote this letter"

We came home   66

And my grandmom say, "Hi, Stacie, how was your trip, Miss   67
    Hoober?"

[laughter]

I was so –   68

I was laughin' so loud   69

I was scared cause my grandmom say, "Well, Miss Hoober, Joanie   70
    has been

goin' to school and I don't think you know who you're talkin'   71
    about"

And then my grandmom called my father and told him what I did   72

My father kept callin' me Miss Hoober   73

[laughter]

Stacie's deceptive letter was not unlike other adolescent forgeries in which an adult's message was copied. The authors attempted to imitate the language of the authorities, to use correct spelling, and to write the letter in the correct format.

Stacie composed the letter with the help of friends; such collaborative composition was common in the adolescents' play with writing and was also found in other writing practices shared by members of a family. These collaborative writing activities turned writing into a face-to-face interaction in which people read aloud and dictated writings to each other. Stacie's account refers to several aspects of writing: the collaborative family effort regarding mail-order sales projects; the ability to recognize someone's handwriting; the recognition among adolescents that they might be recognized by their handwriting even more than by the content of their writing; and an attempt to find the correct spelling of an unfamiliar word by asking a friend. In addition, the name "Miss Hoober," the authority in Stacie's letter, was borrowed from a book read by the class.[5] The revival of Miss Hoober for the purpose of the letter was especially humorous to Stacie and her friends. Stacie had directed plays in which the characters in the book were played by classmates during lunch, and the use of Miss Hoober's name in the letter was an extension of the oral play.

Deceptive letters such as Stacie's were rare; play writing, which was shared only between adolescents, rather than involving parents or other authorities, was more prevalent. (It is possible to argue that Stacie's letter was intended for her sister and did not knowingly involve her grandmother.)

Figure 3.1, "The Constitution of Love and Ammenmants," is an example of the adolescents' play with writing. Play with writing characteristically involved writing by adolescents for each other and involved a face-to-face exchange. (Examples of a non–face-to-face use of play with writing among

The Constitution of Love

We the people young in heart order to form more perfect kisses, enable the mighty hug more the popularity of love is to establish contribution of love.

#1 Method of love

① Not to kiss whom you please but to please whom you kiss.
② If you love him or her say yes, if you don't say yes anyway.
③ If kissing is your language we have to talk.

#2 Method of love

① A kiss on the hand - I like you
② A kiss on the ear - fun and games
③ A kiss on the neck - I want you
④ A kiss anyway - don't get carried away
⑤ A kiss on the cheak - friendship
⑥ A kiss on the lips - I like you so
⑦ A very personal kiss - I love you
⑧ playing with your hair - cain't be without you
⑨ Kissing and holding hands - we can learn to like eachother
⑩ Arms around your waist - I love you too much to let you go
⑪ Looking in each others eyes - kiss me you fool
⑫ Arms around your shoulder - stay with me baby

* Hints *

① If a girl slaps a boy he has the right to kiss her and hold her as he pleases.
② When you kiss close your eyes, its not polite to stare.
③ Never give up on a person, he or she may be shy.

* Laws *

① Always respect love.
② Never end with a kiss always start with one.
③ Practice make perfect, so practice.

* Ammenmants *

① Thou shalt not squeeze hard.
② Thou shalt kiss at every opportunity.

P.S. After this document is read you **must** kiss the person who gave this to you only if her or she is of the opposite sex and not related to you.

Figure 3.1 "The Constitution of Love" and "Ammenmants."

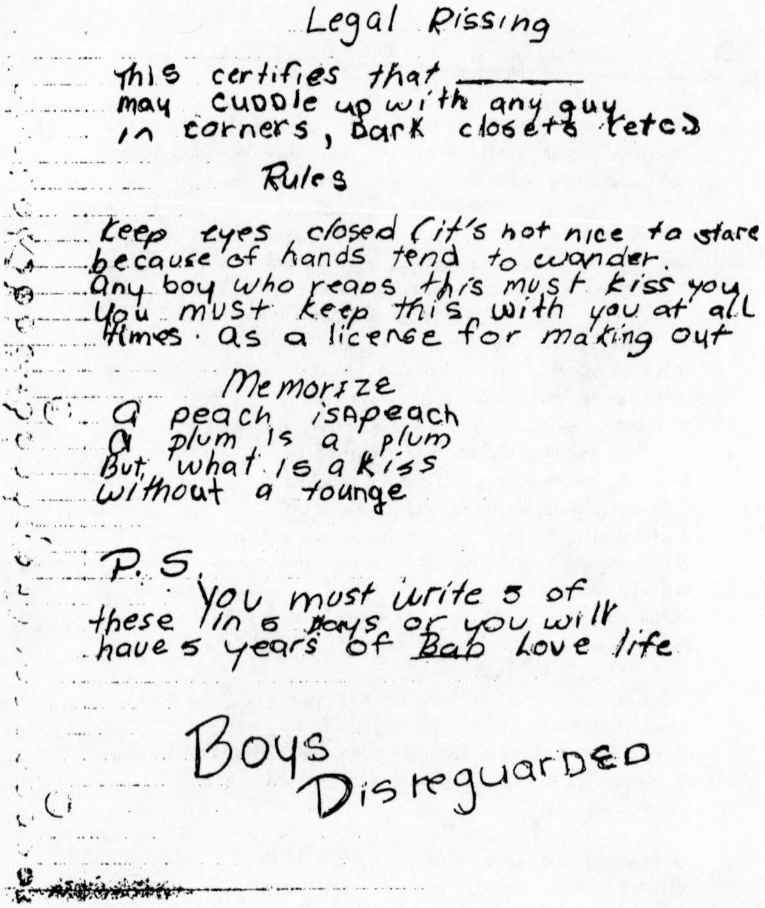

> *Legal Kissing*
>
> This certifies that _____
> may cuddle up with any guy
> in corners, Dark closets tetc)
>
> **Rules**
>
> keep eyes closed (it's not nice to stare
> because of hands tend to wander.
> Any boy who reads this must kiss you
> You must keep this with you at all
> times. as a license for making out
>
> *Memorize*
> a peach isApeach
> a plum is a plum
> But what is a kiss
> without a tounge
>
> P.S.
> you must write 5 of
> these in 5 boys or you will
> have 5 years of ~~Bad~~ Love life
>
> **Boys**
>   **Disreguarded**

Figure 3.2 "Legal Kissing."

adults are chain letters and especially play with parodies of chain letters.)[6]
The adolescents did not use the mail for their play (Stacie's letter is an
exception). Both the writing and reading of playful texts involved collaborative and face-to-face interactions. Writing often involved copying other
written texts, and reading often required filling in forms, from the insertion of
a name, as in Legal Kissing (Figure 3.2), to more comprehensive question-
naires about personal experiences.

The boundaries between adolescent serious and playful writings are not
clearly defined. Someone caught in an embarrassing situation could always
claim that a missive had been a joke, and sometimes it was. Furthermore,
some letters were intended as serious but were received as a joke. This was

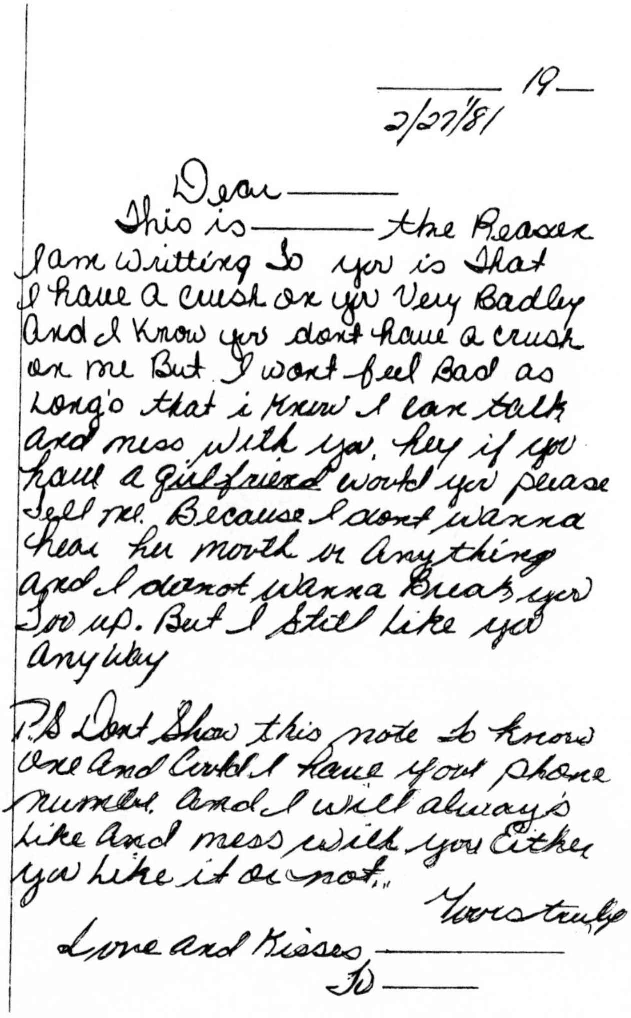

Figure 3.3 Love letter.

often the case with love letters. The love letter in Figure 3.3, for example, was written as a serious statement, but the response of the recipient was to laugh and give the letter to me "for your book." The boy did not respond to the girl's requests, except by explicitly not responding. Even when a letter was accepted in the same spirit in which it was sent, the exchange was not necessarily serious. In one sense, the love letters were the most playful of messages.[7] Consider Figure 3.4, a scrap of paper with "I would want to go withe you" written on one side and "I wouldn't go with you for nothing not

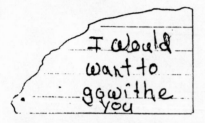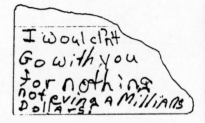

Figure 3.4 Both sides of a scrap of paper.

eving a millians dollars'' on the other side, written by a boy and girl who were courting each other. The playful writing frequently followed a question-and-response pattern. For example, the love letter requested a reply, the constitution of love required a testimonial signature, and Stacie's letter requested a meeting. In face-to-face interaction involving writing, collaborative in either the composing, the reading, or both, adolescents wrote for each other rather than for adult authorities. The format of the writing, the letter or the form, was borrowed from adult writings, and in a sense, the adolescents were playing with adult activities.

The exception to all of these examples of adolescent writing was graffiti. Graffiti did not necessarily involve face-to-face interaction or collaborative work, either in reading or writing, did not mimic an adult form of writing, and did not demand a response. As public displays or signs, graffiti are not the same as writing. The adolescents were able to identify the graffiti in their neighborhoods, but such acts of identification could not actually be called reading. They knew each other's signatures, and if they did not know the particular identities of signatures on foreign walls, they knew which group of neighborhood boys claimed the wall and signed it. (Girls wrote also, but boys claimed the walls.) Groups sometimes competed for space, and in this sense their signature demanded a response. However, this competition was rare among the junior high school students, who maintained the boundaries of their territories and vied for space only at school, the one place where they could not identify most of the signatures. Boys signed primarily on walls; their graffiti consisted of names and what they called "curse words." Girls wrote signatures, "curse words," and rhymes, and did not write as often on walls as in notebooks, on pieces of paper, and in the school lavatories. Both boys and girls were aware of differences between boys' and girls' graffiti in the lavatories.

Graffiti are most important for understanding the significance of names and, more specifically, of written documents as forms on which one places one's signature. Most of the adolescents had nicknames that they used for graffiti and other name-signing occasions. The following story describes signing one's name, and Figure 3.8 provides further illustration.

23

I wrote my name	1
I wrote Candy and David	2
I wrote like this with a pen	3
where he could see it	4
he's always working that desk . . .	5
and he see my Candy right there	6
and I say "it wasn't me" [change of voice]	7
heh heh	8
there're plenty of Candys around	9
I'll say uh "Candy came up with a pen and wrote it"	10

As stated previously, many of the adolescent forms of play with writing involved face-to-face interaction, including speech. The adolescents did not necessarily write as they spoke in their playful use of writing. However, most of their writings could be spoken. This was not true of graffiti, which did not have an easily translatable spoken equivalent.

3.4 Writing as one talks

The writing activity that most closely reproduced speech was the girls' diaries, an example of writing that did not involve face-to-face interaction, was not produced collaboratively, and was not read aloud.[8] Many of the diaries included entries with a large amount of quoted speech. Figure 3.5 is an entry from Stacie's diary. It describes a dispute, but unlike oral accounts of disputes, it was not part of an ongoing argument. Whereas the oral accounts were often offered to provoke disputants, to instigate accelerated quarrels, or to resolve disputes, the written account of what happened did not play a role in the interaction. Further, Stacie often wrote in her diary that she had to delay writing because she was upset. For example:

> . . .
> I think Marie and Linda
> is going to fight with Rose. I'll get
> back with you. Rose is going to get
> it bad. I'm only writing for a little
> while. Okay. Rose has scratches
> and they are realy red.
>
> I'm a little up set
> over Marie and Rose fighting.
> That's why I haven't been writing.

Whereas fighting encouraged talking, and disputes did not help to enhance or discredit reputations unless they were talked about, writing was not at all essential for disputes. Disputes were a familiar topic for writing.[9] Earlier, I discussed the role of fight stories as essential to the fight itself (in fact, in

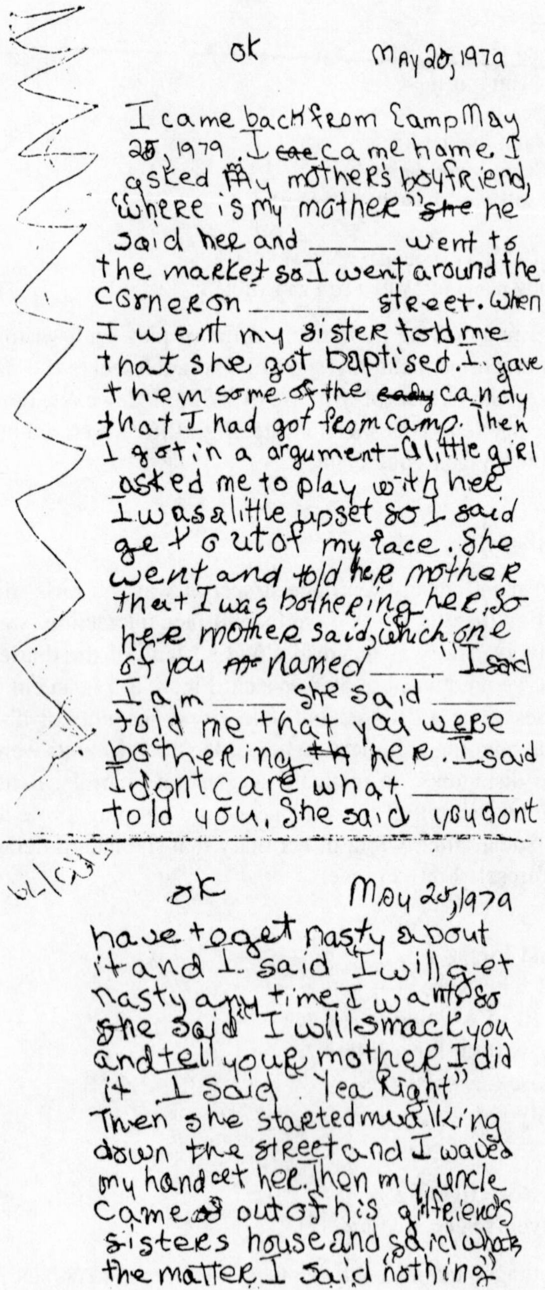

ok   MAY 20, 1979

I came back from Camp May
20, 1979. I came home. I
asked my mother's boyfriend,
"where is my mother" he
said her and _____ went to
the market so I went around the
corner on _____ street. When
I went my sister told me
that she got baptised. I gave
them some of the candy
that I had got from camp. Then
I got in a argument. A little girl
asked me to play with her.
I was a little upset so I said
get out of my face. She
went and told her mother
that I was bothering her, so
her mother said, which one
of you named _____ I said
I am _____ she said _____
told me that you were
bothering her. I said
I dont care what _____
told you. She said you dont

ok   May 20, 1979

have to get nasty about
it and I said I will get
nasty any time I want so
she said I will smack you
and tell your mother I did
it. I said. "Yea Right"
Then she started walking
down the street and I waved
my hand at her. Then my uncle
came out of his girlfriends
sisters house and said what's
the matter I said nothing.

Figure 3.5 Diary entry.

he said "why did you move
your hand at ____ (piching
my arm harder and harder)
"She is a grown lady my
uncle said, I said she is
no grown lady she is a
free bee, the my uncles
girlfriends sister e said
was talking to me about
not talking back to grown
people, then when she
was finished I started to cl
- ean a stick. Then I got tired

Ok
　　　　MAY 25, 1979

and went home when I got
in the house I started to est
tell my sister what happend
then I said to my sister
she thinks she's grown,
My mothers bayfriend said so do
you then I said get out of my face
he said leave me alone or
I will smack the shit out of you,
I said got any more good
jokes. Then when my mother
came home he told my mother
and she said ____ after your
long trip , you must be
exausted and sticky why don't
you take a warm bath and
cool down, I went up stairs
and went in my room to get
a towel and under gamet.
I went in my room and it
was a disceace. Every
thing arranded different,
My books were allees around
my sheets were on the floor. E
- verything was a mess. And

MAY 23, 1979

I went down stairs and told my two brothers and my little sister to clean that room the way I had it or I am going to punch you in the face. My mother told them to go up stairs and clean her room. They went up stairs and started to clean it. Then I came up stairs and told them to get out because they aent cleaning the way they want to. when I put them out they told my mother and called me names. My mother came up stairs I said Don't hit me mommy dont hit me. I grabbed the pill pillow and ran in the closet. She said clean this Room. I didnt clean it I went to sleep. Early that morning 5/24/79 My grandmother woke me up.

Figure 3.5 (*cont.*)

many cases they are more essential than the physical conflict). In contrast, written stories did not play a role in the interaction. (Many of Stacie's diary entries concerned disputes.)

Written notes were sometimes used to send threatening messages and were stuffed anonymously into school lockers. The recipient usually claimed not to be concerned with notes written by people who would not take responsibility for their words. Even signed notes were considered cowardly, since the challenge was not delivered face-to-face. Whereas notes were discredited for their indirect channel of communication, rumors, also involving indirect channels, had great credibility. The adolescents took more notice of a third-party report that someone wanted to fight than they did of a note that said, "Meet me after school."[10] The notes were often thrown away, as if disposing of the paper disposed of the threat.

Third-party reports were met with counterchallenges, orally stated, following the oral challenge. Written challenges were never met with written responses.[11] In most cases, one or both parties failed to appear at the chosen place for the fight, and when someone challenged the failure to appear, the person claimed that she or he was there after all. Both parties claimed to have missed the other. Although writing was not used to resolve fights, differences between boyfriends and girlfriends were occasionally negotiated through letters. In this case, the purpose of the letter was to say things that could not be said in person.[12] For example, a girl sent a boy a valentine on Valentine's Day that said, "I'm sorry." The boy who received it said to me, "I'm gonna be cool about this." Apologetic letters between boyfriends and girlfriends were used to make unspeakable remarks.

As discussed earlier, face-to-face and mediated communications had different consequences in the adolescent community. Using writing to say things that could not be said in person was an important form of mediated communication in which confrontations were minimized and hostilities often shifted from one of the disputants to the person bearing the message.

Saying things that could not be said in person was only one purpose of letters. Some letters, in a manner similar to diaries, used conversational conventions for communication. For example, the following letter, written as part of the National Letter-Writing Week class assignment, from one white girl to another, ended with a statement of affection that would not be conveyed face-to-face:

> Dear Josie,
>
> Hi. How are you doing. Do you go
> with John yet or are you
> still metting him he is cute
> what do you and John do
> do you go to his house yes
> aint his father Little when
> I first seen him I said who
> is he. and his mother said
> Tina this is you cousin John
> This is Tina and when he
> came up he said Look who
> I meet Mona. This bigger
> nurse came in chewing like
> a cow and he said Look
> at that cow. does he know
> your teacher is a nut. I
> hope you's two go together. you
> and John will make a good

match. I think Kitty likes
you a lot. One day I want
to hang with you. If
you want to hang with me

P.S.	Your Best
write	Friend
back	Tina
	Thomas

Tina's letter used many of the conventions of the white female adolescents' speech. Everything in the letter except the salutations and last line could have been said as part of the daily conversation in the lunchroom. The last two lines – "One day I want to hang with you. If you want to hang with me" – are a statement of great intimacy and betray the incongruity of the closing "Your Best Friend." "Best friends" could be defined as people who said things to each other in confidence. Tina's use of the same sentence structure in her letter as in speaking could be attributed more to her lack of awareness of the rules of standard written grammar than to a deliberate choice. Those students who did know how to use the rules of standard written grammar made a great effort to do so.

3.5   Standardization: writing for adults

The issue of standards for writing involves more than a comparison of grammatical usage in speaking and in writing. Thus far, the written examples provided here were produced primarily by adolescents for adolescents. The adolescents also did a great amount of writing that was intended for adults, and this writing followed different standards and attempted to meet the expectations of another, yet familiar, audience. The adolescents were very aware of their audiences in nonclassroom writing. In their play writings, they often imitated adult forms. These writings characteristically adopted more formal conventions; they were not written the way the adolescent spoke. The diaries and letters often reproduced in written form what could have been said orally. In order to understand the constraints that characterized these different forms of writing, and thus to see the writings as using different standards for different purposes, rather than as ill-formed or awkward in comparison to an adult standard, it is useful to investigate each type of adolescent writing as following a format. Each format involves a particular understanding of the relationship between sender and recipient. The writings exchanged between adolescents exhibited several formats for both reading and writing, including the question–response, collaborative creations, playful documents read aloud to an audience of listeners, and recordings of actual occurrences.

The identification of a format combines investigations of the form of production with the form of exchange of texts. The term "format" rather than "genre" is used here, since I am concerned not with types of texts but with the uses of standard or nonstandard grammar, oral or written channels of communication, and face-to-face or indirect exchange. The primary concern here is to demonstrate that standardization and decontextualization are dependent upon patterns of exchange, notions of audience, and situations of use of texts. For the adolescents, the situations of use vary most widely between texts exchanged between adolescents and texts either created by adults for adolescents or created by adolescents for adults.

The adolescents engaged in a great variety of writings for adults. In one sense, it is possible to see these writings as the prototype for all writing, and thus to consider the writings by adolescents for adolescents as takeoffs or transformations of the system. According to such a perspective, the writings by adolescents for adolescents always appear to be imitations of an established order. This is one of the overriding perspectives in literacy discussions and is, in part, advanced by the predominance of situations in which people read and write for others rather than for themselves. (Writers and readers, more often than not, belong to different circles; consider the writers and readers of romance novels, textbooks, operations manuals, and advertisements.) This producer–consumer model of literacy[13] may provide the most pronounced forms of standardization, but it is not necessarily the umbrella under which all textual exchanges must be considered. In another sense, the adolescent writings for adults may be seen as an example of the contextualized use of written texts. Writing, in this case, may be seen as a channel used out of necessity.

The adolescents wrote for adults most often at school. Most of their classwork was in written form. Oral performances could not be turned in and saved for evaluation, and thus were rarely counted in the assessment of a student's work. Much of the written work for teachers consisted of forms. Teachers distributed worksheets that usually consisted of sentences with blank spaces to be filled in. The teachers composed some of the worksheets themselves; many were supplied by the textbook companies and were printed on mimeograph masters to be duplicated.

The teacher whom I observed most frequently used worksheets for almost every class, and much of the lesson was devoted to filling in the worksheet as a collaborative effort. The teacher read the questions, and students raised their hands or were called upon to supply the answers. Many of his worksheets involved puzzles, and figuring out how to use the worksheet was itself part of the work. Certain kinds of writing activities dominated the class (writing sentences including spelling words, filling in blanks on worksheets, summarizing newspaper articles, writing answers to specific questions, answering true/false questions, doing puzzles) (see Figure 3.6).

Comprehension Through Context

As you read the following sentences, you will find some unfamiliar nonsense words. Considering the clues in each sentence and using the picture, identify each nonsense word. Close attention to context will help you improve your comprehension and expand your vocabulary.

1. The zagasaurus is going into the splinx.

   Zagasaurus is number _1_

   Splinx is number _6_

2. The mertz is flying into the henth.

   Mertz is number _3_

   Henth is number _5_

3. The derps are not in the splinx.

   Derps are number _#4_

   Splinx is number _6_

4. The snophtic is going to eat derps.

   Snophtic is number _#3_

   Derps is number _#4_

5. The glinko is under water hiding from the hungry zagasaurus and the immense snophtic.

   Glinko is number _7_

   Zagasaurus is number _#1_

   Snophtic is number _#3_

6. The henth is shading the splinx.

   Henth is number _5_

   Splinx is number _6_

Answer the following questions.

1. Is the snophtic closer to the splinx or the henth? __Henth, splinx__

2. Which two objects could be plants? __Derps, Henth__

3. Name the two smallest creatures. __Mertz, Glinko__

4. Which creature can fly? __Mertz 2__

5. Which creatures are in the water? __Glinko   Zagasaurus__

6. Use descriptive words to tell about the snophtic. __immense, predatory, has   antenas, has a tail__

WORK

Scientific Work = Force × Distance

$$\text{Work} = \begin{array}{c}\text{Effort or} \\ \text{Resistance Used} \\ \text{(in Pounds)}\end{array} \times \begin{array}{c}\text{Distance Moved} \\ \text{(in Feet)}\end{array}$$

Work = 10 lbs. of effort × Moved 3 feet

Work = 30 foot-pounds

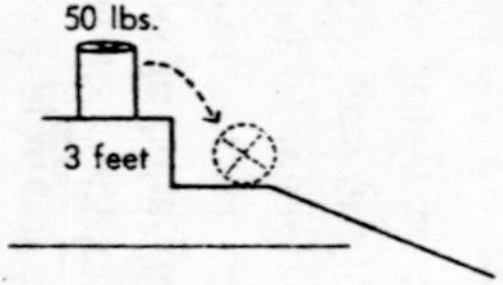

50 lbs.   3 feet

Fig. 1   18 lbs.   6 inches

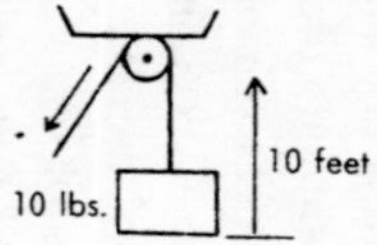

10 lbs.   10 feet

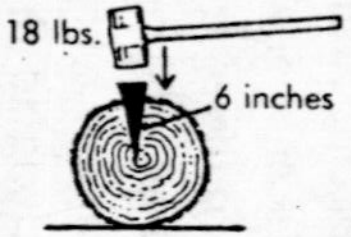

Fig 2   12 lbs.   1 inch

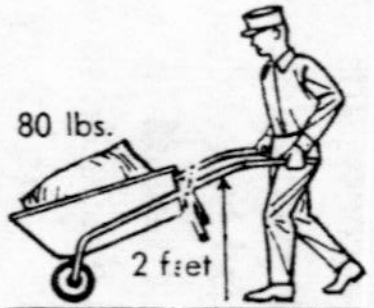

80 lbs.   2 feet   Fig. 5

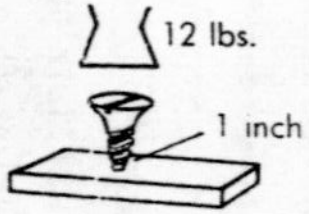

Fig. 3   Fig. 4

STUDENT ACTIVITY

1. Find the amount of work shown in each Figure and write the answer in the spaces provided.

2. In the spaces provided, write the type of simple machine seen in each Figure. Fig-

ures 3, 4 and 5 show two types of simple machines.

3. Scientific work is expressed in the unit of _____

98

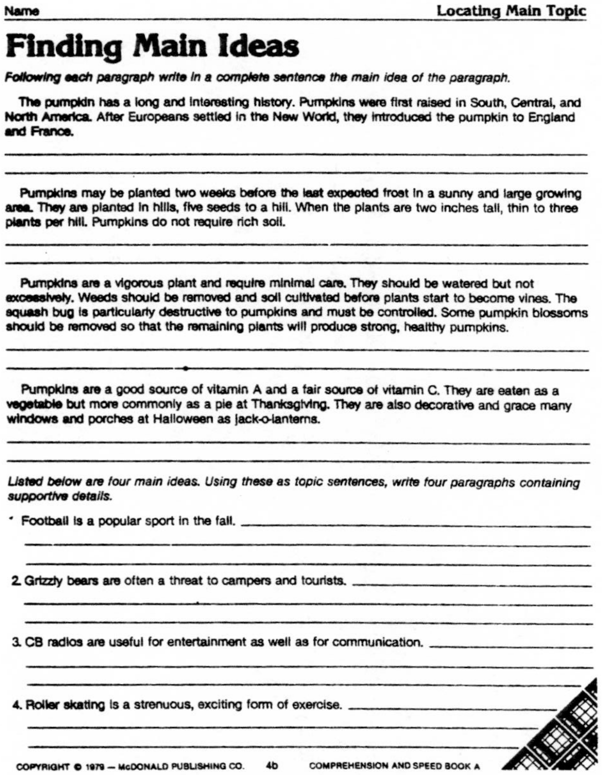
Name Locating Main Topic

Finding Main Ideas

Following each paragraph write in a complete sentence the main idea of the paragraph.

The pumpkin has a long and interesting history. Pumpkins were first raised in South, Central, and North America. After Europeans settled in the New World, they introduced the pumpkin to England and France.

Pumpkins may be planted two weeks before the last expected frost in a sunny and large growing area. They are planted in hills, five seeds to a hill. When the plants are two inches tall, thin to three plants per hill. Pumpkins do not require rich soil.

Pumpkins are a vigorous plant and require minimal care. They should be watered but not excessively. Weeds should be removed and soil cultivated before plants start to become vines. The squash bug is particularly destructive to pumpkins and must be controlled. Some pumpkin blossoms should be removed so that the remaining plants will produce strong, healthy pumpkins.

Pumpkins are a good source of vitamin A and a fair source of vitamin C. They are eaten as a vegetable but more commonly as a pie at Thanksgiving. They are also decorative and grace many windows and porches at Halloween as jack-o-lanterns.

Listed below are four main ideas. Using these as topic sentences, write four paragraphs containing supportive details.

1. Football is a popular sport in the fall.
2. Grizzly bears are often a threat to campers and tourists.
3. CB radios are useful for entertainment as well as for communication.
4. Roller skating is a strenuous, exciting form of exercise.

COPYRIGHT © 1979 – McDONALD PUBLISHING CO. 4b COMPREHENSION AND SPEED BOOK A

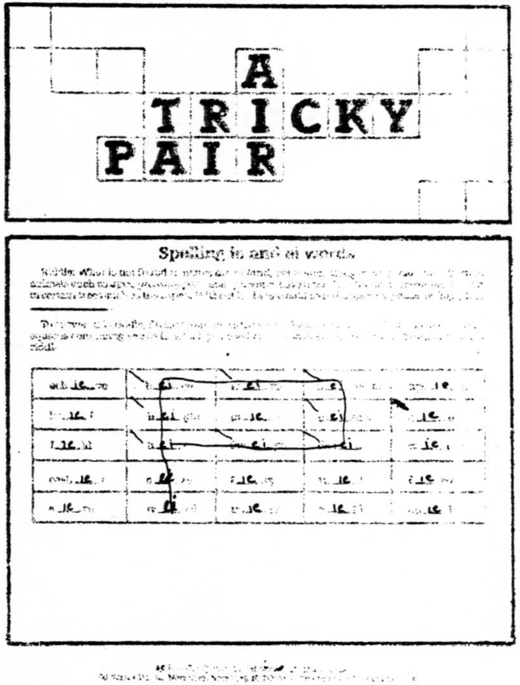

COPYRIGHT SCHOLASTIC BOOK SERVICE.

Figure 3.6 School classwork mimeos. Copyrighted. All rights reserved. Reproduction permission must be requested from original publishers.

Fill-in forms teach a certain mode of writing and require certain kinds of understandings of writing. They also require a particular sort of interaction. The purpose of the worksheets, according to the teacher, was not so much to measure the students' understanding of the material as to ensure their participation in the lesson. The worksheet gave the students something to do and paced their work throughout the lesson.

Worksheets control not only the subject of a lesson but also the time spent on each subject.[14] Like turn-taking, fill-in forms involve a question and a response; however, the response is preestablished, not only in content but in the space allowed for it. Each question on the worksheet represented a segment of time; the amount of time spent answering the question corresponded to the amount of time spent on the subject. Further, the worksheets involved a logical progression from one point to the next. Although it was not always necessary to answer one question before proceeding to the next, the questions were organized according to the sequence of the lesson. One of the benefits of the worksheets, according to the teacher, was that they set up a situation in which individual students could offer oral answers to the teacher's questions and in which all of the students could write the answers on their own worksheets.

The teachers' preferences for using worksheets were based on the quality of student participation rather than on the kinds of thinking or writing demanded by the worksheet. These preferences included the conceptualization of answers in the form of single words or brief phrases rather than long explanations and the formation of answers rather than questions. The students' oral answers were treated as guesses, and guessing was always welcomed. The wrong answers were given no attention and were simply acknowledged by the teacher's response, "No; does anyone else have an answer?" Often the teacher wrote the entire worksheet on the blackboard and provided the answers as the lesson unfolded. Students could fill in their answers without attempting to answer the questions on their own. In a class in which holding students' attention was the major problem, the teacher found that he could encourage full participation by giving students the worksheet to fill in. If he could keep their attention, he felt he was doing all he could to encourage them to answer the questions on their own. Thus all of his lessons were composed of worksheets with missing pieces. Since he could not ensure attention to lecture-type lessons, he lectured through his worksheets. All of his statements were turned into rhetorical questions, and the students were asked to anticipate the correct answer that would fill in the missing piece of a statement. The teacher encouraged guessing in certain directions by offering clues, and the students who gave correct answers exulted in their omniscience.

A characteristic quality of forms is that the purpose of writing is to make an incomplete piece into a complete piece whose completeness is defined a priori by the author of the form. The person who fills in the form is not the author but rather the instrument of completion. Further, forms allow no room for equivocation or ambiguity; they discourage tangential questions. In filling in a form, it is not possible to answer a question with a question. In their own writing, in contrast to the writing produced for teachers, the adolescents were often the authors of their forms. Still, the form dominated much of the adolescent writing, whether the adolescents were the authors of forms in their play with writing or the instruments of completion for an authority's form.

The kinds of writing most frequently found in the homes differed among the Puerto Rican, black, and white families. Puerto Rican adolescents who could read and write English performed many of the official writing tasks for their families. They accompanied their parents, relatives, or family friends to welfare, doctors', or other business offices. In some families, the same child, most often an adolescent girl, was repeatedly assigned these responsibilities. One girl who complained about how frequently she was absent from school because she was needed by someone for such visits said, "Sometimes I wish I didn't know so much English." (She did not complain about her knowledge of Spanish, which she took for granted. She recognized that her knowledge of English was the decisive factor in her being chosen as the family interpreter. She also associated English with filling out forms, both at school and in public offices, in contrast to Spanish, which was associated with letters from Puerto Rico.)

In the visits to public offices, in some cases, the adolescents read English and translated texts into spoken Spanish. In other cases, they read the English aloud. The parents usually responded in Spanish, and the adolescents often used both English and Spanish in their interpretations. The choice of language was determined by both necessity and propriety, although necessity was often the overriding factor.[15]

An adolescent's ability to read and write English was highly valued in the Spanish-speaking homes. Spoken English was primarily used to deal with English speakers on the telephone. Most of the adolescents learned English in the neighborhood before they went to school, since most of the Puerto Ricans lived on streets inhabited by both black and Puerto Rican families. However, the English used for the purpose of interpreting interactions with English-speaking adults was not necessarily the vernacular English learned on the streets.

3.6 Writing and reading in the family

In addition to the frequency of interpretation tasks, which primarily involved reading and filling in forms or government documents, the Puerto Rican adolescents frequently wrote letters to relatives in Puerto Rico. The letters had a prescribed format and illustrated the significance of social conventions as well as writing abilities. One girl described her letters as follows:

24

E:	First you say "Dear whoever you're writing	1
	querido tia" or something	2
	You say "God willing you are well"	3
	and you ask	4
	"How are you?	5
	Presente de esta decirte par saber como tu estas"	6
	You say "thank God everyone here is well"	7
	and you promise to write soon	8
	Sometimes you tell about something that happened	9
	or you say you are working hard in school	10
	and going to church and all that	11
	That's all	12

The students had not received instruction in written Spanish in school, and this limited their ability to write letters in the language. Some of the adolescents who frequently wrote letters to relatives in Puerto Rico said that they did not know how to write Spanish and, when asked about the letters, said, "Oh, my mother helped me," or "Yah, I can write letters okay." Not all of the adolescents corresponded with relatives, and in some families the mother or an older sister handled the correspondence and read the letters received from Puerto Rico in Spanish to the rest of the family. Few of the bilingual adolescents had received formal instruction in written Spanish, with the exception of certain students who had lived for a few years in Puerto Rico and a few others who attended a Jehovah's Witness church where they read the Bible and wrote lessons in Spanish.

The black families I visited had many more reading materials than the Puerto Rican families. In interviews, family members claimed that the reading materials were sharply divided according to age and gender. The adolescents categorized the magazines read by people in their households. They said that men read sports, car, and pornographic magazines, as well as *Ebony;* women read fashion magazines and *Ebony;* boys read sports magazines; and girls read movie magazines. The only magazine reading that I was able to observe was adolescent girls reading the words to songs from teen magazines. They used the magazines to decipher the words rather than to memorize them. Once the words were deciphered, they learned the songs by listening to them on the radio or on records. Many black families had collections of books, and some had sets of encyclopedias. The books were typically stored in an upstairs hallway or in a child's bedroom. For the most part, they consisted of reading material for junior and senior high school girls, and the subject matter often concerned career choices and adolescent experiences. The books in one adolescent's hallway were primarily novels about teenagers and books about the experience of being black in the United States, including stories of heroes and heroines and stories of people with troubles:

I Am 15 and I Don't Want to Die	*A Raisin in the Sun*
Crooked Arm and Other Baseball	*Pork Chop Jones*
Stories	*Sounder*
3 Loves Has Sandy	*Angelita Nobody*
Julie's Heritage	*I'll Get There; It Better Be*
The Miracle Worker	*Worth the Trip*
Don Martin Drops 13 Stories	*Autobiography of Miss Jane*
A Hero Ain't Nothin' But a	*Pittman*
Sandwich	*Shadows in the Light*
Escape on Monday	*Catcher in the Rye*
Sisters	*Mystery of the Old Jalopy*
Jean and Johnny	*Touch of Magic*
On City Streets	*Hardy Boys*
Romeo and Juliet	*To London with Love*
Durango Street	*First Aid*
Leo the Last	*Go Ask Alice*
Go Tell It on the Mountain	*Amy and Laura*
Marian Anderson	*The Jacksons*
A Crack in the Sidewalk	*Short Stories*
If I Ever Marry	*Alice in Wonderland*
New Girl	*Fifteen International One Act*
The Deep	*Plays* (falling apart)

The books had been purchased by older brothers and sisters when they were in high school. Many had been bought through the Scholastic Book Service at school.

None of the white families in the study had collections of books. A few of the adolescent girls owned a copy of the *Girl Scout Handbook,* and some had copies of old textbooks. The most evident reading material in the white homes was newspapers (both the city newspapers and the free local newspaper), as well as calendars and framed (often religious) quotations on the walls. Of course, these observations reveal book-collecting habits rather than reading habits.

Many of the adolescents saved past school work including tests, whether or not they had done well, homework, and particularly special projects. All of the homes had a Bible and a telephone book, and all received mail. However, in many homes, the reading materials consisted of expendable writings rather than collections of books or writings. Except for the things saved by adolescents and the Bible and telephone book, writings were not collected or accumulated in book form. Writing was sometimes hung on the wall, but it was not stored on shelves. Shelves were used for family photographs and knick-knacks. Many of the adolescents, black, white, and Puerto Rican, checked out books from their local libraries or from the school library. The school provided access to the Scholastic Book Service, which offered inexpensive books and posters; the students bought posters far more often than books. They also bought movie or teen magazines in local stores.

The collection of reading materials or the accumulation of books cannot be used as an index of the uses of literacy. Saving written materials is only one use of writing. Just as the possession of books does not indicate that people read, their absence does not indicate that they do not read. However, books are one representation of the consumption of written texts; newspapers and official business transactions are other examples. All of the families had some contact with such texts, although not all family members had equal ability in reading and writing. As discussed, the Puerto Rican families often designated representatives who took primary responsibility for exchanges involving written English (and sometimes spoken English as well). These designations also applied to personal writing, and some members of the family, usually not the same as the English writers, took responsibility for corresponding with relatives in Puerto Rico. Many of the mail-order sales projects in black, white, and Puerto Rican families were joint enterprises involving several members of the family. Also, the white adolescents often entered mail contests. Many of the home business activities involved some form of correspondence. For example, some of the women sold Avon cosmetics. The adolescents said that they were not old enough to sell these products, but their mothers shared the work with them and they were able to select products for themselves in exchange for helping to correspond with Avon.

These observations are not based upon a representative sample of the community; they rely upon observations of the homes of the children from two particular classrooms. The purpose of the preceding sketches is not to characterize the black, white, and Puerto Rican literacy habits in general, but to provide some insight into the uses of literacy of the particular adolescents observed. The Puerto Rican reliance on adolescents as interpreters, the prevalence of letter writing in Puerto Rican homes, the collections of books in black homes, and the placement of words on the walls in white homes are not equivalent observations. They provide the most striking differences; observations of similarities were more prevalent, especially those concerning the adolescents, who were observed more closely than other family members.

3.7 Collaborative literacy

Much of the reading and writing in which the adolescents participated, both in school and at home, involved what may be called "collaborative literacy." The model of collaborative reading and writing suggests an alternative to the assumed model of one person reading alone. Collaborative reading situations call attention to the possibility of reading as a face-to-face experience in which people read aloud to each other rather than as a solitary act. This does not imply that the face-to-face exchange involves the presence of the author of the text. In collaborative readings of business documents, the author and readers were often far removed in both physical space and social distance. It is not possible to assert any necessary relationships between the uses of literacy and social relationships between authors and readers. However, some possible relationships may be noted. For example, greater distance between authors and readers may correspond to collaborative reading – for example, in efforts to figure out income tax forms or in study of the Bible. However, the distance between authors and readers is created in many ways, including social status, time, and space. Each of these involves several means, some that do not implicate authors, such as the distance created in time by saving writings from the time they were received until a later review or the distance created in time by passing materials on from one generation to another. The relationship between an author and a reader or readers is only one relationship involving written texts. This relationship is not the sole determinant of the reading experience, and the expendability or accumulation of texts in particular may depend on other relationships, especially between readers.

The authors of business materials received by mail in the adolescents' homes were most often either anonymous or strangers. The texts were often saved for a time as records of transactions, but they were ultimately expendable. They had limited temporal meaning or usefulness. The anonymity of the authors can be compared to the familiarity of the correspondents in letters to relatives, which, in the Puerto Rican homes, involved collaborative reading. However, this collaborative reading only extended to family members and was consistent with the domain of privacy for family matters. Although the letters, especially those written by adolescents, involved formulaic statements used in every letter rather than intimate disclosures, they were regarded as personal and private, in contrast to the public nature of the mail-order business correspondence. In the Puerto Rican homes, collaborative writing was often a necessity rather than a preference, and some collaborative readings and writings invaded privacy. This occurred particularly when adolescents or neighbors assisted in reading and filling in government or medical papers. Such papers often requested information that was considered private and that became less private only because people needed help in filling out the forms.

It is important to distinguish between collaboration in which everyone participated equally and collaboration in which skills were hierarchically differentiated. For example, in the Puerto Rican collaborative efforts in filling out government forms, adolescents were often given status beyond their age. They were granted access to information that they might not otherwise know. Writing became a medium through which adolescents entered the adult world.

The privilege of participating in adult transactions was often qualified, and parents sometimes limited their requests to "just read the English." However, the adolescents were asked to demonstrate abilities that exceeded those of their elders. Although this has been a common situation, especially for immigrant families, its frequency historically has not necessarily made it more acceptable or manageable.

Equal participation and hierarchical participation in collaborative literacy may be termed a difference between "duplicative" and "complementary" uses of literacy. These terms are borrowed from Van den Berghe's (1973) ethnicity studies, which distinguish whether domains of social life are shared or segregated across ethnic groups.[16] According to Van den Berghe, if each ethnic group has its own bakery, its own laundry, and its own grocery store, each with different products or customers, then one would say that such institutions are duplicated in a multiethnic population. If the bakery is run by Italians, the laundry is run by Chinese, and the restaurants are run by Greeks, he would say that the institutions are complementary. In any community, reading and writing may have either a duplicative or a complementary distribution of skills, or both. That is, either everyone knows how to read and write certain kinds of texts and people do their own reading, or some people do reading and writing of certain kinds for others. Reading and writing may be differentially assigned according to categories of texts, categories of people, or both. People are ideally designated as readers because of both their abilities and their social positions. However, they are sometimes expected to be able to read certain kinds of material because of their social position, and their abilities and position do not necessarily match.

The adolescent uses of literacy involved a hierarchical and complementary system in many of the collaborative writings with teachers and parents, and a duplicative system in the collaborative writings of adolescents among themselves. In writing with adults, the adolescents had a specific role. Particularly as interpreters in Puerto Rican families, they performed specialized tasks that were not duplicated by other members of the family. Typically, the adolescent read an English text and translated it into Spanish for an adult. In some cases, someone recognized by the family as an expert in dealing with public offices was also present to explain what information was required or to suggest ways of managing complex exchanges. The adolescents were not supposed to be involved either in the exchange of information or in the management of the exchange. Some of them were frequently asked to participate in such transactions, and they became somewhat expert in understanding what was required and what alternative arrangements were possible. Such involvement of adolescents in adult transactions occasionally disrupted the social conventions for appropriate age behavior in the community.

Adolescent girls were involved in business transactions far more frequently than boys. This choice corresponded somewhat to their responsibilities in the home, where they took care of younger siblings and did the family cooking, laundry, or shopping. (This was common in the black, white, and Puerto Rican families in the neighborhood surrounding the junior high school.) Adolescent girls were expected to have responsibilities centered on the family. However, these responsibilities were often assigned to girls who did poorly in school and who willingly stayed home. These girls were not necessarily competent in reading English (although they spoke it well). When such poor students were taken to medical clinics or other places of business to aid in translation, the transactions were especially difficult. (Also, these girls were sometimes needed to babysit at home on occasions when their mothers were required to be at the medical clinic or welfare office.)

Public offices often supplied translators, but they were not necessarily available for all stages of the transaction. For example, one mother was accused of assaulting a teacher and was summoned to court. At the court waiting room, when her name was called, she was asked in rapid English, "Do you need a translator?" When she did not answer, she was not provided with one. When I insisted that she needed a translator, the court clerk questioned her slowly in English. At first, the court was unwilling to provide the translator, since she was able to answer the questions. As it turned out, the translator, who was eventually called, was helpful to the woman not only in translating from Spanish to English but also in explaining the meaning of the court jargon. Since no free legal assistance was provided at that stage of the trial, the translator also acted as an interpreter (in the sense of providing legal interpretation) by elaborating the significance of the specific words spoken by the judge and court personnel.

In many public transactions, translators were helpful not only in translating written English to spoken Spanish but also in explaining the meaning of a "sublanguage." As defined by Naomi Baron, a sublanguage provides precision, brevity, or exclusion (1981:123–5). It requires a mastery of the purposes of the group that uses the language. Although not specifically addressed by Baron, sublanguages often involve collaborative reading. When outsiders are involved in reading a sublanguage produced by a specialized group, complementary collaborative reading may be necessary; the help of experts may be required to interpret the sublanguage to an outsider, and the expert may not necessarily be a member of the subgroup. The expert may be an intermediary. In some cases, the Puerto Rican adolescents took the role of intermediary.

In duplicative collaborative readings, the participants often assume that everyone has access to the skills required not only to read a text but also to interpret it. In such readings, participants often assume that they understand each other. The adolescents often expected each other to be able to read everything if they read at all. Writings produced for teachers were often expected (by teachers) to be done individually rather than collaboratively.

However, in a few cases when written communication with authorities was necessary, the adolescents often worked collaboratively. The letter in Figure 3.7 is typical.

The school principal commented on the "perfectly written" letter and agreed to the request. He did not respond as favorably to another form of collaboration: a petition presented to him. He had ruled that a certain play could not be performed during the annual talent show, and the students petitioned him to reconsider. The petition (Figure 3.8), called "Don't Let the wall fall" (the show was called "The Wall"), included twenty-three signatures, signed by twenty-one students and two teachers. It also included the following statements, all made by students:

> "It should stay in because it was good, and won't affect the kids."
> "Don't Let the wall fall because that part was good."
> "It should be left in because it's the funniest show in the show"
> "We the student think is not a bad script because we know right from wrong!"
> "See thats whats wrong with the teacher now they don't give us a change [*sic*] they must put the show on the rold. I'm all for you!"
> "the Show must go on please I beg of you please let the Show go on"
> "It was the best."
> "The Show has to go on"
> "I really like the show which doesn't make me do that to any of my teachers because none of them does any thing to make me do that to them. I really like it and I don't think noone will do that and its only a show"
> "Come on give us A Nother Chance?!! Principals"
> "Leave the show on that's whats wrong now use [*sic*] don't give us a chance and it won't affect the teachers either."
> "I think the show should stay in because it is just a show. I think the students from Paul Revere have enough sense to know how to control thereself during school. It is the high light of the show. Alot of people enjoy it. But it really should stay in. It is just a record. I really think you shouldn't take it out. All the boys and girls who practice and stayed after school and word hard. Why would you take this priviledge away from them. If you take it off they would have did all that hard work for nothing. People really enjoy the show. They even sign pentition. For them to do this they must love it."

The final and most lengthy statement, written by the first signer of the petition, demonstrates the remarkable nature of the petition, a form of written

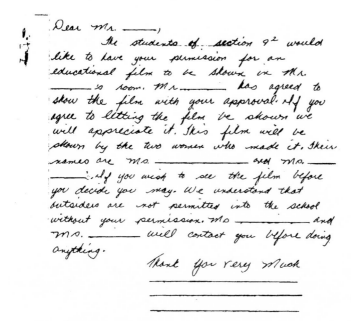

Dear Mr. _____,

The students of section 9² would like to have your permission for an educational film to be shown in Mr. _____'s room. Mr _____ has agreed to show the film with your approval. If you agree to letting the film be shown we will appreciate it. This film will be shown by the two women who made it. Their names are Ms. _____ and Ms. _____. If you wish to see the film before you decide you may. We understand that outsiders are not permitted into the school without your permission. Ms _____ and Mrs. _____ will contact you before doing anything.

Thank you very much

Figure 3.7 Letter to the principal.

communication rarely used by the adolescents. She points out, "They even sign [this] pentition." The protest concerned the removal from the program of a play that was performed to a record by Pink Floyd, popular at the time, which said, among other things, "Hey, teacher, leave those kids alone." In accompaniment to the music, four white girls, dressed as boys in rolled-up jeans, T-shirts, and baseball caps on backward, sat at desks with their feet on the tables, chewed gum, and shouted abuses at a girl dressed in a skirt and representing a teacher. "The Wall" was the only piece in the talent show that involved white students, and the irony of their identity – four white girls without discipline records – suggested one of the few possible roles whites could play in a show dominated by very talented black and Puerto Rican dance groups. The principal responded to the petition in a letter to the teacher who coordinated the talent show.

> Alice,
>
> I appreciate the students' concern, but unfortunately, a principal at times must make decisions which are unpopular or even unjust in an effort to accommodate the general welfare.
>
> I feel that this song is inappropriate at this time and in this place.
>
> I hope they can substitute another number.
>
> M. L. O'Malley

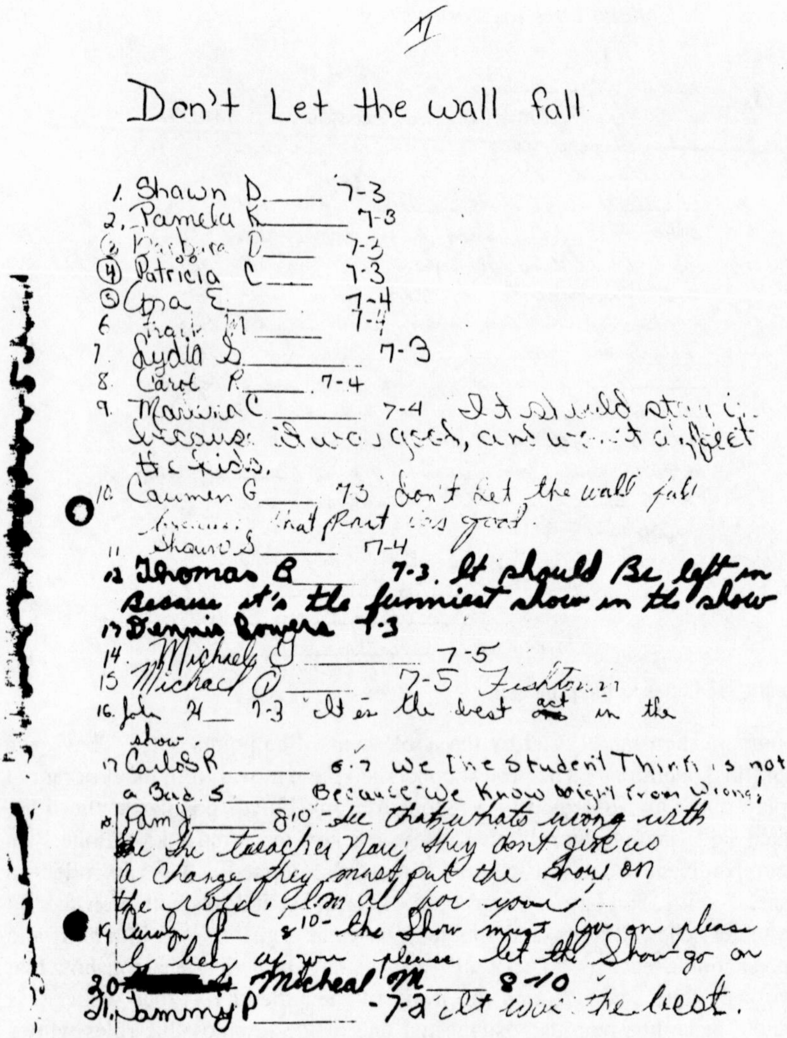

Don't Let the wall fall

1. Shawn D._____ 7-3
2. Pamela K_____ 7-3
3. Barbara D_____ 7-3
4. Patricia C_____ 7-3
5. Gina E_____ 7-4
6. Jiquir M_____ 7-4
7. Lydia S_____ 7-3
8. Carol R_____ 7-4
9. Marivia C_____ 7-4 It should stay in because it was good, and went affect the kids.
10. Carmen G_____ 7-3 Don't Let the wall fall because that part was good.
11. Shawn S_____ 7-4
12. Thomas R_____ 7-3. It should Be left in because it's the funniest show in the show
13. Dennis Bowers 7-3
14. Michael J_____ 7-5
15. Michael D_____ 7-5 Fushtown
16. John H_____ 7-3 It is the best act in the show.
17. Carlos R_____ 6-7 We The Student Thinks is not a Bus. S_____ Because We know Right from Wrong!
18. Pam J_____ 8-10 Lee that whats wrong with the The teacher Now they don't give us a Change they must put the Show on the rotal, I'm all for your
19. Carol J_____ 8-10 the Show must go on please its hey as you please let the Show go on
20. _____ Michael M_____ 8-10
21. Tammy P_____ 7-2 It was the best.

Figure 3.8 *(here and facing)* Petition: "Don't Let the wall fall."

Colener f____ 8:10 the Show began to go
on. Mon b____

Cheryl B____ 7:13.
I really like the show which
doesn't make me do that
to any of my teachers because
none of them does any thing to make
me like that to them I really
like it and I don't think
noone will do that and its
only a show

COME ON GIVE US
A NOTHER CHANCE?!
PRINCIPALS

Tina L____ 7:13.
leave the show on that's whats
wrong you use don't give us
a y chance and it won't affect
the teachers either.

Larry A. H____ — ENGLISH TEACHER. / 5-23-80
Peter J. M____ — English Teacher / 5-23-80

_____ 7-3

I think the show should stay in because
it is just a show. I think the students
from _____ have enough sense
to know how to control thereself during
school. It is the high light of the show.
Alot of people enjoy it. But it really
should stay in. It is just a record. I
really think you shouldn't take it out.
All the boys and girls who pratice and
stayed after school and work hard.
Why would you take this privledge
away from them. If you take it off
they would have did all that hard work
for nothing. People really enjoy the
show. They even sign pentition. For
them to do this they must love it.

111

The principal's options in responding to the students included the following: no response, since he had already stated his decision; an oral statement on the public address system, which was used for announcements every morning and evening; a written statement in the daily bulletin, which was distributed to all teachers with messages to be communicated to students before classes began every morning; or the method he chose, a letter to the teacher. His letter, although addressed to a specific individual, was itself a formal statement that could have been made publicly. The statement directly addressed the students' request for a reconsideration, but he made it not directly to them but indirectly through a teacher. The students could have chosen a spokesperson to write for them as a group. This person might have been the one with the neatest handwriting or the best grammar. The spokesperson could have assembled all of their ideas into one statement, as in Figure 3.7. The last entry on the petition (Figure 3.8), written on a separate piece of paper although there was room on the paper containing others' comments, was in a sense such a statement. An individual statement might have involved complementary rather than duplicative efforts. Instead, the students chose to submit all of their statements together, many with grammatical errors, and the teachers added their names near the end of the document. The teachers saw the grammatical errors and presumably could have pointed them out or corrected them, but they too participated in the duplicative effort in which all signers wrote, as equals, to an authority.

The petition is also remarkable in the students' use of grammatical structures found in their spoken statements. Their statements were written as they would have been said, a demonstration of writing the unspeakable. The statements were very contextualized and demanded a reader's familiarity with the situation. They had a known addressee, the principal, although he was never addressed specifically, and they assumed a shared knowledge both of the matter in question and of the principal's complaints.

Statements such as "It should be left in because it's the funniest show in the show" assumed that the subject ("It") was familiar to the reader. However, this comment followed "Don't Let the wall fall because that part was good," and in a sense, the use of "it" was justifiable in a cumulative comment. Many of the comments can be considered as parts of a whole. For example:

> "We the student think is not a bad script because we know right from wrong!"
> "See that whats wrong with the teacher now they don't give us a change [sic] they must put the show on the rold."

The first statement claimed that the students knew the difference between right and wrong (and therefore would be mature enough to watch a show in which teachers were treated with disrespect). The second statement claimed that the teachers were not willing to give the students a chance (in terms of knowing right from wrong). When read as a cumulative statement rather than as the statements of individuals, each of whom signed his or her name after a statement, the petition can be seen as a coherent statement that presented a logical argument and as grounds for the principal to reconsider his decision. The major points of the students' position were as follows:

1. "The Wall" was a performance of good quality. Students would like it.
2. Students had worked very hard to produce "The Wall," and their hard work had earned them a place in the show.
3. Although the students liked the show, they would not necessarily behave like the characters in the play. They know the difference between right and wrong.
4. There is a difference between a talent show performance and everyday behavior.
5. The fact that many people care about the fate of "The Wall" is attested by the petition.

The students' position was most succinctly summed up in the statements "It was the best," "The show must go on," and "Give us another chance." The most subtle part of their argument was the suggestion that knowing right from wrong was related to knowing the difference between art and everyday behavior. The students did not agree that the performance demonstrated "wrong" behavior; the performance was "just a show," and was not an index of their understanding of the difference between right and wrong.

The similarity of the adolescents' written statements to their verbal arguments is evident, and the writings can be compared to oral complaints concerning the cancellation of the talent show performance:

25

Std:	They says "freedom of speech" so you should let 'em do the play	1
Tchr:	Why do you think they should have let them do it?	2
Std1:	Cause it's a good play	3
Std2:	It wasn't no harm bein' done	4

The petition entries can be seen as incoherent writing that did not provide referents for pronouns, or it can be seen as a coherent collaborative statement in which one statement refers to a previous one. It should be seen as writing appropriate to its context. The adolescents were familiar with their principal's attitudes and complaints, and they knew he was familiar with the talent show program, so they addressed their remarks to him without unnecessary explanations. The petition had a specific purpose.

Although teachers did not necessarily see such specific purposes for their classroom assignments, it is possible to view the students' work as responses

to a similarly familiar individual who knew the subject at hand and thus to see
the students' classwork as appropriately contextualized. Very few class assignments required "decontextualized" writing, or writing that would be
understood by an unfamiliar audience. The principle of writing for a distant
reader was not explained. Teachers occasionally asked students to address
themselves to people on other planets and to write essays about their homes
(including essays on how they spent their summer vacation). Such assignments encouraged students to provide descriptive details that would make this
account intelligible to an outsider. However, such audiences were so unfamiliar to the students that they had "nothing to say." One teacher frequently asked his students to write letters to people interviewed in *Scholastic
Magazine*. In the letters, students often referred to the interviewee's life with
a sense of shared knowledge (between the interviewee and the magazine
reader), as though the interviewee knew what had been said in the magazine
about him or her. In addition, however, the students sometimes made statements about themselves, written to an outsider who might not be familiar with
their world. For example:

Dear Stephen Hawking

How did you find out or how did you know you was so smart? I
read about you in the Read magazine. I'm in the eighth grade and I
can't even figure out math problems like that one in the Read
magazine.

How is a curve line shorter than a straight line. I'll be looking for
your letter and please send me one of your mile long math problems
to see if I could do it.

Thank you
A friend in
Philadelphia
[address]

The following letter fulfilled an assignment to write to Anne Frank. The final
statement, "I don't have anything else to say," provided closure and expressed a common feeling. Such a letter, in which the author feels at a loss to
find a message, is strikingly different from the petition's purposefulness.

Dear Anne Frank

My name is rosita. I'm 13 years old. I read your diary. I think it
was interesting. I wish I could off [*sic*] seing you in person. I go to
Paul Revere junior high school. I do have alot of friends. When we
were reading your diary we didn't know who was Kitty. Until we
heard the rest of it. My friends, Anna, Sylvia, and Priscilla have a

diary. When we read a story we have to listen very careful. I don't have anything else to say.

Yours truly
Rosita Sanchez
Good bye

Write back
Soon

The selection of the intended audience, of the form of communication (essay, letter, or petition), and of the author's purpose (revealing or concealing information) are essential in any assessment of the appropriateness of contextualization in writing.[17] The interviewee of a magazine is a different audience than the teacher; the hypothetical Anne Frank, in a letter to be read only by the teacher, is an ambiguous audience.

The letters consisted primarily of the student's name and grade, the name of the school, and greetings. As Rosita wrote, "I don't have anything else to say." What could the students write? The disclosure about difficulties with math problems in the letter to Dr. Stephen Hawking was both relevant and personal, as was Rosita's statement about diary writing among her friends. Such statements reveal the students' attempts to communicate with an unfamiliar audience, as well as their ability to use the standard letter format.

The petition demonstrated the adolescents' ability to state an argument in writing.[18] They occasionally wrote letters to the principal or teachers to complain about specific incidents, but they rarely wrote petitions. Letters were designed to inform the principal or teachers of something the students wanted them to know. The petition did not provide information on "The Wall"; it presented an argument and demonstrated support for it. As a form, a petition is a contextualized text in which support is metonymically represented by signatures. In the adolescents' petition, statements about the performance of "The Wall" were presented as if in anticipation of the principal's grievances. The petition required a sophisticated understanding of context.

In their duplicative collaborative writing, the adolescents assumed that everyone could write and could understand what others wrote. Such writing experiences encouraged the adolescent perspective, which assumed that everyone knew and understood what every adolescent knew. The central feature of decontextualization (however unrealizable) is that one writes with an understanding of what it is like to read from another person's perspective. The adolescents often assumed their world to be commonplace and given.

Further, they rarely evaluated the success (in terms of mutual understanding) of their own writings. They often evaluated each other's ability to speak or to hold the floor. They especially evaluated each other's ability to sustain a monologue or to keep up an argument. Writing did not involve such contests, and the goal was not the extension of a turn at talk. Further, to criticize someone else's writing would have been to criticize, by implication, one's own ability to read.

The adolescents often used speaking to conceal rather than reveal information, but they rarely used writing for this purpose. The only parallel in writing was anonymous letters. (Forgery, as discussed earlier, involves deception but not concealment.) In speaking, they developed elaborate ways of reading meaning into each other's words, and their exchanges involved constant misinterpretations, especially of orally conveyed third-party messages. Such metacommunicative systems of interpretation and reinterpretation were not part of writing and reading exchanges. In reading and writing, the adolescents did not separate understanding from decoding, but rather assumed that one skill went along with the other.

3.8   The appropriate uses of literacy: context

Learning to read and write specific kinds of texts involves learning the ropes and becoming indoctrinated into a particular system of interpretation. Although many of the adolescents were able to write well for themselves (for example, in their diaries), many did not recognize that there are several ways to write, just as there are several ways to speak.[19] The type of writing required for achievement in school depends on an awareness of the potential multiple purposes of texts. Many of the adolescents demonstrated more abilities than they were able to recognize. They were able to write as they spoke, but they did not manipulate the categories of written texts to the same extent that they played with categories of utterances. Their written communication rarely utilized the complexities of their spoken interactions, which were dominated by multiple interpretations, concealment, and evaluation. For the most part, writing was treated as undigested communication that was to be converted into face-to-face speech.

The adolescents' writings can be divided into those produced for adults and those produced for other adolescents or for themselves. These two kinds of writings provided two kinds of contexts. Each context had different demands.

The demands of adult writing, as perceived by the adolescents, were neatness and certain formalities, determined by the particular type of text. For example, consider the formalities of greetings in the adolescents' letters, of rhetoric in the petition, and of filling in blanks in classwork. For the adolescents, writing for people unfamiliar with one's situation or for an audience of authorities or adults separated, if not by culture, then by social status, was dominated by formalities. The petition, letters to the editor of the local newspaper (see Chapter 4), and letters to the principal were instigated by the adolescents and written for authorities.

Most of the writing instigated by adolescents was intended for other adolescents as readers. Such writing often parodied the adults' assignments, as in the kissing form and the constitution of love, but was guided more by the appropriate uses of oral communication in the adolescent interactions than by formalities that belonged to the domain of written texts. Writings instigated by the adolescents often duplicated the spoken style of similar statements. This was the case in the adolescents' narratives, diaries, and some protest letters. Most of the writings instigated by the adolescents themselves were what have been termed "unofficial writings" (Fiering 1980:131).

One central characteristic of the adolescents' unofficial writings was their close tie to oral communications. The expectation that written texts would be collaboratively written in exchanges dominated by oral communication, and that they would be collaboratively read or read aloud, sustained the contextualization of the written texts.

Literacy scholars have used the term "decontextualization" to refer to the creation of written texts that can be understood by audiences unfamiliar with the contextual details familiar to the author.[20] Ideally, decontextualized texts provide the contextual details necessary for a message to be understood without the explanations provided in face-to-face communication. The text supplies its own context. The basic premise of decontextualization is that certain kinds of literacy require texts that can be read far from their origins (in both time and space) and that supply the necessary explanatory information to be intelligible to their readers. The implication is that oral texts do not decontextualize.

The notion of decontextualization is essentially concerned with the communication of information. If a text is considered to contain a message, then the purpose of decontextualization is to make the message intelligible. The question is, where does the message end and the context for understanding it begin? As Gregory Bateson has stated, all communication is about relationship (1972:137). The context in which a message is placed is a statement of relationship as well as a means for contributing information. Discussions of decontextualization focus on intelligibility, that is, how a message is understood or whether it is understood in the intended context, rather than on the functions of the message. However, intelligibility is not the only function of messages.

The concept of decontextualization places the burden of analysis on the texts themselves rather than on the process of creating texts, the performance of reading, or the relationship between texts. In analyzing texts in terms of decontextualization, one must ask, how does this text communicate information, and does it rely upon the performance context to supply explanations of its meaning or directions for its interpretation? Texts that rely upon the performance context are "contextualized." However, as long as analysis of texts relies only on texts that do decontextualize, we are left wondering exactly how context supplies the necessary supplementary information.

For the adolescents, decontextualization was not necessarily a matter of the ability to produce abstract texts; they were able to translate experience into elaborate texts, both oral and written. The adolescents had few occasions to produce decontextualized texts.

The adolescents' written texts were rarely what would be called decontextualized, but they displayed an understanding of context. The relationship between text and context is complex; a decontextualized text is not possible; every text has a context.[21] Part of the problem in understanding the relationship between text and context in the adolescents' writings lies in difficulties with the term "context." Erving Goffman has discussed the problem of viewing context as an undifferentiated residual category. He says that utterances have multiple possible meanings, partially attributed to multiple contexts: "To find an utterance with only one possible reading is to find an utterance that can occur in only one possible context" (1983:67). The notion of contextualized writing suggests that texts may be understood only in certain contexts. Contextualized texts allow the possibility that "taking something out of context" means distorting its meaning. However, every rendering of experience into texts, oral or written, takes experience out of context. Such renderings can be unsuccessful, as illustrated by the assessment, "I guess you had to be there." Notions of decontextualization and contextualization both concern the rendering of experience into written texts. The ability to decontextualize involves the elaboration of experiences unfamiliar to readers. Decontextualization assumes the reader's unfamiliarity with the experiences described. Contextualization suggests not only the reader's familiarity with the experiences described but also his or her familiarity with the writer. The notion of contextualized writing suggests that the writing is limited to one particular context in which it is meaningful. The general concern in either case is mutual intelligibility. The notions of decontextualization and contextualization are not opposites; they are two of the many means for achieving mutual intelligibility in written texts.

Decontextualization refers to an impossible ideal. Even written texts that are intelligible independently of any oral context for communication depend upon other written texts to provide contextual clues for their interpretation. The appropriate term is "recontextualization,"[22] which implies that written texts take messages out of their oral communicative context and place them in the context of writing. Recontextualization allows communication through written texts across time and space, to unknown audiences, and in the absence of face-to-face interaction. Recontextualization involves the communication of context, and the context is itself a message.

Several conflicting forces operate in establishing the relationship between text and context in written texts. For the adolescents, speaking was an explicit context for writing. Also, categories of experience, such as fighting, were general contexts for specific incidents, such as a fight, and understanding the general context was necessary for understanding a particular account, oral or written.

One purpose of recontextualization in written texts may be to discriminate between messages and metamessages where the latter provide a context. In other words, written texts provide embedded messages, as do oral texts, but since written texts cannot rely upon face-to-face interaction to frame messages, they must utilize literary conventions, understood by the reader through familiarity with other written texts.

Discussions of decontextualization are concerned with the clarity and comprehensibility of written texts in the absence of face-to-face communication. In contrast, discussions of literary devices deal with concealment and play with readers' expectations. These are really just two different ways of talking about the same thing; both can be understood as problems of interpretation involving the relationship between text and context.

Many literacy discussions have raised a vague notion of context as the circumstances surrounding a recounted incident. However, a close examination reveals that what is missing from contextualized texts is not circumstantial details but appropriate literary conventions. The essential context for recontextualized texts is other written texts. Recontextualized texts create the possibility of written communication in the absence of spoken communication. One kind of recontextualized text can be read in the absence of the author, the author's circumstances, and the circumstances related in the written account.

The question of context concerns the indexicality of texts. As Garfinkel and Sacks (1970) have stated, all utterances are essentially indexical. This is not to say that an utterance is made "in" some particular context, but rather that all utterances have multiple possible meanings and any particular meaning is an understanding of context. Further, context is indefinite; it is not possible to pinpoint the contexts of an utterance.

This indefiniteness of context is an especially important consideration for written texts. Speaking is indisputably contextualized; each utterance contains Jakobson's (1960) six factors of addressor, addressee, context, message, contact, and code. Writing, however, can conceal the identities of addressor or addressee and, through emphasis on what Jakobson terms the "message," or poetic function, can obscure the context. In speaking, many channels other than the verbal one (what Jakobson terms the "contact") are available for communication of the message; in writing, this responsibility rests entirely on the written channel, and multiple contexts are created by the channel itself, by the relationship of the texts to other texts.

The relationship between texts, the understanding that writing exists in the context of other texts, is essential for an understanding of the category of literature. Literature presents one kind of relationship between texts. Literary language changes the nature of indexicality from a concern with true and false to a concern with the text's own illusions.[23] The adolescents' texts concern neither the facticity of the text (true and false) nor the production of illusions; rather, the adolescent writings are constrained by the opposite possibilities of expendability and preservation of written texts. For the adolescents, these opposing possibilities are essential characteristics that differentiate the uses of speaking and writing as channels of communication. This is not to say that the adolescents preserve their writings; far more frequently, they discard them. Writing permits the destruction of utterances, which is far more difficult in speech. For example, consider a practice frequently observed in the classroom in which a student received a test or piece of classwork marked with a failing grade. After briefly noting the grade, the student ostentatiously (without permission) got out of his or her seat, crumpled the paper into a ball, and dropped it into the trash can. The most frequent excuse for missing homework was that the student lost the worksheet. The appropriate response to a threatening note found in one's locker was to show it to a friend and immediately throw it away. Written communications could thus be destroyed.

Thus one context for adolescent writings and readings was writing as a tangible record. This context encompassed the official written forms that had to be filled in for governmental or medical records; writing turned in to a teacher as the primary index of a student's performance; formulaic letters to relatives that recorded the state of affairs in various households and affirmed the well-being of family members; statements of protest, including letters to authorities and petitions that attempted to set the record straight; the adolescents' diaries, which were the only personal record and one of the only forms of preserved writing, in addition to the often saved letters from relatives; and certificates of accomplishment, such as diplomas and even graffiti, the territorial record. As discussed earlier, most readings in the adolescents' homes were thrown out rather than preserved. Each home had a Bible and a current telephone book, but most reading matter, including newspapers, magazines, and church bulletins, were either discarded soon after being read or saved for a time, whether read or not, and eventually discarded.

Expendable writing (or what is perceived to be expendable) has currency and temporal limits. This temporal limitation constitutes an orientation toward literacy that may be contrasted to the "book orientation" (Heath 1977). Currency was one context for the adolescents' texts, and what might be labeled contextualization can also be seen as a present-oriented context. The adolescents did not transcend the context of the familiar here-and-now relationship between themselves and their teachers in their writings and did not write letters or essays that elaborated or specified referents for an unfamiliar outsider.

One final issue requires examination: the relationship between indexicality and expendability, two constraints on the orientation to written texts. The relationship is this: The recognition of indexicality admits the possibility of multiple interpretations of texts; the recognition of expendability admits the possibility of limited interpretations of texts. Both recognitions are plagued by similar paradoxes. The recognition of multiple interpretations is plagued by the question of whether the text is an artifact or whether it exists only in its readings.[24] The recognition of expendability raises the question of whether or not the utterance is destroyed when it is thrown away.

This chapter has suggested several ways in which the adolescents recontextualized writing. They transformed written exchanges into oral face-to-face interactions through collaborative reading and writing. They adapted formulaic patterns of speech as standards for producing formal writings intended for authorities, and they established the relevance of written texts to their lives by choosing to discard rather than to preserve them.

4
RETELLINGS

This chapter focuses on multiple tellings, oral and written, about a fight. Unlike most of the fight stories told at the junior high, these stories concern a fight that actually occurred. The multiple tellings provide an opportunity for the close examination of differences between oral and written versions and between versions told among adolescents, among adults, and told (and written) by adolescents for adults.

A few points elaborated in earlier chapters have a bearing on this discussion. First, the story is not the same as the event described; further, events are categories of experience, not to be confused with the experiences themselves. Stories are one way of categorizing experiences as events. Second, stories build shared knowledge by creating categories of experience as tellable. Fights are one such category. Third, clarity is not necessarily the professed or assumed goal of storytelling, and stories may conceal as well as reveal. Mutual intelligibility involves more than clarity and depends upon shared means of communication (codes, narrative devices, framing devices) rather than upon pieces of information.

Rarely are so many versions, oral and written, told by adolescents, teachers, and reporters available for research. Although retellings are a common phenomenon in everyday storytelling, custom decrees that ordinarily one may not be the audience for more than a few versions. The versions presented here were not solicited; rather, they were collected as they were told, as part of everyday conversations. I begin by offering my own version of the event, since for the purposes of intelligibility, a general familiarity with the events of the fight is useful. However, please keep in mind that this outline of what happened is just another version and conveys its own point of view.

The stories concern a fight between two black girls at the school. For weeks before the fight, the girls had had disagreements. As told by their classmates, one of the girls, Linda, constantly antagonized the other, Cindy, characterized as a shy girl who avoided conflict. Cindy brought a knife to school or was given a knife by one of her friends, and at the end of an afternoon class when Linda somehow provoked Cindy, she pulled it out. They ran out of the classroom; Linda threw a trash can at Cindy, and Cindy followed her to the stairwell. At this point a crowd gathered, composed of students from Linda's and Cindy's class as well as other students on their way to the next class. Some of the students tried to take the knife from Cindy but failed, and Cindy stabbed Linda in the back. Linda ran down the stairs to the nurse's office, where the authorities took care of her.

Stories about the event proliferated and were told orally by students, teachers, and parents and reported in writing by the newspapers, which provoked written responses by the students. In one sense, the oral and written versions shared the same functions to account for a serious and frightening event or to take stock of the situation. All of the stories shared a point of view: that violence in school is terrible. However, the students and newspaper reporters did not account for the event in the same way. The students saw the fight as an unusual episode in which things went too far. They did not perceive the event to have consequences that would affect anyone other than the two students involved. The newspapers reported the event as a sign of racial tension in an inner-city integrated school. What did not concern the reporters was the relationship between the two girls, their previous antagonisms, and the perception on the part of both students and teachers that Cindy was a shy girl who ordinarily avoided conflict and who had been pushed too far. In other words, the newspapers did not place the event in the same context as the students. The students protested (in their letters to the editor) that the newspaper had no right (no entitlement) to report on the fight unless they told the whole story.

The question of what constitutes "the whole story" involves the relationship between recontextualization and entitlement. In the simplest sense, the whole story depends upon the determination of when the event begins and ends and whether or not events are recorded in the correct order. An appropriately recontextualized text provides whatever contextual details are necessary for intelligibility and either presents the events in order or recovers the order. However, not all tellers are entitled to the same pieces of information; specifically, the reporters did not claim to know about the relationship between the girls before the fight or about the general atmosphere in the school. In claiming that the fight was worth reporting, however, they implied that it was more significant than other events at the school. They claimed to have the right to determine which events of school life were storyable for the newspaper.

Constraints on entitlement and recontextualization do not necessarily match. Entitlement is usually a constraint on face-to-face communication and suggests that the appropriate telling of a story depends upon the relationship of the teller to the events and to the other participants in both the event and the telling. Recontextualization, usually a constraint on written communications by absent authors, demands that information be presented in its appropriate context. In the retellings of the stabbing story, the adolescents claimed that the reporters did not include the appropriate context and therefore were not entitled to report on the event.

The retellings of the stabbing story included oral and written versions told by both insiders and outsiders. Written versions by outsiders for outsiders place the most demands on recontextualization. Communication between insiders and outsiders, whether oral or written, offers the greatest possibility of challenges to entitlement. Newspaper reporters and other public media personnel usually consider themselves immune from challenges of entitlement, and the adolescents ordinarily do not pay attention to whether or not contextual details have been included. Texts are constrained by both recontextualization and entitlement only when the storytelling context involves both insiders and outsiders.

4.1 The versions

One purpose of the many retellings was to account for how such a thing could have happened. The fight ended when one girl stabbed another with a knife. This occurred at the end of the school day, before the last period, and stories told the following day during lunch at school and during subsequent lunch periods involved attempts to make sense of the incident. The following story is Marsha's account of what happened. She presented the fight as the logical outcome of an unjustified provocation and a justified retaliation. As discussed earlier, the sequence of provocation and retaliation was familiar in the adolescent world. Marsha told the following story in the school lunchroom on the day following the fight to her friends who had not been present during the fight:

26

M:	Okay, well we came out of science	1
	that was between eighth and seventh periods	2
	and we walked down to our lockers	3
	They was in room 406	4
	and our lockers are next to 406	5
	and then they came runnin' out	6
	that's the one that had the knife	7
	tellin' her not to mess with Linda	8
	But she say that Linda's been messing with her ever since she started	10
	and she was fed up	11
	So then she pulled out her knife	12
	And then Linda picked up the trash can and threw the trash can at her	13
	and then –	14
	So Linda turned around and ran down the hall	15
	and Cindy was right behind her, right	16
	so they got down to the end of the hall	17
	um Linda must have turned around	18
	at Cindy because Cindy was	19
	Linda kept runnin'	20

and but a lot of people came down there	21
it was a lot of people tryin' to take the knife away from Cindy	22
and while they was tryin' to take the knife she was cryin' 'cause she said that um	23
she ought not to be messin' with nobody but she kept messin' with her,	24
'Cause Cindy she's not the type that messes with people 'cause she nice	25
They kinda shocked that it was her who stabbed her so the girl must of *really*	26
been messin' with her for her to do somethin' like that	27
So, um, Linda, so she kept runnin' after she got stabbed and she got out on the second floor you know and rushed her into the um nurse's office	28
They took Cindy downstairs and um everybody, the principals and all, was tryin' to act like nothin' did happen	29
But that's somethin' to talk about	30
Because you know we was all in the hall	31
We was there when it was going on	32
And everybody was talking about "what happened? what happened?"	33
They, the teachers and the principal	34
They know what happened	35
But they tryin' to act like nothin' happened, tryin' to cover it up	36
They did wrong 'cause everybody find out anyway	37
and everybody was talking about it	38

T:	Where did she get the knife?	39
M:	Cindy had the knife on her	40
	I think she got it from home	41
	Somebody could have gave it to her but I think she got it from home.	42

Jeanine then told her version of the story:

27

M:	Did you see what happened after class?	1
J:	I saw, I saw when they, when they first started fightin'	2
	When the break came they went outside	3
	They started talkin' and she took out the knife	4
	And then she picked up, the other girl picked up a trash can	5
	And threw it at her	6
	She went and she stuck the knife	7
	And um she ran	8
	And the girl took off her shoes	9
	And she ran after her	10
A:	Were they fighting in class?	11
J:	They were arguin' and when they got outside they started fightin'	12

Stories were told about the antagonism between the two girls long before it erupted. Some of the stories told after the fight referred to these earlier stories. For example, the teacher made the following claim:

(30)

Tchr:	Linda was the instigator	22
	She did have a big mouth	23
	And she told one of the friends of Cindy	24
	that Cindy was uppity	25
	and didn't want to be friends with her anymore	26
	or something to that effect	27

Although the teacher presented Linda's remarks in the lunchroom as statements rather than a story, her story does refer to a he-said–she-said conversation and thus follow a typical mode of presentation for stories about fights.

Stories were told about the fight within moments of its occurrence, both before it was terminated and before the tellers had determined exactly what had happened. Stories were told as part of the ongoing incident, and stories about how it started circulated rapidly through the constantly growing crowd of onlookers. For example, John (see oral narrative 28) said that he was in his classroom when a friend came in and told him that a fight was going on in the hallway. His friend said that a girl had approached him with a knife, but it turned out that she was not chasing him.

Stories about the fight were told in continually widening circles. Before the stabbing, only those people who knew the two girls involved had talked about their daily quarrels. During the fight, anyone near the location of the fight, in the fourth floor hallway of the school, talked about it. The circle then widened to include everyone in the school. For example, when the incident was later reported in the newspapers, one reporter interviewed a girl who had been on the second floor of the school when the fight occurred. Although the newspaper account mistakenly said that "Paula Crockett, 15, was in the school counselor's office when the fight started right outside," in actuality Paula saw only the final moments of the fight, when one of the girls ran down the stairs from the fourth to the second floor and came out of the stairwell immediately outside the counselor's office. As one of the girls wrote in a letter to the local congressman (see Figure 4.2 in Section 4.4), students went home and told their parents about what had happened. The newspaper reported a wider circle in asserting that parents in the community met to discuss what had happened. The newspaper itself was a vehicle for bringing the story to a wider circle. Letters to the editor corrected accounts of the story and entailed a public exchange between people inside the school and newspaper reporters. And this discussion, although maintaining the anonymity of the participants in the fight, the tellers, the school, and the newspaper, carries the story to people far removed from the incident in time, geographical space, and social distance.

Many of the students and teachers considered the stabbing incident to be inconsistent with what they believed to be the characters of the two girls. In Marsha's story, as in other stories about the incident (Stacie's oral narrative 29 and the teacher's oral narrative 30), Linda was depicted as a troublemaker, someone who "messed around" with other students and was "not to be messed with." Linda was a discipline transfer from another school; she had been involved in trouble there and had been transferred to prevent further problems. This was a common practice in the school system. For example, Cindy was transferred to another school as a result of the stabbing. Discipline transfers were not always identified as such by students, although teachers were often informed of the reason for the transfer. Students did not necessarily know that Linda was a discipline transfer. When Marsha stated, "But she [Cindy] say that Linda's been messin' with her ever since she started," she referred to the fact that Linda was new to the school in the spring term.

Marsha and others depicted Cindy as a nice girl who was pushed too far. In the stories, students and teachers said:

(26)

  M: Cause Cindy she's not the type that messes with people cause she   25
     nice
     They kinda shocked that it was her who stabbed her so the girl must   26
     of *really*
     been messin' with her for her to do somethin' like that   27

(29)

  S: I know the girl was tired of everybody keep on botherin' her   12

(30)

  Tchr: And Cindy was getting egged on by everybody else, you know,   38
      "Linda's always doin' this and Linda's always doin' that."
      And uh Cindy supposedly being egged on   59
      I really assume that she was being egged on   60
      That's my bias   61
      The crowd around them was really saying "get her get her get her"   62

According to both students and teachers, Cindy was repeatedly provoked by Linda. People said that Cindy tried to ignore Linda when Linda bothered her. However, the provocations could not have been entirely ignored, especially according to the many people who later claimed that they had seen Linda bothering Cindy. No one identified the people who "egged on" the fighters. The teacher identified one of them, the girl who had given Cindy the knife, and depicted her as someone who appeared innocent while quietly instigating other people's fights. Many said that people had tried to take the knife away from Cindy or told her, as Marsha reported "not to mess with Linda." The crowd had a definite, although retrospectively ambiguous, role in the incident.

The seeming discrepancies and ambiguous characterizations of the people involved in the fight can be seen as part of the typical girls' fighting scenario at the junior high school. Although the stabbing was atypical, other fights were similarly explained as the result of a troublemaker provoking an innocent party. Usually, both sides claimed to be innocent. A girl's friends told her of the other girl's insults, and these friends were generally present during any fights that actually occurred. The same network of friends who relayed threats and insults from one antagonist to another also attempted to stop fights that got out of hand. They were rarely successful. However, they were usually able to restrict the quarrel to messing around and to prevent combatants from hurting someone seriously. In the fight between Cindy and Linda, the boundary between messing around and fighting was not maintained. The students explained this by saying that the person they characterized as the innocent party, the nice girl, was pushed too far.

Stories about the fight between Cindy and Linda were rarely limited to accounts of the physical fight itself. Most of them recounted the days of provocation that preceded the fight and the justice meted out by authorities afterward. The following stories were told by a white boy and a black girl in a classroom before class began several weeks after the fight. The first story, told by John, is an example of a story that does not conform to the scenario for girls' fights. John's purpose was to testify to his proximity to the events. The second story, told by Stacie, who patiently listened to John's story before correcting him, filled in the details.

28

J:	When the stabbin' took place I was –	1
	I was goin' into my art room and and when	2
	and when	3
	and I heard lots o' yellin' and screamin'	4
	and when I went out I seen girls runnin' all over the place	5
	and one of my friends was comin' in sayin' that one o' them girls just passed him with a knife	6
	and then I seen cops yellin' all over the place	7
	and then he told me	8
	and then he was at the fight	9
	and she was like – he was runnin' from her	10
	but he wasn't what she was runnin' at	11
	a girl was fightin' another girl	12
	and then	13
	and one of the girls' friends picked up a trash can	14
	and threw it at her	15
	and threw it at one of the girls that was in the fight	16
	and somebody handed that girl a knife	17

and ran after her	18
I think they were at the steps	19
and she got her	20
she stabbed her in the back	21
then they put the girl and	22
I forgot what happened	23
they took her down to the station	24
and I think	25
she ain't back in the school no more	26
I think she went to a what d'you call it?	27
S: She is right back in school	28
not in this school	29
J: Oh	30

At this point, Stacie corrected John and offered her own account of what happened.

29

S: Now *I* know what happened	1
Okay, there's this girl, I forgot her name	2
She was a light skin girl	3
And there was another girl; I know her	4
Her name is Linda	5
um Her name is Linda	6
Linda Stevens is her name	7
And she um	8
She bothered this other, the light skin girl	9
I forgot her name	10
So she um	11
I know the girl was tired of everybody keep on botherin' her	12
So she musta said that whoever bothers her again, she gonna hurt em	13
So um, they were arguin' upstairs	14
So um I think the fourth floor	15
They were arguin' in the hallway	16
And so one o' the – the girl that was –	17
The girl got mad	18
And she just	19
Her girlfriend	20
gave her a knife	21
So she started –	22
So she started um runnin' after the girl to stab the girl	23
and the girl had picked up a trash can	24
you know the lunch trash can?	25
She just threw it at the girl	26
And then she started runnin'	27
She started runnin' down the hall	28

And then she fell	29
She got back up and the girl stabbed her	30
in the back	31
And then she just, she got up	32
And she ran more, she kept on runnin'	33
And she got downstairs to the second floor where the nurse's office is	34
And then she passed out	35
They took the girl to the police station	36
And they took the other girl to the hospital	37
And she was um	38
The other girl was arrested but I don't know what –	39
Concealed weapon, I don't know what she had	40
And the other girl who, who gave her the knife was accused of um	41
I know she gave the girl the knife so she must of been accused of somethin' cause it was part her fault	42
And after she did that she just stopped	43
She just stopped and didn't say anything	44
And now the girl Linda Stevens	45
Then they put it in the papers and things but it's all wrong	46
They say that the girl was stabbed in the um chest	47
Which they know that in the chest and the back, two different places, the front and the back	48
and she said that the girl was stabbed in the back I mean in the chest	49
So that was the tale they said in the papers	50
And now Paul Revere is gettin' even worse	51
Everybody think they can bring knives to school and this school goin' down down down	52
they write up all over the boards	53
it's out in the halls	54
there's graffiti, graffiti all over the walls	55
they curse anytime they feel like it . . .	56

One of the major differences in the stories told by different people was in the coda, the statement that usually came at the end of the story and brought the situation up to date.[1] When Marsha told her story the day following the stabbing, Cindy's fate had not yet been decided. Marsha's story did not dwell on what would happen to Cindy but rather discussed how the situation was being handled by the authorities at the school. Marsha said:

(26)

They took Cindy downstairs and um everybody, the principals and all was trying to act like nothin' did happen	29
But that's somethin' to talk about	30
Because you know we was all in the hall	31
We was there when it was going on	32
And everybody was talking about "what happened? what happened"	33

They, the teachers and the principal	34
They know what happened	35
But they tryin' to act like nothin' happened, tryin' to cover it up	36

At the time that Marsha told her story, the current issue was how the authorities were handling the situation. When Stacie told her story several weeks later, the issue was how it had been handled by the press. Also, Stacie was concerned with what she perceived to be the decaying situation in the school.

(29)

And now Paul Revere is gettin' even worse	51
everybody think they can bring knives to school and this school goin' down down down	52

Stories told by parents and teachers had quite different assessments of the impact of the incident. Parents warned that they would take their children out of the school. The newspaper reported one parent's comment: "I'm pulling my two boys out of school after today – that could have been my boy!" The point was also made in two of the protest letters:

> "Everyone went home and told their mother about it so their mother say it is a bad school so you will be get out there before April." [See Figure 4.2]
>
> "But really to get to the point, We really think that the [ ] and other known papers should really find out how it happened and what went on. Because we don't want our school to begin to loose [*sic*] population." [See Figure 4.1(a)]

The teacher's story was particularly concerned with how the authorities handled the punishment of those responsible for the incident. As she states in her story, she attempted to find out how Cindy got the knife, and her story included a characterization of the girl who was probably responsible. The teacher told the following story to another teacher many months after the incident:

(30)

Tchr:	They were both in my advisory	1
	Anyway they were both pretty new to the school	2
	One of them had come at the beginning of the term	3
	And that was Cindy and she was the quiet one	4
	And the other one	5
	I don't remember her name	6
	was a new admit	7
	And she was a transfer from another school for disciplinary reasons	8
	She had been in trouble in another school	9
	I think Beacon but I'm not sure	10
	And every day in advisory	11

Tchr2:	Linda Stevens?	12
Tchr:	Linda, yah	13
	Linda was the new person	14
	and Linda didn't get into any groups yet	15
	She had a cousin in that room	16
	And she was kind of into that group	17
	But basically, Cindy had her little group of friends	18
	And Linda	19
	was with her cousin	20
	But somehow or another, what I heard was, in the lunchroom	21
	Linda was the instigator	22
	She did have a big mouth	23
	And she told one of the friends of Cindy	24
	that Cindy was uppity	25
	and didn't want to be friends with her anymore	26
	or something to that effect	27
	and Cindy heard about it	28
	She was really egged on by the crowd	29
	And one of the other girls in the – in the –	30
	in their advisory, 9-4	31
	was Nora, a real real instigator	32
	and she was the sweet innocent looking type	33
	but she was really a nasty-hearted person, I mean she was nasty	34
	And she'd turn around and like and she was just a nasty person	35
	And somehow or another, she told Cindy about a friend of hers who had a knife	36
	And she told –	37
	And Cindy was getting egged on by everybody else, you know, "Linda's always doin' this and Linda's always doin' that."	38
	"This is what Linda said about you," kinda stuff	39
	so, um during science that's seventh period in the afternoon	40
	She asked to be excused and Linda had been messing with her the whole time	41
	Really, I don't know if she did any kind of physical stuff	42
	She's continually harassing Cindy, who's a quiet person and doesn't say much	43
	So Cindy got excused to go to the bathroom, where she went	44
	And with Nora's help	45
	Nora told her where to find the girl	46
	She went to the girls' room	47
	Borrowed the knife	48
	came back	49
	and during the break of classes between seventh and eighth period	50
	they all went out for a drink of water or whatever	51
	and Cindy and Linda had another confrontation	52
	And at that point Cindy took out a knife	53
	and something happened in there where a trash can was thrown	54

	I think that Linda ran back into the room	55
	and got a trash can	56
	and threw the trash can at her	57
	and then she started to run down the hall?	58
	and uh Cindy supposedly being egged on	59
	I really assume that she was being egged on	60
	That's my bias	61
	The crowd around them was really saying "get her, get her, get her "	62
	And Cindy got her	63
	She stabbed her in the back	64
	She ran after her	65
	And after that I think that one of the teachers grabbed Cindy	66
	But I'm not really sure what happened	67
	And the kids were really quiet the next day	68
	They didn't want to tell me about it	69
	They didn't, you know, they just didn't want to talk about it	70
	And a few, one of the kids, one of the boys, he's a quiet type came in earlier and I asked him what had happened	71
	And he said something like "Well"	72
	I said, "Who was involved; where did the knife come from?"	73
	And he said, "I heard Nora had something to do with it "	74
	Then during class I was asking probing questions like "What happened	75
	Did anyone know anything about it? Does anybody know where the knife came from?"	76
	And Nora turned around and just looked the other way and started talking to her friends	77
	And she, you know, had I not known from Simon that Nora might be involved, I might not have noticed	78
	But I was definitely noticing her reaction	79
Tchr2:	Did anything ever happen to that?	80
Tchr:	Yah, they were both sent to different schools	81
	As a matter of fact	82
	Something ironic	83
	I think that, uh,	84
	Cindy was at Beacon, the school that Linda came from	85
	And Linda went to Broadway or somewhere like that	86
Tchr2:	What happened to Nora?	87
Tchr:	Nothing, nothing happened to Nora	88
	It wasn't investigated	89
	I don't know of any kind of fact-finding commision to find out about the knife	90
	or who gave the information to find the knife	91
	Other stories I've heard say that Cindy brought the knife to school	92
	So a lot of people don't know that part	93

Many of the people in the school saw the fight between Linda and Cindy as involving injustice. Student friends of Cindy believed that Cindy had been pushed too far and that the true injustice lay in Linda's provocations. Many of the teachers agreed with the characterization of Cindy as a nice girl and of Linda as a troublemaker. No one suggested that Linda deserved to be stabbed, but at the same time, people were more worried about what would become of Cindy than they were about Linda's recovery from her wound.

Fight stories usually focused on beginnings and establish endings, especially on who started a fight and how it was resolved or, if not resolved, its status at the moment of the telling. Retellings can be compared on the basis of the details each provides concerning what happened or on the basis of where the story cuts into a situation. In fight stories, the details of what happened during the dispute were secondary to the more overriding concern about how the dispute fit into other incidents. As discussed earlier, fight stories were not always preceded by physical disputes; far more of them were told about quarrels that had not and would not come to blows.

Fight stories were told as part of current situations. One purpose of the telling was to establish current alliances, to realign or to confirm friendships. The insertion of an incident into the larger situation could be managed in many ways; in particular, the depiction of a character as provoked depended upon when the incident or provocation purportedly began. According to the adolescents, responsibility for a fight between girls fell heavily on the person who started it. When the instigator was identified, the blame shifted from the antagonist in the dispute to the instigator herself (for example, see oral narrative 9).

In the retellings of the clash between Linda and Cindy, the primary concern was the characterization of the two girls in terms of who started the fight and who would start a fight. The only person to speak in Linda's behalf was Linda's sister, who, when interviewed for a newspaper story, reportedly said that her sister was involved in a fight at her old school and added, ''But she's not the kind of girl who would start a fight.'' The teacher's story attempted to shift the responsibility from Linda to Nora, whom she perceived to be the instigator of the fight. If the adolescent tellers knew that Nora had provided Cindy with a source for a knife, they did not include this detail in their stories. To do so would have been to begin a new dispute between the teller and Nora. Stacie included the person who provided the knife in her story, but as long as she did not know the person's identity or could not be expected to know it, she could safely make such statements.

In addition to the attempt to portray Cindy as the victim of a fight in which she was pushed too far and as someone who would be further victimized by the punishment she would receive for stabbing Linda, there was also an attempt to identify the authorities who were somehow responsible, if not for the fight, then for the general situation at the school. In the stories, this attempt appeared in the closing remarks, in the way in which the teller resolved the situation in terms of the present. The girls who told their stories (oral narratives 26 and 27) on the day following the fight discussed how the authorities at the school were "tryin' to act like nothin' did happen." A few days later, when the same girls saw the newspaper account of the incident, they discussed how the newspapers had slandered their school with sensationalist reporting. Weeks later this was also the concern in Stacie's story. Students and authorities at the school felt victimized by the newspaper account, and this account, like the fight itself, became the basis for further retellings.

On the day following the fight, a newspaper carried the following story (names changed to maintain anonymity):

PAUL REVERE WARS LEAVE GIRL BLOODY

A 14-year-old girl was in critical condition last night after being stabbed in the chest by another girl at Paul Revere Junior High School in Welmont. Linda Stevens, of the 600 block of N. Park St., transferred to Paul Revere from Broadway Junior High only two weeks ago . . . because her mother thought she was hanging out with a bad crowd and heading for trouble. "Her school work was suffering," Mrs. Adele Stevens, a mother of nine, told the *News* last night. "I thought she'd be better off at Paul Revere. But she hadn't even had time to settle down before this happened." The stabbing occurred at 1:30 P.M. after Linda and another unidentified girl had gotten into a fight and Linda had apparently swung at the other girl with a garbage can. "That's what I was told, anyway," said Mrs. Stevens. "I don't know if the other girl had pulled the knife then or not. Linda swung the garbage can at her and tried to run. She got stabbed in the chest." Linda was listed as critical in the intensive care unit of St. Frances Hospital, Park and Latimer Sts., with a chest wound and internal bleeding. Doctors were waiting to see if surgery would be necessary. She lost five pints of blood. A 15-year-old classmate of Linda's was arrested at the school and charged with aggravated assault, simple assault, reckless endangerment and weapons offenses. Police recovered a paring knife with a four-inch blade. The girl was released to the custody of her parents. She will have a hearing today at the Youth Study Center. Paula Crockett, 15, was in the school counselor's office when the fight started right outside. "Me and my girlfriend were there. We heard a bang against the wall. When we went out, this black girl was lying on the floor. They sat her up and there was blood down the back of her shirt. They tried to get her in a wheelchair but she couldn't sit up. She was spitting blood from her mouth. Some of the kids who saw the fight said they

tried to grab the knife from the other girl's hand. I heard she was a
Puerto Rican. They said she was real strong, they couldn't hold her
back." Paula, of the 400 block N. Patterson St., said she went
straight home and wasn't going back to Paul Revere until something
was done to make the school safer. "Even the counselor said he was
shook and that he would like to live a little longer," she said.
"There's always fights, the black kids make wise-cracks at us but
it's best to just ignore them. You can smell pot all over the school but
the principal doesn't seem to even try to do anything. It's like he's
scared. I don't like it there at all. How can you learn when you're
worried the whole time about what might happen to you? But there's
no other school I can go to." Linda's sister, Yvette, 15, who still
goes to Broadway, said Linda had had her arm broken in a fight there
before she transferred. "But she's not the kind of girl who would
start a fight," she said. "She was always good in school." Mrs.
Stevens said she had been allowed to see Linda briefly. Her daughter
was conscious but unable to talk.

On the same page, the newspaper had a photograph of Linda, with the caption
"Linda Stevens was critical last night after being stabbed at Paul Revere
Junior High in Welmont. She was a casualty of apparent ongoing wars between blacks and whites at the school." A photograph of Linda's mother and
sister had the caption "Mrs. Adele Stevens and one of her other daughters,
Lisa, 8, talked to the *News* about the stabbing of Linda, 14, at Paul Revere
Junior High School." The full-page report included an interview with a group
called "Concerned Parents of Paul Revere Junior High School" (a group of
white parents).

The full-page tabloid story contained many discrepancies. As the students
pointed out in their letters, and as Stacie pointed out in her story, the newspaper incorrectly stated that the girl was stabbed in the chest rather than in the
back. The newspaper listed its sources for this fact as the girl's mother and the
hospital. Also, the newspaper incorrectly reported the location of the fight and
interviewed, as a witness, someone who had not seen it. The newspaper also
incorrectly presented the dispute as a fight between girls of different races. In
actuality, both girls were black. According to the teacher's story, a Puerto
Rican who may have given Cindy the knife was also involved, but, as the
students argued in their letters, the dispute in this particular fight was not
racially motivated.

The discrepancies between the different versions include not only mistaken
facts but, more importantly for this discussion, different contextualizations.
Whether or not the fight was reported as a racial incident is a contextual issue.
Was the context racial violence in the schools or a dispute between two girls?
For the students, the appropriate context was the general atmosphere of the

school, which they criticized as antagonistic but not violent. They saw the fight as taken out of context in the newspaper reports and therefore distorted in its point of view.

Point of view and context are often related in storytelling, but in the adolescents' stories, disputes over point of view rarely focused on the presentation of facts in their correct context. When presented with what appeared to be an authorized version in the newspapers, the adolescents challenged the entitlement of the reporters for taking the story out of its context.

4.2 Entitlement

Students at the school were outraged about the newspaper coverage. They were angry that the story was covered at all; they were angry at what they perceived to be a distortion of the facts; and they were angry about the depiction of their school as a violent place.[2]

The newspaper coverage of the stabbing concerned an undeniably actual incident, but the students' complaints concerned the accuracy of the account and the entitlement of the newspaper to defame a school that, the students claimed, they were trying to improve and that, according to them, was inaccurately portrayed. In both cases, complaints were made by insiders against an outside medium.

The junior high school students wrote letters to the editor of the newspaper and to the local council representative. All of the letters were written by ninth graders who knew the people involved in the fight and who were present when it occurred. Some of the letters related the right to speak about the school with the accuracy of the reporting:

> We really think that the [ ] and other known papers should really find out how it happen and what went on. . . . So would you really think about it and stop putting Paul Revere down in many ways. [Figure 4.1(a)]

> I feel as though the newspapers should get the facts straight before informing the public incorrectly about any situation or incidents. [Figure 4.1(b)]

> I do not think our school should be categorized the way you did. You projected our school as if it's a very bad and brutle school You should have gotten the bare facts before you assumed what you thought may have happened. [Figure 4.1(c)]

> I am very disapointed because of what the news and the newspaper about my school which is Paul Revere J.S.H. . . . to get to the point on March 9, 1979 the [ ] had in bold type PAUL REVERE BLOODY WAR. That makes it look like there was a war at my school and in my three years in PAUL REVERE I have never seen or heard about anyone beeing stab.

To whom this may concern

We the students of (_____) school know that a bad incident happen the other day. We think that it was bad, because this was the first time for a knife incident to happen at the school, since we have been attending _____. But really to get to the point, We really think that the _____ and other known papers should really find out how it happen and what went on. Because we don't want our school to begin to loose population. So would you really think about it and stop putting _____ down in many ways.

Worried friend,

a   _____

Dear Mr. _____

March 8, 1979 we had a fight at _____ High School in _____ The fight involed two 14 year old black girls They were fighting the hallway and one girl was chased down the hall and she feelled backward and was stabbed in the back. The next morning there was article in the _____ about the incident, in bold face typed "_____ Bloody War." the headline make it seem as if there was a big fight and everyone was carrying knives and were going around stabbing each other. My feelings toward the article are we ones of dissappointment and outrage. I have been attending _____ for 3 years and there have never been A STABBING AT _____ SINCE I HAVE been ATTENDING. I feel as though the newspapers should get the facts straight before informing the public incorrectly about any situation or incidents. I as President of _____ would like your help. Your help would be appreciated by all who attend _____

Sincerely Yours

b   _____

138

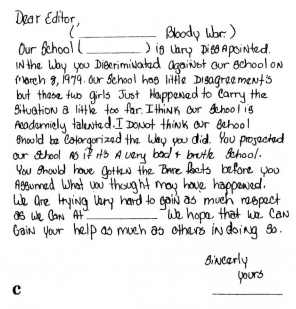

Dear Editor,
(_____ Bloody War)
Our School (_____) is Very DissAppointed.
IN the Way you DiseriminAted agaiNst our school on
March 8, 1979. Our School has little DisagreemeNt's
but these two girls Just HappeNed to Carry the
SitvatioN a little too far. I think Our School is
AcademicIy talented. I DoNot think our school
should be Categorized the Way you did. You projected
our school As if It's A very bad + brutle School.
You Should have gotten the Bare facts before you
Assumed What you thought may have happeNed.
We Are trying Very hard to gaiN as much respect
as We CAN At _____ We hope that We CaN
GaiN Your help as much as others iN doing so.

Sincerly
yours

C _____

Figure 4.1 *(here and facing)* Letters to newspaper editors.

The students objected most of all to the newspaper headline, which magnified the fight between two students into a fight between many. One way in which the letters to the editor and council representatives commanded entitlement was to assert special knowledge of what happened. Here the issue of what happened became entwined with the issue of who saw what happened and who heard about it from whom. The focus on the facts involved both the social role of the teller (entitlement) and the mode of presentation (contextualization).

The students' protests concerning the newspaper account of the fight illustrate the difference between several contexts, including the stabbing as a particular incident, the school as a place that exists apart from the particular incident, the context in which the story was told to the public, and the context for communication within the community. This understanding of different contexts made it possible for the students to protest the newspaper coverage of the school as a bad place and, at the same time, to complain about the school themselves.

Shifts in attention to recontextualization or entitlement are particularly important for understanding the relationship between stories and events. "Accurate" or "original" versions or the "core story" are basically forms of entitled versions. All versions claim some entitlement, and all recontextualize the experiences they describe. Barbara Herrnstein Smith argues against a two-level model of narrative in which a core or basic text "is independent of any of its versions'' (1980:215–16). What one person identifies as the core is essentially another variant of the story. Smith's alternative proposal is to consider narratives as part of social transactions. She suggests attention to "the social and circumstantial context of the narrative and the structure of motivation that sustained the narrative transaction between the teller and his audience" (1980:234). This proposal focuses attention on the context in which the story is told rather than the context in which the events supposedly occurred. When listeners argue that a story has not been told correctly, they are usually referring not to the context of the telling but to the context in which the events occurred. Stories do not duplicate experience; all stories are versions that recontextualize events. Entitlement and recontextualization are both ways of understanding the fact that people may argue about correct versions and that a correct version does not exist separately from the person asserting it to be correct.[3]

Katharine Young proposes a model for the multiple contexts of narrative, including the tale world, the world inhabited by the characters in a story; and the story realm, which corresponds to Smith's model of social interaction, the things listeners and tellers bring to bear upon a storytelling situation (1983).[4] Young's model provides a solution to the problem of confusion between experience and literary representations of historical events, or what I discussed earlier as the relationship between experience, event, and story. The "historically real universe," as Smith terms it, is one kind of "story realm" (using Young's term). The close proximity to tale world representations in narrative texts sometimes persuades readers that historical events deserve a special nonfictional status when rendered in texts.

Young's distinction between tale worlds and story realms enhances our understanding of how the adolescents viewed outsiders' representations of themselves in the media. They rejected the representation of the newspaper. They did not dispute the fact that the school had problems, but they did not grant the reporters entitlement to portray the school as a problem school. In one sense, the problem of entitlement can be seen as relevant to the story realm. It involves who tells what stories in what situations. In another sense, it involves the characterization of tale worlds. The adolescents disputed the tale world that had been assigned to them.

Erving Goffman has discussed the relationship of persons to the stories they tell in his discussion of frames of talk (1974). Goffman considers the circumstances in which people tell stories about unfavorable situations in which they are or were a part. He suggests that in telling such a story, the narrator separates himself or herself from the situation being described. Goffman's discussion of the narrator who reports unfavorable things about himself or herself primarily concerns playfulness; he suggests that by using playfulness, the narrator can mitigate responsibility for the incidents described. "Playfulness and other keyings may be involved which sharply reduce personal responsibility . . . what the individual presents is not himself but a story containing a protagonist who may happen also to be himself" (1974:540). Whether playful or not – and for the adolescents the negative narratives were not necessarily playful – this separation between narrator and main character grants the narrator a status separate from his or her deeds. The narrator of such incidents is someone privileged to stand in two worlds, as participant and as observer.

When people relate negative incidents about themselves, one implication of the narrative is that they are the entitled spokespersons for their own lives. The adolescents used this form of commentary on their worlds far more often than the authorities whom they challenged realized. In their petitions to school authorities and in their letters to the newspaper editors and council representative, they disputed who had the more accurate view of the situation. When participants challenge others who spoke for them, as the students challenged the newspapers, they step outside and become spokespersons for their worlds.

The adolescents based their challenges to entitlement on the accuracy of the outsiders' perspectives.[5] They claimed that the outsiders did not get "the bare facts" before writing their stories. This claim implies a distinction between the relationship of the story to the incidents described and the relationship of the story to the occasion on which it is told. Although the adolescents disputed the reporters' access to accurate information, the newspaper version was not discrepant with their own versions in terms of the fact that the two girls fought and one stabbed the other. The adolescents offered their own versions as a challenge to the newspapers; they were anxious to correct the record of how the incident should be portrayed.

The adolescents' complaints revealed a concern not only with what happened but with the text, the mode of expression. Their greatest disputes with the newspapers concerned the sensationalist reporting of the incident and the fact that it was reported at all. Their dispute primarily concerned the story realm rather than the tale world, the circumstances in which the story was reported in the newspaper rather than whether or not a fight had occurred. The dispute was essentially a matter of entitlement.

In this case, as in many cases concerning entitlement, the issue was who could claim to represent the situation. Disputes over entitlement often began with the claim that someone "got the story wrong" and often turned into arguments over either the way something was said or the form in which it was said. Especially in the reporting of negative incidents, the issues of what actually happened and of who has the right to report it can be intertwined.

The adolescents' challenges concerned not only a version of events but also a version of reality shared by insiders and unknown to the outside reporters. The insiders knew the tale world to be different from that presented by the reporters. However, their challenges were directed not only at the facts of the tale world but also at the rights of the reporters in the story realm.

4.3   The noninformative nature of retellings

Since many of the people who listened to or read stories about the fight knew that a fight or a stabbing had taken place at the school, it can be argued that those listeners were hearing retellings. They had already heard the "news." Of course, many of the details were new to these listeners, but then, retellings often present new details or fuller descriptions. Details are an important warranty for retellings, although not the only warranty.

Goffman has discussed the prevalence of what he terms "replays," which can destroy the novelty necessary for suspense. He is particularly concerned with suspenseful outcomes, and he points out that suspense may be preserved in retellings if a member of the audience is hearing the story for the first time. However, the warranty to retell stories does not depend entirely upon suspenseful outcomes. If the outcome of the fight was the stabbing, then most people in the community who heard the story of the fight already knew that someone had been stabbed. They wanted to know how it happened. Goffman points out, "Indeed, it seems that we spend most of our time not engaged in giving information but in giving shows . . . the point is that ordinarily when an individual says something, he is not saying it as a bald statement of fact on his own behalf. He is recounting. He is running through a strip of already determined events for the engagement of his listeners" (1974:508). In each retelling, a teller demonstrates his or her relationship not only to the fight but also to the text. Such orientations were often provided at the beginning of the narrative. Marsha began her account as follows:

(26)

They was in room 406	4
and our lockers are next to 406	5

Jeanine merely acknowledged that she saw the fight:

(27)

I saw, I saw when they, when they first started fightin'	2

John's account was oriented entirely to his presence in the general area where the fight occurred. Since he did not actually see the fight, the most he could do was to testify to his proximity to it and to claim that someone who was his friend was even closer than he (although the friend too did not see the entire fight):

(28)

When the stabbin' took place I was –	1
I was goin' into my art room and and when	2
and one of my friends was comin' in sayin' that one o' them girls	6
just passed him with a knife	
and then he was at the fight	9

and she was like – he was runnin' from her   10
but he wasn't what she was runnin' at   11

Stacie was not present during the fight, but she claimed to know one of the participants:

(29)

And there was another girl; I know her   3

The teacher was not present during the fight but similarly claimed to know the girls involved and also recounted her attempt to learn about the fight from her students, her special source.

(30)

They were both in my advisory   1

The written accounts, all prepared by people who were present during the fight (although some were closer to it than others), did not assert their special access to information about the fight (although one letter recounted the fight), but rather presented more general information about the school and especially the lack of frequent violence there. For example:

> "I have been attending Paul Revere for 3 years and there has never been a stabbing at Paul Revere since I have been attending. . . . I as President of Paul Revere would like your help."

> "in my three years in Paul Revere I have never seen or heard about anyone beening stab. In my three years I have made lots of friends like Johnnie Stone who is Black, Jose Garcia who is Spanish, and Mike Pilot who is White."

> "Some people like people color matter what color are you Black white or Spanish and some dont like I like any color long I got friend with me to play color dont matter what color are you."

Goffman's point might be rephrased to state that although information may not be the central concern of narrative, the "information state" is. Goffman uses the phrase "information state" to refer to the perspective of the teller as provided in the orientation to the narrative.[6] The information state of the tellers who told their versions to each other or to members of the community who heard that there had been a stabbing and wanted to know what happened depended on the proximity (in terms of either time, space, or friendship) of the tellers to the fight. The information state that the writers of letters to editors and council representatives wanted to project concerned their knowledge of life at the school. The letter writers protested the narrow (synechdochal) perspective of the newspapers, which allowed one event to represent the general situation at the school (in the eyes of the students).

The oral tellings shared within the community shaped the perspective toward what happened in another way. All of the people at the school who knew the girls involved in the fight were shocked by the stabbing. They were shocked that a fight between girls had resulted in a stabbing, they were shocked that a stabbing had occurred at all, but most of all, they were shocked that a girl who was known to stay out of trouble had done the stabbing. Many of the stories conveyed characterizations of a nice girl who had been pushed too far. These characterizations were an essential part of the information state provided by the tellers.

A central warranty for retellings is interpretation. In the case of the stabbing story, the outcome was known by most listeners. People wanted to know how it happened, and by this they meant more than details. In actuality, few details were provided in any of the stories, and many of them were discrepant and never confirmed. Listeners wanted to hear interpretations that would account for how such a thing could happen.

Relationships between retellings are perhaps most evident in the pairing of tellings in a single occasion. Oral narratives 26 and 27 and oral narratives 28 and 29 were told in single occasions. Oral narrative 27 was a confirmation of oral narrative 26. Jeanine arrived at the table where the story was being told after Marsha had finished telling about the fight and while she was telling about how it was handled by the school administrators. Jeanine filled in the part of the story she had missed. Oral narratives 28 and 29 offered two different perspectives. Stacie patiently listened to John's account and then gave what she perceived to be the accurate version. John's account ended with his admission of not knowing what happened to the girls involved in the fight. Stacie elaborated upon John's story. His sketchy, incomplete account gave her a warranty to do so. John did not present any of the reasons for the fight. Stacie presented the same justification presented by Marsha:

(26)

    M: But she say that Linda's been messin' with her ever since she started   10
           and she was fed up

(29)

    S: I know the girl was tired of everybody keep on botherin' her [7]   12

Marsha's and Stacie's similar statements had become part of the information state attributed to the stabbing incident. The two stories were told weeks apart, for nonoverlapping audiences, by people who may have recognized each other and certainly had networks in common (both tellers were black girls; Marsha was in the ninth grade and Stacie was in the seventh grade), although they did not know each other by name. The stories demonstrate the possibility that retellings share not only details but also information states.

In the process of retelling, the adolescent community built a shared interpretation of the stabbing story.[8] The letters of protest to the editor and council representatives all stated that the newspaper account was sensationalist and damaging to the reputation of the school. The oral accounts conveyed the belief that the incident "got out of hand" or, as some teachers said, "something which shouldn't have happened happened." In their retellings, none of the tellers credited someone else from whom he or she had heard the story. These were not retellings of someone else's story; rather, the shared interpretations allowed the teller to appropriate the story and to insist upon special access to the knowledge of what happened. Each of the tellers claimed, from some specified distance, special access, if not witness status, to the events described. Even the challenged reporters could claim that they had spoken firsthand with some of the people involved.

Rereadings and retellings may be considered part of the same processes. Readers may quarrel over the accuracy of their interpretations, each asserting that his or hers is the right one, and retellers may quarrel over their right to tell a story in their own words. These quarrels may share the same fallacies in their claim to authenticity, but their grounds for authenticity differ. This difference can be seen in the contrasting approaches of folklore and literary scholarship in defining their domains. Literary scholars require a demonstration that a particular text belongs to the world of artistic works. Texts must conform to certain standards and, at the same time, must transcend them. As Pierre Macherey has pointed out, the texts that most closely reproduce or conform to the standard are precisely those that are rejected as simplistic and popular (1978:28). In contrast, folklorists have chosen the nonstandard as their domain.[9] In recent years, in refuting past assumptions, scholars in both areas have come closer to a middle ground. Literary scholars have realized that each text creates new standards, that standards are the effect and not the cause of literary works; folklore scholars have realized that standardization is at the center of any community aesthetic. Some literary scholars and folklorists are beginning to sound remarkably similar. Consider Fish's statement:

> All aesthetics, then, are local and conventional rather than universal, reflecting a collective decision as to what will count as literature, a decision that will be in force only so long as a community of readers or believers (it is very much an act of faith) continues to abide by it. Thus criteria of evaluation (that is, criteria for identifying literature) are valid only for the aesthetic they support and reflect. This history of aesthetics becomes an empirical rather than a theoretical study, one that is isomorphic with the history of tastes. (1980:11)

Retellings are one way for tellers and listeners, as well as scholars, to build shared understandings of standards.[10]

4.4   Oral and written retellings

The oral and written stories about the stabbing had very different audiences. However, they illustrate adolescent uses of written and oral texts, and, more particularly, they demonstrate some of the processes involved in scripting and performing narratives.

One of the major differences between the oral and written accounts of the stabbing was that the oral ones described what happened from the initial provocations to the final disciplinary actions, whereas the written ones mentioned only particular phases of the incident that were relevant to the author's argument. Only one of the letters (Figure 4.2) told what happened (original spelling and punctuation kept throughout):

> Her how it happen two girl was figthing in the room One name is Cindy and the other girl name was Linda Stevens the one try to get the knife from Cindy so Linda try to get it with the trash can So the trash can roll over and so she ran down the hallway So Cindy ran up to Linda and Stave her on the backside our some way elese and Linda went to the nurse and them the nurse told the principle about it. then they to called the policeman came and lock here up and took Linda to the hospitol and she was crying was bad She could not breathe got and then it was time to go home the first bell ring veryone went home and told theire mothe about it so thier mother say it is a bad school so you will be get out thier before April because it is so bad school But it is not a bad shoool it is nice it because the fight to much not thier this the first time some one got stave went I was thiere some Paul Revere sould not be catorgized for that every one like Paul Revere some white peop like black people and Spanish people and black like But they dont now how it is Some people like people color matter what color are you black white or spanish and some dont like I like any color long I got friend with me to play color don't matter what color are you. Because dont got the same color dont go the same color But the in side is the sam we are sister and brother to the leader
>
> Shelly Franklin

Shelley's letter did not include any of the standard letter forms found in the other students' letters. In her description of the fight, her letter was closer in content to the oral narratives of the students. However, Shelley's closing remarks were unlike those of the oral narratives, and in making them, she identifies her audience as adults or authorities.

Differences between versions of the stabbing event were less a matter of the distinction between writing and speaking than between context and function. Not only did the oral and written versions set up different relevant contexts, they also displayed a different relationship between text and con-

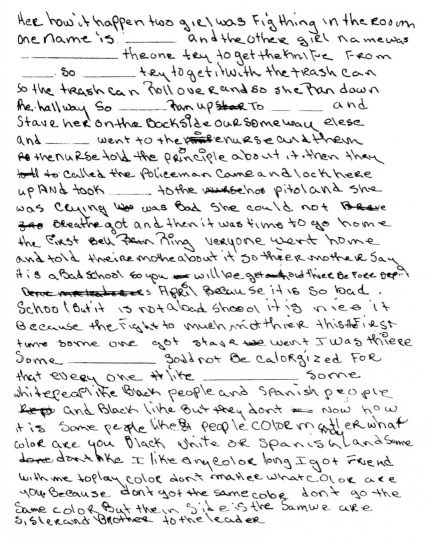

Figure 4.2 Shelley's letter to a newspaper editor.

text. The relevant context of the oral narratives was the relationship between the girls who fought. The relevant context of the written accounts was the reputation of the school. The oral narratives used details about the girls' prior relationship rather than explicit discussion to convey their point of view. In contrast, the letters, written in response to the newspaper account, provided few details about the event and explicitly discussed a point of view. The function of the oral narratives was to formulate an understanding of what happened. The function of the letters was to protest the newspaper's entitlement to what the adolescents considered to be an erroneous point of view. This difference – between the concealed point of view of oral narratives and the explicit argument of written texts – is consistent with other adolescent uses of writing, both as an accumulative communication (a response to another text) and to express a protest. Writing was not used to present accounts but to dispute or settle them. In the adolescent world, there was little room for explicit argument, and face-to-face disputes could easily lead to physical fights. Writing, in contrast, allowed adolescents to protest without facing the consequences of face-to-face retaliation.

In a classroom exercise designed to improve the students' writing ability through increased awareness of the difference between speaking and writing, students were asked to write stories about fights in which they had participated or that they had witnessed. The written stories had more clearly defined closings. For example, consider the following endings:

> "Even the boy that he was fighting with seen it. Soon everybody in the neighborhood knew it."
>
> "then they broke it up and we lived mad ever after."
>
> "And for now those girls does not mast with us for now on. And that the end of my store [*sic*]."
>
> "The men broke it up and it was over."
>
> "I took her to the nurse and then I dont know what happened after that. The End."
>
> "When he tried to get up he got leg chopped off he's still in the hospital."
>
> "My cosin punched him in the face and beat him up and now he leaves me alone."
>
> "He beat Carlos up. And Carlos never never messed with Wendy again."
>
> "We start to fight and then she start to cry and that's the end of the fight."

The written stories were designed for an audience unfamiliar with the people involved in the story; they were written out of the context in which such stories were most often told. Many of the students added fairy-tale endings to their stories; after all, they were asked to write "stories."[11] The stories provide examples of written narrative conventions.

In the adolescent world, there was no context in which adolescents wrote fight stories for each other. On rare occasions they did write stories in letters to authorities, such as the letters written to the editor of the newspaper, as well as stories in their own diaries. The assignment to write fight stories distorted the context for telling such stories. However, it was helpful as a classroom assignment. It resulted in the longest written works produced by the seventh graders in response to any classroom assignment. The students learned that they could extend writing as they extended speech. The assignment gave them something to write about.

Some of the written fight stories had a structure very similar to that of oral fight stories. As discussed earlier, fight stories told by the adolescents among themselves followed a script that included how the fight began, what physical acts were involved, and the relationship between the participants at the time of the telling. The sequence of presumed offenses and retaliations was familiar to all of the adolescents. Anyone could provide an abstract model for how fights happened. Girls' fights involved the claim that someone was pushed too far; boy's fights involved the claim that a boy "went all kinds of crazy" and lost control of himself. Some of the written stories mentioned the offenses as the basis for the fight. Consider, for example, the following two stories:

A fight that I saw

One sunny day in the school yard some boy named Anthony was making fun and embarrassing this boy named Vincent. He told Anthony to stop talking about him and his family, but he just kept on bussing on the boy, so he pushed the boy and the boy punched Anthony in the face, then they started fighting. And so happen a man that knew Anthony's father was walking by and he saw Anthony fighting so he ran and told Anthony's father. Anthony's father came and beated him all the way home with an extinction [*sic*] cord. Then when he got home his father beated him with extinction cord and one belt and everybody saw that he was back naked when he beated him. The whole crowd had followed him and his father home while his father was beating him. His father beated him until the blood came out of him. Even the boy that he was fighting with seen it. Soon everybody in the neighborhood knew it. The End.

One day I was fighting with a girl name Claudia because she said that when I cam to Paul Revere that I start to show of [*sic*] and I told her that when she stike with her girlfriend that she's the one to start to show of [*sic*] and we start to fight and then she start to cry and that's the end of the fight. The End.

Both stories describe the offenses that precipitated a fight. However, one of the elements often missing from the written narratives and essential to the oral ones was the depiction of a character as a victim. The written narratives for the teacher often depicted the central character, especially when this character was the author, as a hero. In letters and diaries, the adolescents almost always depicted themselves as victims. Whereas the letters were part of a protest and the diaries were part of an ongoing text, the narratives for the teacher were not told in the context of an ongoing situation. They fictionalized the stories by providing fairy-tale endings and beginnings (such as "One sunny day in the school yard") and removed them from the ongoing situation.

The central difference between the oral and written accounts of the fight between Linda and Cindy was in the genre (letter versus storytelling), not in the written or spoken channel.[12] The channels for telling personal narratives can be spoken or written; writing and speaking about familiar experiences can be quite similar – for example, in the congruence between the adolescents' oral stories shared in the school lunchroom and written in their personal diaries – or the contexts can be more distinct – for example, the difference between the oral stories and the written letters. Each genre carries rules for appropriate use, including rules about which categories of experience can be appropriately communicated in a genre. Fight narratives were a category of experience for the adolescents. This category also imposed constraints upon the chosen channel of communication. In telling stories among each other, the adolescents were aware that the teller might become an antagonist in the fight by overstepping the boundary of entitlement. In the letters, the students took on the authorities as antagonists who had injured the reputation of the school. Both performances concerned entitlement. In the oral narratives, the tellers avoided antagonism by announcing their alliance with Cindy, the favored victim. Antagonisms could have developed if someone had spoken out in favor of Linda. In the written letters, the students challenged their audience by presenting themselves as the victims. They chose to communicate their challenge in writing in part because they had no opportunity to speak to their audience and in part because they wanted to speak as representatives of the school. Further, the letters stood as proof of their arguments; they demonstrated that the adolescents could act responsibly.

The adolescents used writing as part of an ongoing situation to say things that they could not easily say orally. Their frequent letters and less frequent petitions broke through a communication boundary between authorities and adolescents. Most of the adolescents' written communications to authorities (not including schoolwork) were protests or complaints. Not all of the adolescents were able to follow the rules of grammatical writing. Shelly's letter to the editor (Figure 4.2) was in sharp contrast to the other letters. Everyone told fight stories as individual performances, but when the written channel of communication was chosen, the adolescents presented their position collaboratively, as in the petition.[13] In the oral fight stories, each teller was responsible for his or her own words, and telling stories could get a person into trouble. Fight stories always emphasized the position of the teller, either as an ally in the oral accounts or as a spokesperson in the written letters. Written and spoken versions did not involve different categories of stories as much as different categories of tellers or different relationships between teller and listener. The difference is not really a matter of decontextualization in writing or face-to-face interaction in speech. The significant difference is the transformation of the potential antagonisms of oral tellings among adolescents into the protests and challenges by adolescents to adults.

The central issue involved in retellings is entitlement. One is entitled to retell a story to a new audience, to retell in order to express a differing point of view, or to retell to claim personal participation. Each of these purposes involves a claim: that the audience is entitled to hear the story, that the teller is entitled to express a point of view, or that one's participation is legitimately relevant. Challenges to entitlement can be made against any of these claims. The first charge is most easily made against oral tellings, although translations can be seen as retellings to new audiences, and, as in the case of the newspaper accounts, a written account often retells oral accounts. The second and third claims are as common to writing as to speaking, although the same things, particularly narrative voice, reported speech, and point of view, are used as challenges to the entitlement of an oral retelling and can be used as justifications for a written retelling. The significance of these issues will become more apparent in the next chapter.

5
VARIETIES OF CONTEXTUALITY

The rules for determining who is entitled to tell what to whom are not explicit but are based upon a continual process of building shared understandings. Shared understandings involve contextual relationships both between addressors and addressees and between revealed and concealed messages. It is especially important that these two contextual relationships be considered together in discussions of oral and written communication in order to avoid the false assumption that writing always serves to present explicit (revealed) messages to distant readers.

Literacy scholarship has often made the mistake of discussing only information, or revealed messages. Scholars have focused on how written communication makes information available to distant readers, and they have argued that writing provides contextual details that are often unnecessary in face-to-face communication.[1] Although the distinction between distant writers and proximate speakers is sometimes valid, it cannot account for the familiarity or distance created by specialized written communications, collaborative writing, concealed oral messages, or diary entries. Familiarity and distance depend not only on the appropriate use of contextual details but also on the relationship between addressor and addressee and on the use of messages to reveal or conceal information.

The appropriate use of contextual details follows certain conventions, and one way of defining distant and proximate communications is to state that distant communication requires that conventions be standardized enough to be shared among people far removed from each other in space, time, or social status, whereas proximate communication relies upon local conventions. (Here the concepts of ''standards'' and ''standardizing'' should not be confused. All conventions, local or authorized, involve standards.) Further, conventions work on all levels of contextuality: The cultural context assigns privileged or stigmatized status to different conventional systems; the situational context determines how the frame of a message will be interpreted; and the textual conventions provide clues for intelligibility.

This chapter examines several conventions for manipulating the distance between addressors and addressees, including the use of pronoun referents and reported speech, the sequential ordering of events, and the presentation of contextual information. The discussion begins with oral fight narratives, includes a brief examination of some of the adolescents' written imaginary stories, and then turns to the girls' written diaries.

This discussion of manipulation of the distance between addressee and addressor also raises questions concerning differences between oral and written narratives. Does oral narration presume familiarity? Does written narration presume distance? Are diaries written version of oral communications (since the addressor and addressee can be the same person and thus can presume familiarity)? Are the conventions for recognizing authors and authorship the same for writing and speaking? Certainly the contexts for writing and speaking differ, but how do the conventions for contextualization (and here we include both concealing and revealing information) differ? Borrowing David Olson's (1977) distinction between meaning in the context of oral communication and meaning in the text of written communication, we can ask, how do contextual and textual displays of information differ?

An outsider would not necessarily understand the stories the adolescents told about their fights. However, the adolescents did understand each other, and their individual understandings overlapped to a certain extent, creating what may be termed "shared understanding." This is not to say that each of the participants in a situation had the same stock of shared understanding or that the agreements were at all explicit, but rather that the overlap was sufficient for some degree of implicit consensus.

Many studies of story comprehension begin from the vantage point of the investigator's assessments of intelligibility.[2] To the investigator, a story may appear unclear in terms of the identity of the characters or the sequence of events, and some investigators have proposed models for measuring the coherence of stories or have discussed children's stories as having characteristics that mark them as undeveloped adult stories.[3] A primary criterion for assessing the intelligibility of standard (Western) adult narratives is the appropriate use of referents. The adolescent narratives did not always conform to the standard, but they did follow conventions that made them intelligible to the adolescents.

5.1 Shared understanding and the use of referents

The use of referents in a narrative, to indicate either people or places, depends upon the listener's familiarity with the characters and places described. One purpose of the adolescents' stories was to identify and sort out the relationships between the participants in a dispute. For example, consider the following interchange between Marie and Stacie:

31
M:	Cornie and Sylvie was gonna fight	3
S:	Who?	4
M:	That girl Sylvie Fox	5
S:	They use to live around our way?	6
	I mean they used to go to our school?	7

M:	She still do go to our school	8
	Sylvie	9
	Not Pearl, Sylvie	10
S:	Who – who the hell is that?	11
	I don't know	12
M:	She used to be with Sonya and them	13
S:	Oh yah	14

The interchange reveals a process for creating intelligibility. Marie explained the identity of the disputants through the already shared understandings of who lived where, who attended the school, and who associated with whom.

Shared understandings are not a fait accompli. They are constantly being built or impeded. Each new recounted incident requires new understandings, and the process of building understandings has various phases, from the brief identification of the participants in a dispute, such as the exchange between Marie and Stacie, to ongoing constructions of shared understandings of expected behavior in various situations such as the classroom, the street, and the family.

Impediments to shared interpretation are also ongoing, constantly undermining consensus. The assumption of understanding can itself impede understanding. The following narrative, told to a group of friends and the researcher, concerns two disputes: The first was between a girl (Shelley) who called another girl a "B" (bitch); the second was between the teller, Marie, and the vice-principal of the junior high, who, she claimed, had no right to interfere in the fight since it occurred off school grounds. In the story, Marie claimed that a teacher at the school told her that the students could kill each other without school interference as long as they were two blocks away from the school, and that therefore the vice-principal was in error. Marie's story did not describe her exchange with the vice-principal, but she later told me that when he stopped the fight, she cursed him for coming to the park and interfering in a fight that was none of his business, and he suspended her from school for cursing him.

32

M	We, um she, we was at Brick Park	1
	and um some girl name Shelley Franklin pushed her	2
	and she took, she came over there and she swung at me	3
	And she called me a "B"	4
	And I was fightin' her	5
	Jeanie was fightin' her first	6
	My niece Jeanie was fightin' her first	7
	and then she was fightin' Jeanie	8
	Next it was, next it was me	9
	Then it was some girl name Shelley	10
	Another Shelley	11

	She was fightin' her and then	12
	And she got mad	13
	And she was fightin' us	14
	And then when Mr. Rork came, she called us another "B"	15
A:	She called you a "B"?	16
M:	Ya and then	17
A:	He came to the park?	18
M:	Yah, he came to the park	19
	He knowed we was gonna get her for callin' us that name	20
	We know we ain't no "B"	21
	but she kept callin' us that	22
	Then she got her butt kicked in front of all those people	23
	And Mr. Rork aint had nothin' to do with it because what's her name	24
	Miss – I don't know her name	25
A:	A teacher or a vice-principal	26
M:	No I think she a teacher	27
A:	Or an NTA or something	28
M:	No a teacher, her name's Miss May, I think	29
	She said that we could kill each other two blocks away	30
	and we was more than two blocks away	31
	But we wasn't trying to kill her or nothing	32
	We was just beatin' her up for calling us a bitch	33
	But we ain't fight her all at the same time	34
	We fight her one by one	35
A:	And they said that you were fighting her all at one time?	36
M:	I don't know	37
	I don't know what they were sayin'	38
	She probably say that	39
	And then she say her mother say that she was going to press charges	40

The participants in Marie's story are named as follows:

> She, her
> Some girl name Shelley Franklin
> Jeanie, My niece Jeanie
> some girl name, Shelley, another Shelley
> Mr. Rork
> those people
> Miss – I don't know her name, Miss May, a teacher
> her mother
> I (Marie)
> We (Jeanie, Marie, and Shelley)

The antagonist of the story was never named but was referred to as "she," and her mother was referred to as "her mother." Mr. Rork, the vice-principal, was referred to by the name Marie used when addressing him rather than by his title. Such terms of reference are typical of the adolescents' narratives. The category "some girl" indicated that the person had no special relationship to the teller outside of the situation described. The category "this girl" or "this guy" or "the guy" often referred to a specific antagonist in the adolescents' stories. In Marie's story, the antagonist was identified in line 3 as the person who "swung at" Marie. The protagonists are those people who also fought the antagonist. The only unclear referents are those in lines 12–14.

(32)

She was fightin' her and then	12
And she got mad	13
And she was fightin' us	14

The "she" in lines 12–14 could be either the antagonist or Shelley. ("She" was the antagonist.) However, the story does not account for a new antagonist, and the adolescents had no difficulty in understanding Shelley's role in the fight.

The devices used for identifying characters are an important part of the distance between author/narrator and listeners or readers. The distance between story characters and storytelling listeners in Marie's story are minimized by involving the listeners in identifying and understanding the roles of the characters. The point of the story was who did what to whom rather than a description of a character as a certain kind of person. A narrator who describes a character as a type of person steps back from the situation and asserts the right to evaluate others, using what Labov has termed "external evaluation."[4] Description of character types is one kind of distance created between author/narrator and listeners or readers.

In Marie's story, the only character description was the antagonists's description of Marie as a "B" and Marie's denial, "We know we ain't no 'B.' " In contrast, the stories told about the stabbing (Chapter 4) identified the antagonist as the kind of girl who wouldn't mess with others, thereby distancing what listeners and participants knew about the characters.

5.2   Firsthand experience and reported speech

The relationship between the fights and the fight stories, as determined scenarios, can be understood in terms of what H. G. Gadamer calls "temporal distance" (1976:124). Gadamer states that understanding requires temporal distance, the "filtering process" that allows one to stand back from experience. Reported accounts imply temporal distance. However, the distance is not an objective stance that allows one to perceive a situation more accurately. Rather, Gadamer states, "We define the concept of 'situation' by saying that it represents a standpoint that limits the possibility of vision" (1976:128). The limited vision not only belongs to the listener, who hears a story without the opportunity of firsthand experience, but also includes the firsthand experience as a limited perspective. Gadamer's term "horizon," referring to the range of a person's perspective or vision, is particularly important for considering the relationship between a narrative and the experiences it describes as a problem of intelligibility.

The problem of shared understandings of narrative is not merely a matter of the difference between the narrator's firsthand experience and the listeners' reliance on a secondhand account combined with their own possible prior knowledge. Narratives do not recapitulate experiences; they convert experiences into a story. It is a mistake to place the burden of understanding the problem of narrative intelligibility on the difference between firsthand experience and secondhand reports. The notion of firsthand experience is itself created by the forms of reporting and is a negotiated category rather than an observable fact.[5] Among the adolescents, the claim to firsthand experience was often disputed as only partial knowledge, and people often claimed hearsay as a firsthand experience. These contradictory claims contributed to a climate in which claims could escalate far out of proportion to the incidents that prompted them.

The notion of firsthand experience refers to the presence of a person in a situation. The fact of presence is often used to assume firsthand knowledge, as though the presence were responsible for the knowledge. The adolescents' narratives reported primarily prior conversations. Thus they posed the problem of a person asserting as firsthand experience the statements made by another person. They require an assessment not only of the storyability of experience in general, but specifically of the storyability of conversational experience. The adolescents' narratives contained a great deal of reported speech. Their intelligibility depended upon the teller's ability to recognize the difference between the voice of the narrator and the reported voice of another speaker.[6] For example, in Joan's story about her fight with Mary, Joan used the following reports of speech:

(1)

and she says that "You want to fight my sister?"	7
she said, "Go do it "	8
so I went down to the office	21
and she said, "Go ahead"	22
and I called my mom at work	23

Hearers (rather than readers) must identify another voice for the words in quotation marks in order to understand the intended referents for the pronouns. "My sister" in line 7 was Joan, the speaker. The implied "you" in line 8 was Mary. The speaker in line 22 was the unmentioned secretary in the office who, in saying "Go ahead" to Joan, gave her permission to use the telephone to call her mother. Joan did not change her voice to indicate reported speech, and a listener who did not recognize the use of reported speech would probably not understand what Joan was saying. Joan's story also included described speech:

(1)

and I called my mom at work	23
and she said that uh	24
just to stay home	25
my sister said that if she touched me	38
she would kick her butt	39

In all cases in Joan's story, described speech was preceded by the statement that a person "said" something. In oral narrative 2, Joan similarly used "said" for described speech – in this case her own speech – but in addition, she used "says" for her own reported speech:

(2)

I started pushin' her, I said how often you [. . .] at the school	2
I says, "Come on, I'll fight you right now"	3

The distinction between the use of reported versus described speech in lines 2 and 3 is that "how often you" was not a quotation of Joan's conversation with Mary; it was a description of the content. Line 3 reproduced the conversation as it might actually have been said.

Other adolescents' stories similarly used "said" for described speech.

(4)

The police came. They said they couldn't take him because	4

(5)

She said she went to City Hall but my mother said she don't think they can do anything	26
My mother she said she going to try to get somebody to go up there	47
and try to straighten him out	48
My mother said she should go up there	55
and my mother said she be glad when he get his car out of the shop	58

(8)

And then he said	12
If I punch him in his face	13
He was gonna stab me, right	14
and I told him if he do that	15
he'd better never come to school	16

"Said" was also used in reported speech. The main difference between reported and described speech, both designated by "said," was the designation of pronouns rather than a change of voice. For example:

(15)

el dice "Tu no me quieres" 20

(14)

and she jumped up in my face and said, 2
"Give me some of that ice cream" 3

(9)

And Ginger said, "I better not be around you 2
or Rose will get in my face" 3
Mary said, "If Rose is bothering you, 4
I'll kick her ass" 5

In all of these instances, reported rather than described speech is indicated by the use of pronouns. Oral narrative 9 is especially interesting since the teller, Rose, reported speech from situations in which she was not present. Moreover, the story is about reported speech or rumor. It refers to a series of conversations that, according to Rose, set the stage for a fight. Whether or not the statements were made as Rose reported them is disputable. In particular, Rose's challenge was more common to fight stories than to fights:

(9)

So I went up to her 7
and said, 8
"I hear you want to fight me" 9

This sequence appeared in several fight stories, always followed by the denial and by the statment "And then she hit me," or as in Rose's narrative, "That's when she slugged me."

These statements illustrate the importance of reported speech in the adolescents' stories beyond their descriptive purpose of telling what happened. They used reported speech as a resource for retrospectively inferring a causal sequence for the fights. Rose may not have known exactly what Ginger said to Allen (and it is unlikely that she did), but she knew how to present their supposed conversation in the style of reported speech. This involved more than a shift in pronouns, and the statements "Rose will get in my face" and "If Rose is bothering you, I'll kick her ass" were both borrowed from the everyday speech of the adolescents.

The adolescent listeners knew the difference between reported speech that merely sounded similar to what someone might have said, as in Rose's reports of Ginger's and Mary's speech, and reported speech that suggested specific and special knowledge of a conversation. Most of the reported speech in the stories was either a first-person report of the speaker's own prior speech or described speech.

The adolescents reserved reported speech, which was intended to represent the other parties' exact words, for reports of insults. Many reports of insults used reported speech. ("Mary called you a 'B'.") Reported speech was used to exaggerate the insult or to confirm or substantiate a described accusation. ("First, Mary said you was stuck up, then she says, 'Terry's a "B"'.") The person who reported an insult could herself be challenged for interfering in someone's else's business, and such challenges often rested on inaccurate reports. Described speech was often considered inaccurate since it was not what the person had actually said. The adolescents understood how to recognize and distinguish reported from described speech, and thus how to identify the referents of the pronouns used and to use both forms in their own stories. They also understood the potential consequences of using the different forms.

This understanding of the consequences, and of the potential challenges that could be made on the basis of inappropriately reported or described speech that invaded privacy, constituted a shared understanding that guided the adolescents' use of pronouns beyond an interest in grammatical clarity. The issue is not the competence of the adolescents to supply the correct referent for a pronoun but rather the shared understanding of how to use past speech in present narratives and conversations.

The adolescents used reported speech in descriptions of ongoing interactions and in fantasy stories and other records of events in a distant world. In the first case, the quoted words supposedly represented exactly what someone said, and the words had consequences. In the case of distanced reporting, the words quoted were what could or might have been said in a particular situation.

Reported speech is part of the larger category of transmitted words, or any discourse that refers to another source (including written sources, supposed sources such as "it is said," and authorized statements). Transmitted speech, whether described or reported, places the author in the position of recontextualizing others' words. This is one of the primary means of establishing (and also measuring) distance between author, teller, narrator, and reader or listener. The reported speech can be contemporary, a recognized part of the speech of the teller and listeners. In reported contemporary speech, the source and the narrator and/or listener belong to the same speech community. Greatest proximity exists when all three share speech. Distance begins when the teller asserts shared speech with the source and excludes the listener or when the teller excuses himself or herself from a suggested association between the source and the listener. The greatest distance between text and listener or reader can be traced to what M. Bakhtin calls "authoritative discourse":

> The authoritative word is located in a distanced zone, organically connected with a past that is felt to be hierarchically higher. . . . The degree to which a word may be conjoined with authority – whether the word is recognized by us or not – is what determines its specific

demarcation and individuation in discourse; it requires a *distance* vis-à-vis itself (this distance may be valorized as positive or as negative, just as our attitude toward it may be sympathetic or hostile). (1981:342–3)

Authoritative discourse is not necessarily lodged in persons as speakers; it may also include sacred words, beliefs, or other fixed texts. Bakhtin contrasts authoritative discourse, which "permits no play with its framing context," to internally "persuasive discourse" – contemporary shared speech, which includes "retelling a text in one's own words, with one's own accents, gestures, modifications."[7]

In the adolescent world, the school, the church, and adult family members represented authorities whose discourse ranged from the contemporary and shared to the authoritative. The he-said–she-said stories rarely reported an authority's exact words; rather, they described them. Reported speech conveyed not only the words but also a sense of their performance; described speech did not insist that the words be repeated exactly as heard.[8]

Reported speech is often called for to reproduce a source's dialect or style that is different from the narrator's – in other words, to reproduce an oral performance. Described speech is more often used when exact imitation of the source's voice would inappropriately disrupt the narrator's voice. This explanation of the difference places emphasis on the social uses of reported and described speech rather than on their linguistic properties (such as the use of pronoun referents and types of speech acts). In speaking, performed imitation of the source can substitute for grammatical constructions that indicate reported speech.

The social implications of imitation are entirely different in writing and speaking. In both cases, "it's not what you say, but how you say it." However, one may have the entitlement to reproduce words, but not necessarily sounds. Of course, sounds can also be reproduced in writing, and reproducing dialect pronunciation or pause sounds may have as much impact in writing as sound imitation in speech. However, the special efforts used to call attention to speech in written forms only further identify them as conventions for oral interaction.

The distinction between the uses of reported speech in writing and speaking suggest that there are fewer constraints on written verbatim imitations, since they are distanced from an ongoing situation with its possible challenges of impropriety. The corollary possibility is that the imitations of reported speech reveal ongoing situations.

Reported speech is one of the main means available to an author for manipulating the distance in time between author, narrator, and listener or reader. It affords the possibility of using multiple voices traceable to distinct time frames. The report of a past conversation locates an event in time, and the narrator, as a mediator between the past conversation and the present storytelling, has the option of further distancing the narration by not accounting for his or her own position in the events. As discussed in Chapters 1 and 2, in the adolescents' oral narratives, the adolescent narrators almost always placed themselves within the events as a first-person witness or antagonist. Only the reports of television soap operas and a few accounts of the nonadolescent world, such as the "ladies killing babies" monologue (Chapter 2, oral narrative 18), omitted the position of the narrator as a witness. Similarly, the position of the narrator in the events of a written narrative depended on whether or not the narrative described ongoing daily events or resolved past events. The latter category included what the adolescents called "made-up stories." Although both oral and written accounts of past resolved events and nonadolescent events omitted the narrator's position and thus created distance between the time of the narration and the time of the events described, they used different mechanisms for separating time. Oral narratives used described rather than reported speech. Written narratives relied upon frames for distance, including the once-upon-a-time frame for made-up stories and the diary for written stories.

The adolescents used reported speech not only in their oral fight stories but also in their written letters, imaginary stories, and diaries. In their oral and written stories, reported speech indicated ongoing action. In fight previews and stories told during an ongoing dispute, what people said to each other was often the substance of the fight, and reported speech consisted primarily of descriptions of offenses, accusations, and threats.

Stories written for classroom assignments always told of imagined events. Exciting or important moments were conveyed through reported speech (see Figures 5.1–5.3).

Similarly, in the diaries, reported speech was used to describe tense moments. For example, the following excerpt from Stacie's diary entry (see Figure 3.5) relies upon reported speech to recount a series of confrontations:

> i asked my mother's boyfriend where's my mother, he said her and shelley went to the market . . . then i got in a argument. a little girl asked me to play with her. i was a little upset, so i said, get out of my face, she went and told her mother what was bothering her so her mother said which one of you named stacie. i said i am stacie, she said dolly told me you were bothering her. i said i don't care what dolly told you. she said you don't have to get nasty about it and i said i will get nasty anytime i want so she said i will smack you and tell your mother i did it. i said, yah, right. then she started walking down the street and i waived my hand at her. then my uncle came out of his girlfriend's sister's house and said what's the matter. i said nothing. he said why did you wave your hand at Mona? pinching my arm

Fighting over A Girl

There once was a boy named
Ricky and another boy named
Andy and a girl named Cheryl S._____
Well Ricky and Cheryl was boyfriend and girlfriends
and they was walking down the street and
they walked right into Andy Cheryl's old
boyfriend But cheryl also had Something to do
with Andy. And Andy called Cheryl but Cheryl
didn't go because Ricky told her not to
Cheryl was about to go anyway Ricky
Said if Cheryl go to Andy He was going
to beat her up. Andy heard Ricky telling
Cheryl this So Andy said man don't
be talking to girl like that way and
Ricky said your girl what you mean your
girl -that's my girl. So they asked Cheryl
Which one She go with Cheryl said both
and Ricky said it isn't going to work that
way and Andy said to Cheryl don't say nothing
Else to me no more so Ricky and Andy started
to beat Cheryl up and the next day Cheryl was
in the hospital for what they did to her.
So Cheryl brothers got Andy and Ricky for doing that
to Cheryl.

Figure 5.1 "Fighting Over A Girl."

harder and harder. she is a grown lady, my uncle said. i said she is no
grown lady she is a freebee . . . then i said to my sister she thinks
she's grown. my mother's boyfriend said so do you. then i said get
out of my face. he said leave me alone or i will smack the shit out of
you. i said got any more good jokes. then when my mother came
home, he told my mother and she said, stacie after you long trip, you
must be exhausted. she said why don't you take a warm bath and
cool down. . . .

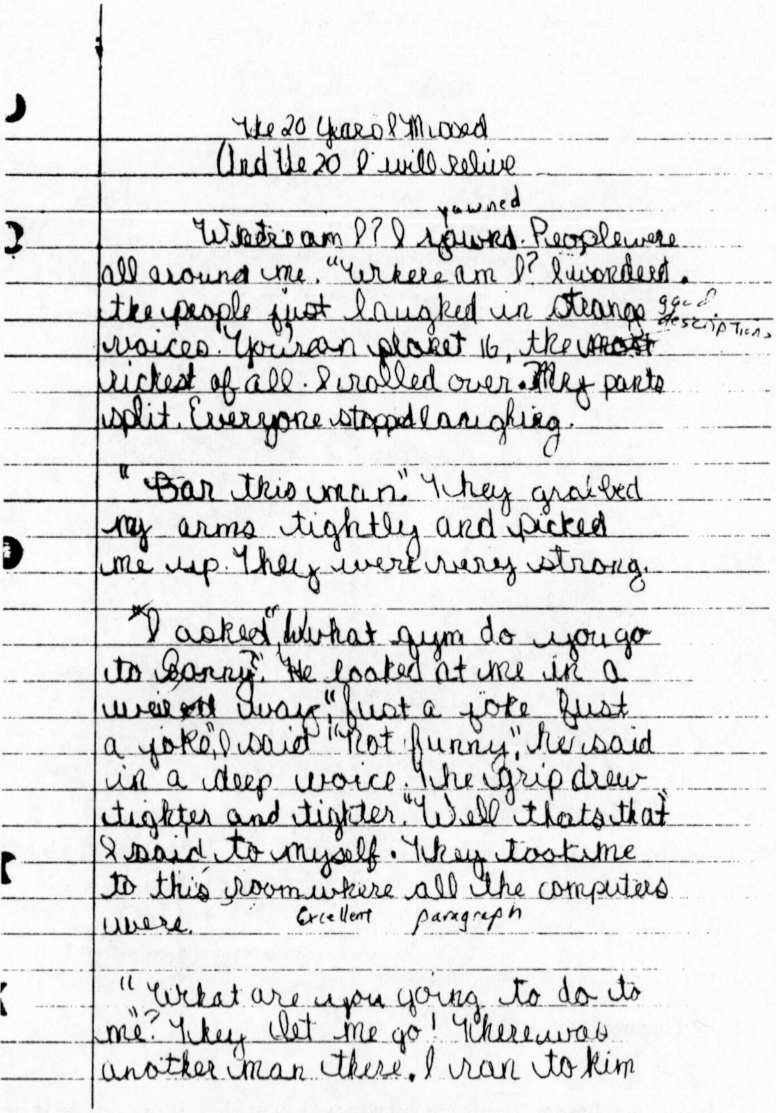

The 20 Years I Missed
And the 20 I will relive

Where am I? I squwked. People were
all around me. "Where am I? I wondered.
the people just laughed in strange *good*
voices. You ran picket 16, the most *description*
rickest of all. I rolled over. My parts
split. Everyone stopped laughing.

"Bar this man." They grabbed
my arms tightly and picked
me up. They were very strong.

"I asked "What gym do you go
to Barry? He looked at me in a
weird way. "Just a joke just
a joke, I said "Not funny," he said
in a deep voice. The grip drew
tighter and tighter. "Well thats that
I said to myself. They took me
to this room where all the computers
were. *Excellent paragraph*

"What are you going to do to
me? They let me go! There was
another man there. I ran to him

Figure 5.2 *(here and facing)* "The 20 Years I Missed. . . ."

The adolescent fight stories told after a fight had been resolved rarely, if ever, used reported speech. It was as if once the events were past, the exact words of the antagonists were forgotten or unimportant.

The made-up stories, written for a class assignment, posited an omniscient narrator who reported events without identifying herself or himself as a wit-

and said " Whats going on? He
couldn't talk for he had no larynx.
I assumed they had Tortured him.

"Ha Ha Ha", a voice laughed
"You are here and youre never
leaving". I fell to my knees and
held my ears for that laughing
was driving me out of my mind.

They took me to the Queen
my knees. I said, Where am I?
She said, "Don't worry Tom
I will keep good care of you".
"How do you know my name"
I am Rebeca". "Don't you remember
me" Sure said Tom

'I love you Tom" she said "Come
here and let us walk out into
the sunset." She grabbed (his) hand
and the loving mist. And I am writing
This story to say don't fall asleep
for over 2 hours. y "ending

ness or other type of participant in the interaction. In ''Fighting Over a Girl''
(Figure 5.1), for example, the reader never learns how the author heard the
story or whether she knew any of the characters. The boys in the story have
only first names; the girl has both a first and a last name and is possibly a real
person. Authors of imaginary stories never differentiated a narrative voice. In

Marisol said,"Thank you."

When they got to the prom, there were all the
senior classes. We all walked over to Priscilla
and Angel. Everyone was there, including Herby,
Frank and Willmel. We were having a good time
when a stranger walks in. Then all of a sudden
the room smelled of a decomposed body. We were
all wondering where the foul odor was coming from,
but just as it came, it left. Well we all started
Dancing. The stranger moved across the floor and
over to where Evelyn and Willard were. He had a
deep voice and a nice smile. He said to then,"Hello,
my name is Bernadino L____ ." Willard said, "Hello,
my name is Willard C____ and this is my girlfriend
Evelyn V____ ." Bernadino said hello to Evelyn.

When the record was over, we all walked

over to Willard and the stranger. We all got introduced
to the stranger. Then we were all talking as if we had
been close friends. Suddenly all of the lights
were turning on and off. Then there was a moaning
and a loud scream. Everyone was thinking that it
was someone playing a joke. So no one payed attention
to it.

We were still talking to Bernadino, when
Marisol asks him," Where do you live?" Alberto gave
her a very jealous look. Then Bernadino said,"Only
God Knows." Everyone looked at him. All astonished
at his strange answer.

Alberto asked Marisol to dance, and she said
yes.He said to her,"What did you want to know where
he lived at?" Marisol said,"I wanted to know, because
I have never seen him around here."I wonder why he
gave me such a strange answer? " Alberto ignored
what she said.

As twelve o'clock came the room became cold.
MArisol asked the stranger for his jacket. He gave
it to her. It was strange though, the jacket smelled
of a rottened body.

At two o'clock the dance was nearly over.
Marisol looked all around the room for Bernadino,
to give him back his jacket, but he was nowhere to
be found. She asked somepeople if they knew where
he lived. Someone said that he lived on _____ street.

When Willard took Evelyn home, I asked him to drive
me to Bernadino's house. Alberto came along with us.
When we got there, Marisol got out of the car and
walked to the front of the house. She ranggthe bell and
out came a lady. She must have been in her fourties.
Marisol said," Hello, does Bernardino L___ live here?"
The women at hearing this name began to cry. Marisol
said,"I'm sorry, did I say something wrong?" The lady
said in a tearful voice,"No, it"s just that Bernardino
is my son. He died 3 years ago in a plane crash."
Marisol nearly feinted at hearing this,Aand she said close
to tears,"He was at my prom today, how can he be dead."
She said in a toneless voice," They say he comes back
on the day he died, which happens to be today.I don't
know beeause if he does come back he never comes here."
Marisol said,"Woll here is his jacket." She handed it
to her and asked where his grave was. The lady told her
and said ,"Thank You for coming by."

As she got into the car she told Alberto and
Willard what the lady had said. She told Willard to take
her to the cemetary. He took her there and they all went
to his grave and saw his name on it. The only thing that
scared Marisol was that the jacket she had given to the
lady was now lying on top of the grave. She told Willard to
take her home. So they left the grave without saying a
word to one another. As they reached her house she kissed
Alberto goodnight and said good-bye. She said to them,"This
will be a night to remember."

The socret about how the jacket got to the grave
has never been known.

Figure 5.3 *(here and facing)* Fragment of "The Unknown Stranger.'

some cases in made-up stories, they situated the events in their own neighborhoods, but unless they were the protagonists of first-person accounts, they did not identify their position as witnesses. The stories created distance between narrator and listener by dealing with unfamiliar characters (although the characters could be familiar and only the events made up), but the author and narrator were not distanced.

Often, written made-up stories shifted between first- and third-person narration. Narrators used a once-upon-a-time beginning, which indicated that the story was to be understood as a fabrication and led to an introduction of third-person characters. Later, signaling a break between background orientation and action, one of the third-person characters shifted to the first person for description but maintained third-person status for reported speech.

Shifts from first to third person might best be understood as slips, but their placement follows a pattern. "The 20 years I missed and the 20 years I will relive" (Figure 5.2), one of the few fabricated stories told by a first person other than the narrator, shifts to the third person at the end, at the moment that interaction changes from conflict to resolution. Only the coda shifts back again to the first person. "The Unknown Stranger" (Figure 5.3, also a familiar legend) shifts from third-person description of background information to first-person plural descriptions of action. The narrator continues to refer to herself in the third person, although she uses her real name, until the final resolving episode, and then only briefly uses the first person, perhaps as a slip, before completing the story in the third person.

The use of either first- or third-person narration did not make the made-up stories substantially different from the personal narratives. The made-up stories conveyed a person's experience largely through reported speech and conveyed action by relating who said what to whom rather than by evaluating situations. As discussed earlier, "Who says?" rather than "So what?" was the primary justification for narration. The interest in "who says" and the concomitant use of reported speech provided covert (or what Labov terms "internal"[9]) evaluations, which were less susceptible to challenges of entitlement.

Constraints on reported speech are often a matter of entitlement. Earlier, I discussed entitlement in terms of challenges, or the consequences of speaking inappropriately, and in terms of recontextualization, or the perspective and point of view of the teller. Reported speech is one device for recontextualizing. The teller claims entitlement not only to use words from another source but also to recontextualize or reframe the words as part of a particular perspective, point of view, or stance.

All of the adolescent narrators of oral and written communications used reported speech to proclaim a stance and to claim entitlement to both the right to report and to take that stance. The letters of protest to the newspaper (Chapter 4) claimed that only the witnesses or participants in the fight were appropriate sources of information and stated that the newspapers were not entitled to comment without reporting the perspectives of these sources. The petition to the school principal (Chapter 3) tried to use many voices (in the form of signatures) to interest him in their point of view. In the oral fight stories, narrators used reported speech to call attention to a prior interaction that, they claimed, had ongoing significance.

Reported speech in the adolescent interactions usually consisted of either protest or parody. Another person's speech was used to express solidarity in a contest, dispute, or plea, or was ridiculed and reduced to empty words without a voice. Diary entries can be understood as both protest and parody. Since a source's words were usually not reported in agreement but rather in conflict with the narrator's position, they could be understood in terms of what Bakhtin has called "parodic stylization" (1981:364), in which the errors of the source are exposed through a report of his or her words. The act of writing in a diary things that could not be said without challenges to entitlement was itself an act of defiance, and entries parodied the interactions they reported by setting up a distance between the author and the ongoing situation.

Any use of reported speech indicates a distance between the source, the current narrator, and the listener/audience. When in orally told fight stories an instigator reported an antagonist's challenge to the supposed offender, the distance was minimized since the person listening to the story and the object of the challenge were the same. In other words, the story was the challenge. Distance was also minimized when an offended antagonist reported an offensive remark directly to the offender and the two quarreled. Whenever reported speech was used in an ongoing situation, the distance between narrator and listener was minimized.

5.3   Shared understanding and the order of events

Another way in which teller–listener distance was minimized was through shared knowledge about the expected order of events. When the listeners know the sequence of events before the story is told, they share knowledge with and minimize distance between themselves and the teller. The most significant differences between shared and unfamiliar sequences correspond to differences between narratives told as part of ongoing situations and narratives told about resolved events. In narrations about ongoing events, listeners and teller share a social context. Narrations about resolved events can describe an unfamiliar context with an unfamiliar order of events.

Shared understanding of the order of events is essential for narratives to be intelligible to listeners. Listeners must be able to follow what happened in what order, and since narratives do not necessarily present events in sequential order, but more often recover the sequence, listeners must either understand the devices for recovery or share with tellers knowledge of the expected order of events. The adolescent fight narratives relied upon the latter, and as discussed in Chapter 1, tellers and listeners shared understandings of an expected sequence of interactions that constituted fights and were recounted in narratives.

Marie's story (oral narrative 33) did not present the incidents in the order in which they happened, but it did recover the order so that the listener could understand the sequence. The sequence in which the incidents occurred is as follows:

1. [The teacher said the students could kill each other two blocks away] sometime prior to the park incident.
2. "She" called Marie and her friends a "B."
3. Mr. Rork heard that Marie and her friends were planning a fight.
4. Marie and her friends went to the park.
5. Shelley Franklin pushed the antagonist.
6. Jeanie fought the antagonist.
7. The antagonist swung at Marie and called her a "B."
8. The antagonist fought another Shelley.
9. The antagonist fought Marie and Jeanie.
10. Mr. Rork came.
11. The antagonist got her butt kicked in front of a lot of people.
12. The antagonist called the protagonists another "B."
13. The antagonist said that her mother said that she was going to press charges.

Three incidents were out of sequence in Marie's story. The vice-principal's knowledge of the intended fight, which had to begin before the fight and continue through and after the fight, and the teacher's statement about fighting two blocks away, which also had to precede the fight (but also applied over a period of time), were both introduced when the characters were mentioned and when the focus of the story turned from the fight in the park to the interference of the vice-principal. Marie's story recovered the order in which these incidents happened, although it did not present them in sequential order. The statements:

(32)
M:	And I was fightin' her	5
	Jeanie was fightin' her first	6
	next it was, next it was me	9

also involved a recovered sequence, though it is not clear from the story whether Marie fought once or twice. (She fought once.) Marie's story can be seen in terms of three distinct sequential units. The smallest unit is Marie's fight with the antagonist, represented in lines 3–5. Marie's fight is part of the larger unit of the fight between all of the protagonists and the antagonist. The exchange between the fighters and the vice-principal constitutes a separate unit. Each of the units is sequentially organized, but to understand the whole, the listener must insert Marie's fight with the antagonist into the larger fight and must assume the vice-principal's prior knowledge of the fight. Understanding the story requires the listener to recover the sequence.

The identities of the protagonist and antagonist and the sequence of incidents are essentially intelligible to the outsider reading or hearing the story. However, several elements of the story are potentially unfamiliar to the outsider, and these elements, if not understood, can obscure an understanding of what happened. Most generally, Marie's story followed a fight sequence that was familiar to the adolescents at the junior high school. No adolescent would question the importance of the park as a location of the fight, the significance attached to the teacher's statement about fighting two blocks away (from the school), or the justification for fighting someone who had called one a "B." Marie's story reported an insult (one girl calling another a "B"), described a retaliation (seeking out the girl at the park), recounted elements of a physical fight, and included a shift in focus from the fight with the girl who called Marie a "B" to a quarrel with the vice-principal about his interference.

Understanding when to provide what contextual information often requires self-reflexive evaluation of a situation from a distance, a perception of the relationship between text and context as an outsider. The adolescents often assumed that others understood them, that others saw the world as they did, and that no explanations were necessary. They did not provide contextual information in their stories, and they rarely asked questions of each other, even when they later acknowledged that they had not understood; they preferred, at all costs, not to appear ignorant. Certain kinds of knowledge identified group membership; those who were affiliated supposedly shared knowledge, and to admit ignorance was to admit being an outcast. Also, denying someone information was a way to deny them membership in a certain group. Information was a source of power.

Shared knowledge of narrative is to a certain extent different from shared knowledge of other forms of communication. In any communicative event, speakers may be differentiated from hearers and intended listeners may be distinguished from those who overhear or listen without being the intended recipient of communication.[10] However, narrative is more than an extended form of talk. The distinguishing features of narration are the use of sequencing and the reporting of experiences from another space and time. Narratives belong to a class of formalized speech genres that are performed. Understanding what is said in such genres is a matter of understanding not only the content but also how to categorize the form appropriately. Most scholarly discussion in this regard has concerned jokes, and especially the negotiation of the category of joking in conversation such that a person may either frame a joke as such or may retrospectively reframe an unintended offensive remark as "only a joke." Narratives are not as explicitly problematic as a category that may be manipulated to reframe information, but in the case of stories on the border between fiction and documentary, such as tall tales, they can involve the negotiation of categories (prompting questions such as "Is that just a story or did it really happen?").

Shared knowledge necessary for understanding narratives includes the knowledge of storyable categories. Among the adolescents, fights or potential fights were storyable. The adolescents expected to talk about fights in which they participated physically or as witnesses, and the question "Were you ever in a fight?" was a legitimate one (for an outsider) that any adolescent could answer with a story. Labov chose the question "Were you ever in a fight with somebody bigger than you?" because it regularly elicited narratives. The phrasing of the question, Labov explained, was designed to allow people to describe fights in which they could justify losing. By asking this question, Labov was able to tap a storyable topic, the justifiably lost fight.

In my research with girls (Labov's questions were primarily directed toward boys and men), I found a storyable topic to be "Has anybody messed with you and pushed you too far?" This question similarly allowed the tellers to present themselves as the victim, although not necessarily the victor, of a fight. The fight stories told by the adolescent girls were storyable as narratives about victimization. Among them, fighting was appropriate as a means of defense. One could defend any number of things (all aspects of saving face), including family reputation, personal integrity, or courage. Part of the purpose of the fight story was to assert that one had been offended in some way, and in the fight as in the offense, the protagonist was the girl who had been pushed too far. Thus the loser of a girl's fight was often characterized as the aggressor who got what she deserved, and the heroine was identified as a victim.

Understanding the criteria for storyability can be important for understanding a story. The criteria for storyability determine which aspects of an experience are relevant for telling, and thus which aspects may be recounted. The adolescents shared criteria for relevance and were able to supply the missing details necessary for understanding each other's stories. They understood a story as referring to a certain category of experience (whether fights or problems with one's family), and understood the general scenario of which the specific story was an example. For example, oral narrative 9 presents a telescoped scenario that combines several episodes. The first episode concerned a possible relationship between Ginger and Allen:

(9)

Ginger and Allen were talking	1
And Ginger said, "I better not be around you	2
or Rose will get in my face"	3

The second episode concerned Mary's intervention in the possible dispute between Rose and Ginger.

(9)

Mary said, "If Rose is bothering you	4
I'll kick her ass"	5

The third episode concerned rumors about a possible fight between Mary and Rose. The possible fight between Rose and Ginger never materialized and was discussed only as a basis for the fight between Mary and Rose. Although the story began with the relationship between Ginger and Allen, their relationship was no longer an issue, and in a sense became nonstoryable. Adolescents understood this piece of the story as the basis for the dispute between Rose and Mary rather than as an issue in itself.

The fight stories often began with descriptions of auxiliary incidents that were understood as partial justifications for the fight. In these stories, the orientation section was often a separate episode involving characters other than those who were eventually involved in a dispute.

34

They threw some stuff on her, right	6
And then I said	7
"Y'all better stop this," right	8
Me and her started arguin	9
So we are gettin ready to fight	10

(1)

Yesterday	3
my sister went over to her	4
and she grabbed her	5
and she pulled her	6
and she says that "You want to fight my sister?"	7
She said, "Go do it "	8
So I went over to her	10

35

well we was in reading	1
And Miss May said "sit down"	2
and she gave me a puzzle to do	3
. . .	
So I sat in Sam's seat	18
because Sam was playing' around somewhere	19
Then he came, he told me to get out of my seat	21

In the fourth and final episode of her story, Rose confronted Mary with the rumor that Mary wanted to fight Rose. Mary denied it but fought Rose for confronting her with a "lie." The actual fights, when they occurred, could be seen as specific replays of the general scenario for adolescent disputes. Each of the disputants played her role and later claimed that she had no choice; once the other person had spoken, she had to respond as she did. Here the shared understanding of the fight story and the shared understanding of the fight experience were indistinguishable. Tellings determined what were perceived as limited alternatives for action.

5.4   Authorship and entitlement in the girls' diaries

Although self-reflexivity and the use of the elaborate contextual detail that would provide a distanced perspective were rare in the oral fight narratives, they were the substance of written diary entries. Diary writing was one of the only ways in which the adolescents could set up a distance between themselves as authors and the ongoing situation. Diaries provide seemingly unlimited entitlement to express a point of view. At the same time, they constrain the author by insisting that the text represent her point of view. Readers expect diaries to be true confessions and diary writers to be reliable narrators whose views coincide with those of their authors.[11] However, this understanding of diaries as representing the actual stance of the author is misleading. All communicators take a stance, and an unconcealed stance indicates only that the entitlement constraints are less blatant than usual.

The adolescent diaries provided a particularly complex example of the possible relationships between reported speech and entitlement, since the diaries were ends rather than conduits for rumors. Further, the diaries potentially reported what one would have liked to say or could not say, as well as what was said. The diaries provided an opportunity for personal disclosure; private remarks written in a diary could be addressed to imaginary audiences or to their authors at a later date and could be read by the authors, illicit readers, or, in some cases, selected privileged readers. In diaries, as in a few other written forms, the questions of address and audience were not necessarily the same.

One of the central issues raised by discussions of oral fight stories and written forms of protest (petitions and letters) and play was the social consequences of communication – specifically, entitlement – within the ongoing everyday interactions of the adolescent community. Unlike the other forms, diaries might be presumed to be safe from challenges to entitlement, since they are heavily guarded by proscriptions eliminating the entitlement of would-be audiences. However, the idea that someone might surreptitiously read one's diary, or the care taken to conceal messages – either stylistically, through cryptic writing, or overtly, by hiding the book – itself involves conditions of entitlement.

The adolescent diaries provide a glimpse of what could not be said aloud or written for others to read. At the same time, they provide an example of authorship, of the act of claiming not only an experience, but also a telling, as one's own.

Unlike the petitions and letters, which were intended for specific current situations and rarely saved as either records or souvenirs, the diaries were not expendable. They were written to be saved. However, the entries did concern ongoing situations – contemporary, even urgent and unresolved – and although not shared with others, they constituted an immediate dialogue between the author and her text. In the diaries, the author wrote for herself; supposedly she understood whatever she wrote, and yet she intended her writings for the future and wrote what she would be able to decipher long after she had forgotten the incidents that precipitated her entries. The entries required recontextualization for future reading.

The diaries add the dimension of history to the adolescents' writings; they are one of the few kinds of texts that were collected rather than discarded. This historical dimension, along with the dimension of argument exhibited in the adolescents' letters of protest, form the beginnings of an understanding of how the adolescents used writing and how those uses match or contradict general assumptions about literacy.

Written and spoken forms can be contrasted in terms of their uses, including expendable or ephemeral versus collected texts; the relative distance versus immediacy of the relationship between listeners/readers and tellers/writers, or between a narrative and the events it purports to describe; and collaborative versus individual productions and performances.

The adolescent conventions for diary writing can be examined in two dimensions:

1. in terms of social interaction, or entitlement – that is, how the entries fit into the patterns of conversational communication among the adolescents, and
2. in terms of narrative device – specifically, reported speech and the positions of the author, narrator, and addressee.

Constraints on interaction often inform narrative conventions. In the case of the diaries, the girls often wrote things that they would not have said to each other. Further, they often described things more specifically in private writing than in speaking. One question is, To what extent is this difference attributable to the act of writing itself, the fact that writing can be preserved and therefore demands more specificity for comprehension at a later date when the events described might not be remembered, and to what extent is the elaboration of details in writing simply a matter of different conventions for communication? To what extent is writing governed by the conventions of the collection rather than those of the expendable, ephemeral conversation, the texts or narratives spoken once and not repeated or stored?

The diaries challenge the boundaries of written and spoken conventions. To a certain extent, this is a property of all diaries. They are as close to conversational narratives as they are to fictional written ones. The adolescent diaries further exaggerated this contrast, since their writings were sometimes indistinguishable in form and content from their spoken conversations. They often wrote as they spoke, though they often wrote things that they would have been reluctant to say.

Talk was one of the greatest sources of hostility among the adolescents in the junior high school. To talk about someone else was considered a major offense justifying a fight. Threats, challenges, and reports of talk behind someone's back circulated as rumors and created a climate in which fights could erupt in any corner between any number of potential antagonists. Actually, much more talking about fighting took place than actual fighting.

In many communities there is an understanding of the difference between public knowledge, which is anyone's right to discuss, and private knowledge, which belongs to the people directly involved in the situation discussed. In the junior high school, information regarding students – from what bus an individual rode to and from school, to the latest boyfriend–girlfriend relationships – was private. Family information was the most private and was rarely discussed among people who knew each other, though people who did not know each other at all sometimes reported their own recent family events as if such information was innocuous when told to someone too distant to use it against the teller. Information about boyfriends and girlfriends was discussed constantly and was accompanied by frequent accusations that someone had violated privacy by spreading the information beyond its warranted boundaries. One way to understand the complexity of the situation is to say that there were few constraints on telling information but that any retelling was a potential offense.

Diary writing provided an opportunity for the adolescent girls to report information they were reluctant to tell, for one reason or another, and information that they could not retell without being charged with talking behind someone's back.

Stacie wrote her entries as a dialogue with the diary itself, which she named Cary. The difference between her stories told during and after school among friends and her diary was that she told her diary things that were rarely shared among friends. She told her stories in the same way that she told stories among friends, and she shared some stories with both friends and the diary. However, other entries were not the kinds of things friends told each other. For example:

28 April

> Today I went to school. I was so hungry I wanted to come home. I
> might play sick tomorrow in school. I hate being in school with no

lunch money. My stomach was growling in class and I was embarrassed. But I'll have money tomorrow because Miss Addie gave me a dollar to braid her hair. Its not much but at least I'll eat tomorrow. Anyhow I did a terrible job. Today I got two books out of the library. I'm going to make a report on one of them. I don't know which one I'm gonna use. When I get my check from the College math program I'm gonna take five dollars out for a weeks worth of lunch. I'm trying very hard to get on the honor roll for the last report period. Well, Cary I'll talk to you tomorrow okay.

Many of the things said in this diary entry could have been said to friends at school. The author could have complained about being hungry, and she could have said, "I was so hungry my stomach was growling; I was so embarrassed!" However, to complain about being hungry, especially about having no money, would have the same effect as asking friends for food or money. Students often borrowed money from each other at school and often shared food, but they rarely if ever complained about poverty. Stacie could not borrow money until she was sure that she would be able to pay it back the following day.

The entry takes stock of the day's activities candidly and tells several things that would not be revealed openly. Stacie was hungry, did a terrible job of braiding someone's hair, and took books out of the library. Neither of the first two comments was a secret; like the third comment, they did not have a proper audience. The entry further makes plans: to play sick in school if she was hungry again, to have money for lunch in the future, to get on the honor roll. It contained private hopes that could not be fulfilled by speaking about them in Stacie's world. Some of the diaries contained entries about family matters, about romances, or about sexuality, topics that involved great discretion when discussed among friends.

April 8

Dear Cary

After tonite I'm going to look for someone else to care about. I need someone thats my speed. Thomas told me that Jarod was a punk and that he sat in between Jarod and his girl and Jarod got mad and walked away. And just tonight he sat and let a boy hit him and all Jarod did was sit there and let him.

I was mad but I just kept talking to Thomas. I don't hate Jerod I'm just mad at him. I have listened to what everybody said and I still like him. Starting Easter vacation week I'm gonna fix my self up and start hanging out. I'm gonna get someone who cares about me. Thank you Cary for letting me talk to you.

Stacie

The content of the April 8 entry was no different from that of many adolescents' discussions. However, in her diary, Stacie stated her feelings as contrary to the opinions of her friends and declared her intention to find someone new. Had she stated these views orally, they could have become the subject of rumor and hostility (between Stacie and Jarod or between Stacie and everyone who offered an opinion). In discussions among friends, and especially in personal stories, the adolescents were greatly constrained by the consequences of their statements. Talk was always a source of potential antagonism. However, in her diary, Stacie could write anything. (Diaries were often a source of controversy between their authors and brothers, sisters, or other intruders who were suspected of reading them without permission.) There are things that cannot be said without accepting the consequences of speaking. They incur obligations of certain reactions on the part of the listeners, and the speaker must take responsibility for having instigated the interaction. Although entries discovered in someone else's diary could be grounds for disputes, the writer could escape liability by placing the blame on the person who read the diary without permission.

5.5 Contextualization

Although the diaries were presumably intended to be read only by their authors, they provided far more contextual detail than narratives told orally between friends. Diaries presented the possibility of totally contextualized writing in which referents were not provided for pronouns, understanding of locations and times was assumed, and behaviors were not explained. However, some of the diaries were written as if intended for an audience who would not know even the most commonplace facts. Entries included details such as "I went to my room. It is at the top of the stairs on the left" or "So I says to Michael, that's my brother . . ." The following entry illustrates the point well:

> May 22, 1979
>
> I woke up 6:30 I got up washed up and put my clothes on. I didn't get done till 7:30 My mother ask Maggie did she have a token. Maggie said "No Mommy" My mother found a token to give me to get to school. The school bus leaves 7:05. I caught the bus and seen a friend of mine named Terry. We were waiting on Bridge Ave. My trolley came and I left for school. I am in Mrs. Stocking class for Math. Next I am going to Mrs. Oliver. The first bell just rang. That was 1st period. It is now 8th period and 1:03 oclock. Mr. Corkran is my teacher. He gave us a review on English. I got a detention from Mrs. Blinker with Mr. Corkran. My grandfathers birthday is today. That is my mothers father. I am down the street after walking Lucas

home from my house. Well I just came home and I go in and see Bruce my oldest sisters boyfriend in my house. I asked him where was Patty last night. Then Bruce asked Patty "Were [*sic*] were you last night when me Joan and Tracy went looking for you. She said "I came home from school about six o'clock and then me and Sharon walked Sharon's sister to the bar." Then Bruce said "You are a damn liar. No matter what I will love you anyway."

Not all of the diary entries provided pronoun referents or explanations that would make the information intelligible to an unfamiliar reader. In the April 8 entry, it is not clear what happened between Jarod and Thomas: "Thomas told me that Jarod was a punk and that he sat in between Jarod and his girl and Jarod got mad and walked away." Apparently, Thomas sat between Jarod and Jarod's girlfriend. But isn't the author, Stacie, the girlfriend? The entry is a highly contextualized piece that fits the mode of oral narratives shared between friends. No explanations are needed because the audience would be familiar with the situation. Neither is the entry especially cryptic; Stacie's brothers and sisters would have no difficulty understanding the entire picture.

Diary entries do not appear to be decontextualized, partly because an entry is never intended to stand alone as a text. Each entry exists within the context of the diary and other "texts," including the oral narratives told in everyday life, yet they discuss commonplaces, facts so familiar to the author that they would ordinarily go without mention in conversation. One explanation for the inclusion of detail in the diary entries may be that the authors approached the diaries as writing, as belonging to the kind of communication that invites contextual detail.

Contextualization in a diary entry is complicated by the fact that the author is also the reader. Instead of seeing the May 22 entry in terms of what could have been omitted or what might be unnecessary for the reader-author, it is possible to see it as a chronicle, a record written by someone who wanted something to write and who may not have been concerned about her audience. Most of the adolescents' writings, including letters and notes, school assignments, and the diary writings, can be seen in terms of what they had to say in particular circumstances and for particular audiences. "I have nothing to say" or "I don't know what to say" was a common response to school assignments. Letters and notes provided an opportunity for the students to say things in writing that they would not say face-to-face. Many of the girls saw the diaries as asking the question, "What did I do today?" and they responded with a chronology of their activities. The diaries imposed the constraint of daily entries, and most of the girls wrote schedules, sometimes as they were occurring and sometimes retrospectively. In most cases, the girls supplied more, rather than fewer, details in their diary entries than in their oral stories. They explained relationships between people; they provided elaborate descriptions of the circumstances in which things happened; and they offered contextual information (such as the regular departure time of the school bus).

5.6   Storyability

The diaries demonstrate that the relationship between text and context must be considered not only in terms of the elaboration of contextual information but also in terms of diary writing as a particular context for communication. Diary writing for the adolescents was a context for elaborated discourse, in contrast to face-to-face interaction, which restricted communication by presenting constant challenges to a speaker's right to speak.

H. P. Grice and William Labov have offered two models for discussing the appropriateness of discourse. Grice's cooperative principle evaluates talk according to four maxims: quantity (be informative), quality (be true), relation (be relevant), and manner (be perspicuous).[12] Diaries are not parts of conversations and, understandably, do not conform to all aspects of the cooperative principle. Specifically, they violate the maxim of quantity by providing both more and less information than is required. However, the cooperative principle can help explain the larger context of communication in the adolescent world and thus help to explain how the diaries play a part not played by talk. A revision of Grice's model is needed to accommodate the adolescent communication. Grice has outlined the maxim of manner as follows: "Avoid obscurity of expression; avoid ambiguity, be brief, and be orderly." Among the adolescents, the central rule in discourse was not to disclose more than one was entitled to tell. The trick was to hold the floor without risking challenges of interfering in someone else's business. For the adolescents, the fourth maxim was entitlement rather than perspicuity.

The diaries offered an outlet for expression free from challenges of entitlement, truth (though there was less reason to violate this maxim), relevance, and informativeness. Whereas decontextualized writing in most cases conforms to Grice's cooperative principle and provides intelligible information, diary writing encourages not detail and clarity, but privacy. The form of the diary encourages elaboration by providing blank pages to be filled with information of current, and not necessarily lasting, relevance. It provides an opportunity to express point of view rather than the truth.

As already discussed, Labov's model focuses on the use of evaluative phrases within narratives to articulate the point being made. A narrative without evaluation is pointless and open to a listener's challenge of "So what?" The April 28 and April 8 entries were highly evaluative, but both included the kinds of evaluative remarks that would be inappropriate in talk among friends. Remarks such as "I was so hungry . . . I hate being in school with no lunch money . . . I was embarrassed . . . I did a terrible job . . . I'm trying very hard to get on the honor roll . . . I need someone that's my speed . . . I'm gonna get someone who cares about me" were complaints about the world as it is, and complaints elicited criticism, not sympathy, in the adolescent world. The May 22 entry had no evaluative remarks, and the information provided appears to be especially extraneous in their absence. Evaluations provide the justification for discourse, and although diary entries do not need any justifications, since there are no listeners to say "So what?", they do utilize evaluative devices to express a point of view. Labov does not discuss the perhaps inappropriate use of evaluations in private writing, since his point is to identify the function of evaluations in establishing meaning in face-to-face discourse. Evaluations function to establish meaning in diaries, but instead of making a story meaningful to an addressee, diary entries record meanings and points of view much as they record the events of the day. Evaluative statements in the diaries do not necessarily justify the enterprise of writing; rather, they were private statements expressed in one of the few appropriate channels.

Discussions of both essay writing and oral discourse have focused largely on the intelligibility of texts.[13] The concept of decontextualization is essentially concerned with how an absent audience will understand a written text. The written text must provide enough contextual clues to be intelligible. Studies of oral discourse similarly attempt to identify those elements that contribute to intelligibility. Intelligibility, however, is not the problem in diary entries. Since the author is the addressee, intelligibility is assumed. A diary can be seen as a record of shared understandings or an account of points of view. Entries that provide more information than is necessary can be seen as attempts to perpetuate the text, to fill in the blank pages. The three criteria for the diary entries – storyability, contextualization, and tellability – sort out some of the characteristics of the diary entries. Storyability is essentially an artistic criterion, as concerned with how a story is told as with its content. Certain kinds of experiences are storyable for their remarkable quality; in a diary any experience, remarkable or not, is storyable as a record of what happened on a particular day. Contextualization involves an evaluation of the function of the text; the notion of writing as decontextualized assumes that the function of written texts is intelligibility. Diaries can be heavily contextualized private documents that explain little to the intrusive outside reader. However, they can also include contextual details that would seem unnecessary for the intelligibility of the reader-author, but that are included to keep a record and perpetuate the text. Tellability is a social criterion; an experience may be storyable in its remarkableness but not tellable in a particular situation to a particular audience. The diaries afforded an opportunity to tell the untellable, to express a point of view without being vulnerable to the consequences.

The adolescent diaries were as strongly constrained by the rules for oral narratives as they were by the conventions for writing. Stories were written in the diaries much as they would be told orally. Further, diary writing was used as an extension of oral discussion to work out ideas in the midst of ongoing experiences. Although the written stories were preserved in the diary, the entries duplicated the most ephemeral of adolescent communications, more expendable even than conversations since they could be produced without the risk of social consequences, without challenges to entitlement, and without the "So what?" response.

Most of the adolescent girls wrote diaries, and people in the community considered diary writing to be part of the culture of adolescent girls. Younger brothers made a game of trying to locate their older sisters' diaries, and elders complained that girls sat in corners of the house and wrote when they were supposed to be watching young children or doing other chores. Diary writing was nonstandard or unofficial writing, traditional as an adolescent female activity, and folkloric, in contrast to the standard writing required in school. It can be seen as part of a larger group of protest writings, including letters written to school and community authorities to complain about specific actions, and petitions written to friends to persuade them to join an alliance against another group.

The adolescent diaries invite questions about the relationship between speaking and writing, ordinary discourse and art, folklore and literature. The diary entries are close to oral discourse; yet some of the properties, especially the extensive details, can be explained only as an act of perpetuating a writing activity, of filling in an empty book. The entries are more than inventories and definitely represent the creative performance of an artistic hand. Close as they may appear to raw experience, they are not the experiences themselves but renderings, transformations of experience.

The greatest problem in categorizing the diaries is the lack of an audience. One cannot speak of the interpretations of the text (as one would of a literary work) if there are no readers to interpret it. One cannot speak of the community aesthetic or shared understandings or transmission of knowledge (as one would of folklore) if there is no audience. Stacie, the author of the entries presented here, has conveniently provided a fictitious audience in her addressee, Cary. Even so, it is clear that a diary is a book to be written and not read; the process eludes the product. Only a written text moves toward decontextualization or the ability to be read out of context. An oral text depends upon context for intelligibility. The diaries are not about intelligibility; they escape the constraints of both the context provided in an oral performance and the ideal of decontextualization sought in written essays.

6

FAMILIARITY AND DISTANCE: TOWARD A THEORY OF ORAL AND WRITTEN PERSONAL NARRATION

6.1 Literacy as a category

Speaking and writing have been contrasted as the epitome of the nature–culture dichotomy. Walter Ong states:

> Speech wells up out of the unconscious, supported by unconsciously organized grammatical structures that even the most ardent structural and transformational grammarians now admit can never all be surfaced entirely into consciousness. Speech is structured through the entire fabric of the human person. Writing depends on consciously contrived rules. (1979:3)

This polarization of conscious and unconscious, contrivance and deep structure, and (stated later in the same essay) history and memory, abstract and concrete, leaves a great deal unexplained. The ability to speak is not the same as the ability to tell stories or to interpret the meaning behind someone's words. Although written standardized texts can often be distinguished from oral nonstandard ones, this distinction is complicated by such phenomena as texts that were written to be read aloud and by the use of ordinary language in literature.

Recent studies of literacy have eroded the absolute differences between writing and speaking. At the same time, in literacy studies, these categories are becoming polarized metaphors for social change, cultural differences, and the impact of technology on communication. Increasingly, literacy studies have provided evidence of a shift in our understanding of the categories of writing and speaking. The question of the impact of writing must be rephrased to address the impact of certain kinds of texts and of specific ways of using texts. Many scholars have pointed out that the boundaries between orality and literacy are not clear. Essentially, the problem concerns the definition of literacy: Does it consist only of reading and writing, or does it also include indexing, archiving, interpretation, the use of standard spelling and grammar, familiarity with certain kinds of texts, the ability to compose as well as to copy, and multiple uses of texts? Literacy is usually defined in terms of its uses, and it is difficult to separate the mechanical skills from their conventional uses.

Searches for the boundaries between the oral and the written have concerned the implications of the differences rather than distinctions between the channels of communication themselves. Each disciplinary approach provides a different set of implications and a different contextual boundary for the category of literacy. Cognitive psychologists and educators, concerned with literacy as a mode of thought, see learning or the acquisition of skills as an important context (Wagner 1982). Historians and classicists have noted the alphabet (Havelock 1977), index systems (Clanchy 1979), and public education (Graff 1979) as contexts that make literacy historically consequential. Linguists have regarded standardization as the key factor that makes written and oral communications significantly different, although they also point out that the use of writing in a society does not mean that a language or that all writing has been standardized (Bloomfield 1964; Garvin 1964). For literacy scholars, the most significant context is contextualization itself, or the relationship between text and context in oral and written communications. Folklorists might also be mentioned here, although they have been less interested in the implications of literacy than in the perpetuation of the verbal arts with the advent of a more literate population. Although the folklorists of the late nineteenth century themselves propounded the view of verbal arts as the survivals of a bygone era, current folklore research focuses on the performance of living traditions as the most significant context for verbal art. Folklore provides an interesting meeting ground for oral performance and written texts, since these can be seen as both compatible and competing channels of communication.

The processes of literacy – writing, reading, and referencing – share some attributes with the processes of oral transmission – composing, performing, and remembering. Referencing, a means of tracking relationships between texts, is an alternative to remembering. Both the reference system and the mnemonic device can be identified separately from the texts to which they refer. Referencing and remembering are contextual concerns, and the identification of either process as a significant factor in determining the difference between orality and literacy suggests a shift in focus from written or spoken texts to categories of relationships between texts and contexts. It is not the texts alone but the contexts of their use that have the greatest implications for the differences between written and spoken communication.

For the most part, research on literacy from each disciplinary perspective has challenged, rather than confirmed, a sharp distinction between oral and written communication. The boundaries have eroded slightly; interestingly, at the same time, some of the disciplinary boundaries have also tumbled as psychologists, historians, linguists, literary theorists, educators, classicists, and folklorists find themselves asking some of the same questions. A group of related issues repeatedly arise, including decontextualization and contextualization, composition and transmission, textuality and intertextuality, variation and performance, ordinary and poetic language, logic and epistemology. These shared concerns do not necessarily lie on the margins of the interested disciplines; often they undercut central premises of these fields.

The boundaries of literacy change with each focus of investigation. When gatekeeping is the purpose of the research, the study of literacy includes not only who reads and writes what, but also the value of reading and writing for participation in a certain group, social class, or occupation. When abstract thinking is the issue, the focus shifts to the kinds of texts produced by a certain group, rather than the kinds of groups that produce texts.[1] When categories of knowledge such as history or science are the claimed products of literacy, the categories include printing, indexing, and archiving as well as reading and writing.[2] In each case, literacy involves both the mechanical skills of producing and decoding written texts and the social skills or conventions for correct interpretation, for shared understanding of either referencing methods or of relations between texts. The development of "civilization," now attributed to the advent of literacy, might more appropriately be attributed to archiving, preserving, and standardizing texts. Literacy is a matter not only of what people know but also of how they use their knowledge.

Perhaps the most elusive consequence of writing concerns the relationship between literature and literacy. The notion of art as a recognizable product that conveys enough of an illusion of permanence to be interpreted by a number of critics, who may then regard each other's interpretations as texts for further commentary, is built into both literary and art historical scholarship. Oral art forms, such as oral poetry, have been largely disregarded in literary discussions (Finnegan 1977). One erroneous assumption is that only "oral cultures" have oral artistic forms and that the perpetuation of oral art forms in a "literate culture" is a mere survival of the past (Finnegan 1977:160–8).

The danger is that the division between oral and written can imply a distinction between ordinary and artistic. Speaking, even spoken literature, is wrongly considered to be closer to the everyday as a less contrived form of communication. An alternative is the study of oral communication and the ethnography of speaking as framed interactions or as "speech acts" in which the poetic is treated as one more device used to convey meaning.[3]

6.2 Literary and literacy understandings of texts

For educationally oriented literacy scholars, written texts may be encyclopedic, exhaustive, independent of face-to-face communication, and self-explanatory. These scholars understand that an exhaustive text is impossible, but they are interested in the potential for exhaustiveness and in the cognitive skills involved in producing such abstractions of discourse.[4] Literary theorists, in contrast, tend to discuss the irreducibility of texts. They are interested in the finite quality of text and the infinite possibilities of interpretation. There is an area of agreement between the two approaches, which seem to have little knowledge of each other, at the point on the continuum at which they each consider a text to be a completed product.[5] However, the rationales for considering a text complete vary from the notion that a completed text is self-explanatory to the argument that a text is complete insofar as it demands interpretation and implies multiple, and not necessarily consistent, interpretations in its readings.[6] Literacy scholars are usually interested in the ability to be explicit. Literary theorists are more often interested in the manipulation of the implicit.[7]

Pierre Macherey proposes a distinction between what the work "refuses to say" and what it cannot say. The silence of what the work cannot or does not say, he suggests, is a condition of language. "The explicit requires the implicit: for in order to say anything, there are other things which must not be said" (1978:85). Literary theorists such as Macherey are addressing the temptation faced by literary critics to explore the unsaid dimensions of a text – for example, facts about the author's life, facts about the political climate in which the writing was produced, potential unnamed referents for characters or places, or other details of possible symbolic or otherwise referential relevance. Macherey cautions against the indiscriminate search for meaning outside of the text, especially against the search for "the meaning," as if there were only one meaning for a text. Macherey's discussion (implicitly) turns attention to the conditions for meaning rather than to the sources of meaning. The central difference between the literary theorists' and literacy scholars' approach to the text is that the former, as in the case of Macherey, do not see the text as a source of information that can be confirmed, and the latter are interested in the completeness of a text insofar as it relays information and is a source of confirmable information.

For the most part, literacy scholars are concerned with written texts in terms of the kind of information they contain. They focus on the adequacy of texts for conveying information and on different ways in which information is more or less adequately conveyed. Mikhail Bakhtin explains that a word can be directed "both toward the object of speech, like an ordinary word and toward another word, toward another person's speech" (1973:153). Reported dialogue in stories is an example of double-directed words.

> Every utterance has its author, who is heard in the utterance as its creator. We can know absolutely nothing about the actual author as he exists outside the utterance. The forms of actual authorship can be very diverse. A given work can be the product of a collective effort, can be created by the successive efforts of a series of generations, etc. – in any case we hear in it a unified creative will, a specific

position to which we can react dialogically. A dialogical reaction personifies every utterance to which it reacts. (1973:152)

In the adolescent fight stories, reported speech is used to substantiate evidence and to remove oneself from authorial responsibility. The he-said–she-said story refers not only to what was said but also to the act of talking about an event. This double-directedness of words is not exclusively a property of literacy; it might be attributed more convincingly to fictional discourse in general.

The relationship between the fight and the fight story in the adolescents' oral and written accounts relies upon a fictionalized sequence of supposed violation, challenge, he-said–she-said story, and fight. The shared understanding of the sequence lends itself to contextualized texts in which one would need to know the entire expected sequence of fights in order to understand the story. Just as a fairy tale does not require explanations concerning the expected relationships between princes, princesses, and villains, the fight story does not require explanations. Of course, both genres could benefit from explanation; one could question the gifts granted to princesses or the type of punishment meted out to the villain, just as one could question whether or not a junior high school student challenged to fight must necessarily respond. These fictions are intertextual contextualizations; they depend more on familiarity with previous fight stories or fairy tales than on knowledge provided by a particular telling.

Fictionalization in texts is not simply a matter of referring to oneself in the third person. Nor are fictions in texts necessarily decontextualized. Rather, fictionalizations may imply specific situational referents not explicitly stated in the text (for example, the suggestion that certain characters in a fantasy refer to political figures). The autobiographical character of a work may be concealed as easily as or more easily than it is revealed, and one of the difficulties of texts is that they are rarely decontextualized. That is, they rarely reveal their referents as explicitly as does the school child's essay. "Essayist literacy" may not exist outside of the textbook, if it can be found even there.[8] When literacy scholars such as Scollon and Scollon write that "consistent maintenance of the point of view is one of the hallmarks of written text" (1981:70), they mean that the author intends his or her point of view and understands that certain uses of point of view will be intelligible and others will be potentially confusing to the reader. They mean that in face-to-face communication, the speaker does not need to account for the fact that he or she is speaking and that in writing the author may attempt anonymity. Anonymity is certainly one of the privileges of writing, but its use permits concealment as much as it demands clarity. Literacy scholars, perhaps in their focus on the speech of children learning the rules of discourse rather than on adult manipulation of the rules, imply that the literacy orientation demands an ability to provide texts that will be intelligible without familiarity with the situations in which they were created and to which they refer. But written texts play with concealment as often as they provide context-independent, explicit, intelligible information and descriptions.

Literacy scholars tend to discuss ellipsis, what is not said in texts, as pieces missing from a complete text.[9] They are concerned with how people learn to provide complete texts and suggest that writing demands complete texts that are self-explanatory and may be presented in the absence of face-to-face interaction. The relationship between oral and written communication or, more specifically, ephemeral discourse and printed writing, is also recognized by literary theorists as related to the dilemma concerning the completeness of the text. Macherey writes, "So the real trap of language is its tacit positiveness which makes it into a truly active insistence" (1978:89). Later, he states:

> By means of its stubborn linearity the discourse of the work establishes a certain form of necessity: it advances ineluctably within its appointed limits. The line of the discourse only seems to be fragile: it cannot be interrupted, or changed, or allied with another discourse from which it might receive that quality which it seems to lack. The text is established in its systematic thinness. Unless we espouse the normative fallacy, there is nothing to be added, nothing to be corrected in the book as it presents itself. (1978:98)

When literacy scholars address the problem of understanding how people learn how to produce such texts, their discussions turn to subjects such as "learning how to take from books" (Heath 1980), or learning an orientation toward literacy, or acquiring "incipient literacy" (Scollon and Scollon 1981). Here it is clear that recontextualization[10] essentially involves the recognition that texts are contexts for other texts (rather than the concept that written texts are contextless).

This point is especially important for understanding the adolescent oral and written fight narratives. What may seem to be incomplete texts to the outsider are appropriate concealments to the adolescents. The skillful use of ellipsis can be seen as a narrative device employed either to assert a point of view, or in contrast, to minimize what could be construed as an opinionated statement in oral and written fight stories. The fight narrative, as a variety of narrative forms, informs the appropriate content and construction of a particular tale. To judge the texts according to fixed standards of intelligibility, and thus find the narratives lacking, would be to ignore exactly what makes them successful in the community in which they are told and written.

A narrative is informed by both the events it describes and the narrative form.[11] When a piece of the event is missing from the narrative, it may be seen as present in the expectations of the form. The recognition of the ellipsis or absence is itself a presence. Decontextualization is an impossible notion when considered in terms of contextless texts. However, the notion of a special kind of independent written text may be possible when the context for such a text is considered to be other texts.

The preference for either literature or everyday life texts involves more than a choice of a domain for study, and the materials chosen reflect basic understandings of what constitutes a text. Oral communication is often treated as a residual category for the ordinary, in contrast to the contrived or "artful" written text, and literacy discussions have rarely addressed oral literature. However, the case for literature as a special example of the use of discourse cannot be made, whether based on distinctions between fact and fiction or on everyday language and literary language.[12]

Although a group may have culturally specific conventions for classifying certain forms of discourse as privileged and for assigning certain forms to their appropriate domains, the status granted to written literary texts (whether journalistic, novelistic, or essayist) is not inherent in literacy. The conventions for written texts in Western literature have been seen as particularly powerful in asserting standards of communication. The privileged status of written narratives is best understood in its cultural historical context; whether or not written and oral narratives are substantially different is a question requiring close examination of both social and textual conventions.

6.3 Standardization

Whereas the concept of decontextualization considers texts in terms of their presentation of information, the concept of standardization deals with the social acceptance of texts and of particular uses of language. The ideal of decontextualized texts in essence refers only to standard texts. Standardization, rather than decontextualization, permits the possibility of intelligibility in the absence of face-to-face interaction. The proposal that standardization rather than decontextualization characterizes contemporary Western literacy is a reiteration, in different words, of the previous statement that recontextualization involves the recognition that texts are contexts for other texts. As stated earlier, it is impossible to distinguish texts on the basis of their potential factuality. Works of "fiction," whether written or oral, may, or usually do, contain facts, and narratives describing actual everyday experiences create fictional frames for recounting experiences as events.

The inability to distinguish texts on the basis of potential factuality presents only one of many problems in claiming the possibility of a decontextualized text. First, objectivity and factuality (or any other way of categorizing a description as an accurate portrayal of the existence of something) are not qualities inherent in texts but rather are the conventions for understanding a text. If decontextualization is possible, it involves not only the detailed presentation of what happened, so that in the absence of face-to-face interaction a listener would understand the referents in the description, but also the use of standardized conventions for writing and reading. Second, these conventions involve a relationship between a specific text and a general class of texts, of which it is recognized to be a part. In other words, a contextless text is impossible; a text must be understood in the context of other texts. This relationship of one text to others provides, in the case of written texts especially, the possibility of standardizing conventions for presenting discourse in order to be understood in the absence of face-to-face interaction.

The notion of standardization in literature or any art form involves a great irony. The discrimination of "classics" from everyday discourse depends on presumed standards. However, great literature is distinguished from lesser literature on the basis of uniqueness and nonconformity to standards. The work that copies the formula may be considered second rate, but it provides perhaps the truest example of the standard.

> This kind of text, the more or less accurate fake, is often the most characteristic of a genre or style. Here is to be found in a pure if not original state all that defines the type. The skilful imitation can be more revealing than the model. (Macherey 1978:28)

Imitation often conjures up the label of "fake," but especially in the case of adolescent narratives, imitations must also be seen as a sign of shared values. The decision to imitate can suggest a kind of communication, a perpetuation of something valuable, and a recognition of community standards.

The classification of standards is further complicated by disputes over the authenticity of versions of texts. Standardization often involves authorization, or the stamp of the authorities that a particular work is recognized as belonging to a certain school of thought. This stamp of authority may, and often does, involve quarrels over the authenticity of a text or the historical debts of an author. The dispute involves both whether a certain author is indeed the author of a work and whether a certain work was intended to mean what critics believe it to mean. Both disputes are casualties of the existence of texts in the absence of face-to-face interaction between author and reader; they are properties of writing.

The dispute over the authenticity of versions of texts is essentially a recognition of the fact that standardization involves the relationship of texts to other texts. Stanley Fish has discussed this point in terms of the prestige attributed to the standard version:

> Some stories, however, are more prestigious than others; and one story is always the standard one, the one that presents itself as

uniquely true and is, in general, so accepted. Other, nonstandard, stories will of course continue to be told, but they will be regarded as non-factual, when in fact, they will only be non-authorized. (1980:239)

Standardization is not only a property of written texts. It may be seen as a property of the popularization of any text, written or oral. Popularization involves the spread of a text across whatever is considered to be a wide audience. It is a means for taking a text beyond the context of its creation to audiences that do not necessarily have face-to-face interaction with a text in always the same circumstances. The standardization or search for authentic versions of oral literature has received as much attention as the concern for standardization in written texts. Whereas standardization has been accompanied by the stamp of authority for written texts, it has been seen as the sign of inauthenticity for oral texts.

Further, the written form of oral texts has itself been deemed potentially inauthentic. This contrast in the treatment of oral and written literature points to the essence of the issues involved in considering standardization, and, although not specifically discussed as such, bears upon discussions of the production of literary works in the writings of both Pierre Macherey and Raymond Williams. Both Macherey and Williams criticize the focus in literary criticism on products rather than on modes of production. Williams discusses the history of the development of a notion of literature and points out that the word "literature" was first used to refer to reading ability and reading experience as a form of polite learning and was later used to refer to "an apparently objective category of printed works of a certain quality" (1977:48). The distinction between literary and nonliterary texts came much later. One of the main bases for distinguishing both between literary and nonliterary works and between oral and written literature is the relationship between a text and the events it purportedly describes, whether factual, imaginary, personal, historical, or otherwise. Williams contends:

> There was a falsification – false distancing – of the "fictional" or the "imaginary" (and connected with these the "subjective"). And there was a related suppression of the fact of writing – active signifying composition – in what was distinguished as the "practical," the "factual," or the "discursive." These consequences are profoundly related. To move, by definition, from the "creative" to the "fictional," or from the "imaginative" to the "imaginary," is to deform the real practices of writing under the pressure of the interpretation of certain specific forms. The extreme negative definition of "fiction" (or of "myth") – an account of "what did not (really) happen" – depends, evidently, on a pseudo-positive isolation of the contrasting definition, "fact." (1977:147–8)

Recontextualization does not make texts more accurate; it makes them more convincing. Thus texts posit certain kinds of relationships between experiences and their rendering. These relationships are not proven in texts; rather, in certain kinds of texts, authors attempt to convince their readers or listeners of the factuality, verisimilitude, or imaginariness of the incidents they describe. The distance created between authors and readers, created by situations in which texts are read in the absence of face-to-face interaction with authors, is directly related to the distance between texts and experiences. However, this process of recontextualization, providing distance between teller and listener and providing contextual information for the sake of intelligibility, is not limited to written texts.

6.4   Personal experience narratives

The notion of standardization has particular importance in considering personal experience narratives. As discussed earlier, personal experience narratives present a problem for the categorization of fiction. They involve a particular kind of distance, both between the teller and the experiences recounted and between the teller's knowledge and the listener's knowledge of the characters or places mentioned. This distance is greater than that in other kinds of narratives. The distance is "particular" because it is a foregrounded concern in such narratives. The distance is a defining feature of the genre and is often different from that of other kinds of narratives. For this reason, the oral personal narrative may be considered the quintessential contrast to the decontextualized written text. In addition, the personal narrative may be considered the least standardizable type of text in terms of authenticity (the text demands uniqueness), and yet may be formulaic in terms of following a familiar scenario for the presentation of similar stories.[13]

Standardization involves the comparison of versions. Personal narratives almost always involve multiple versions. However, this involves a standardization of content, in contrast to the concern for the standardization of form in what is authorized as "literature." The existence of multiple versions of texts (and every text is a version)[14] provides an opportunity and a necessity to examine the process of literature as a process of standardization. However, different sets of standards may exist, and this variation may be the key to a difference between oral and written uses of texts.

This approach to literacy challenges notions of decontextualization as discussed by literacy scholars. Literature is itself a challenge to the notion of decontextualization, since what is recognized as literature is not what anyone can write or read. The notion of literature places texts in the context of other texts. The notions of decontextualization and of literature each give priority to kinds of texts; further, each gives priority to a different kind of text. The notion of decontextualization asserts a distinction between texts that are shared in the absence of face-to-face interaction (and that therefore must be self-explanatory) and texts that are shared as part of face-to-face interaction (and that therefore can be highly contextualized). Both situations are possible, but they are not necessarily mutually exclusive. It is not texts, but relationships between texts and contexts, that determine the way a text is contextualized. The notion of literature asserts a distinction between ordinary language and literature, a distinction that has not been demonstrated.[15] Rather, recent discussions of literary theory have concerned the closeness of literature and ordinary language. The often stated comment that the most difficult thing is to write as one speaks further complicates the issue.[16] An implied distinction between decontextualized writing and literature suggests that the purpose of decontextualized writing is to convey information, whereas that of literature is to express meaning. If anything, literature is a reminder that ordinary language is not ordinary in a mundane sense, or, in any case, that literature does not use out-of-the-ordinary language.[17]

Once the relationship between ordinary language and literature has been considered, the question of the relationship between oral and written communication, whether literary or not, remains. What are the uses of decontextualized and contextualized writing? Further, if the notion of standardization is used in place of the notion of decontextualization, thus shifting the burden from the text to the relationship between writers who use standard procedures and readers who can recognize them, how are standards used and manipulated?

The categories assigned to writing can be recast in terms of categories assigned to speaking, so one can begin to look at literature in terms of communication, and such a recasting alone can provide new perspectives on the categorization of writing. However, the new categories are no less restrictive and are not necessarily more suitable. The point is not just to substitute one category for another but to probe the foundations of the categories in order to determine the dimensions on which differences are most significant. Here conversational narratives can be particularly useful in the exploration of the categories of writing and speaking. A next step in the move from formalism to a sociology of literature, from new criticism to reader-response theory, from historic-geographic to performance theories of the transmission of traditions, from structural linguistics to the ethnography of speaking, or from literacy as types of texts to literacy as uses of texts, is the examination of conversational narrative.

Conversational narrative demands that we focus on context as well as on text, and on the relationship between narrative and event – not as a matter of referentiality but as a matter of relationships between speakers and listeners and, correspondingly, between the story world and the storytelling situation. Because conversational narratives are on the boundary between verbal art and literature, they provide a good ground for examining some of the issues central to assumed differences between writing and speaking. The category itself defines a contextualized genre, a narrative within conversation, and thus provides an opportunity to examine ways of contextualizing, including familiarity, performance, storyability, and tellability, and to determine the extent to which these concepts are a factor in face-to-face, in contrast to absent-author, communication.

The adolescent fight narratives were a product of daily interaction. Their focus was not the events purportedly described but the claims made by the narrator. These claims included the entitlement to tell the story and the challenges that the stories often implied. The central difference between the adolescents' fight narratives or personal narratives in general and other traditional genres of verbal art such as fairy tales or ballads was in the relationship between the narrative and the experience it described. The fight narratives described familiar experiences. However, here it is important to differentiate between levels of familiarity. One can be familiar with form; for example, one can be familiar with the type of ending in a fairy tale and thus can have certain expectations about a story that appears to be a fairy tale. Alternatively, one can be familiar with the tale world; for example, a listener can claim to be as knowledgeable, or more so, than the teller about the events described in a story. One can claim familiarity with characters, types of texts, genres (forms), the works of particular authors, or alternative versions.

On another level, familiarity can refer to familiar language forms. Both writing and speaking involve the use of well-worn phrases or clichés, language that calls attention to itself as another and more traditional voice than that of the narrator, the taken for granted – language that is uncritical of itself. Familiar language can also be strange, and includes the understood as well as the seemingly meaningless.

The larger umbrella categories of the storytelling situation and the tale world further classify kinds of familiarity. Familiarity with the tale world's characters, events, and sequences of events is distinct from familiarity with the storytelling situation's form of presentation, the listener's prior knowledge, and the consequences of communication. In a sense, attention to the storytelling situation involves familiarity with familiarity (familiarity with the participants' familiarity with the tale world). Familiarity with the tale world represents one level; familiarity with the storytelling situation represents a second, metalevel on which the first level can be evaluated. A third level involves familiarity with the relationship between the tale world and the storytelling situation and the examination of the flow of knowledge between them. (Whether or not the third level requires familiarity with the storytelling situation is a matter of dispute.[18])

As I claimed earlier, a central difference between writing and speaking as modes of communication is the situational difference between absent authorship and face-to-face communication. In other words, as Olson (1977) has pointed out, writing involves attention to the properties of the text and speaking involves attention to the context. Distance can be associated with absent authorship and familiarity with face-to-face communication, but this is an oversimplification of familiarity. In terms of the three levels of familiarity previously identified, both absent authorship and face-to-face communication involve the first level, familiarity with the tale world, but only face-to-face communication provides familiarity with the contextual details of the storytelling situation and only absent authorship enables an examination of the third level, a kind of familiarity that is more often recognized as distance.

Personal narratives are potentially the most familiar, the least distanced, of narratives. However, their familiarity is not, as one might suppose, in their content; rather, it is attributed to the close alignment between the storytelling situation and the tale world. The problem with the notion of widening circles of familiarity or different kinds of conduits or tale processes as a factor distinguishing personal narratives from other kinds of narratives is that a personal experience story may be told to a small group of people within a short time of the experiences recounted, or it may be told many years afterward to a group of people familiar with the teller but totally unfamiliar with the experiences. Personal experience stories are told just as often to strangers as to friends, and may be told just as often years after as immediately following an occurrence. The only claim for familiarity as a distinguishing criterion may be that the teller of personal experience stories is necessarily familiar with the experiences recounted and that the listeners may also be familiar with them. That is, such familiar stories may be categorized as personal experience stories; however, personal experience stories may also involve a great degree of unfamiliarity.

In personal narratives, the teller claims an experience as his or her own. Harvey Sacks comments on the personal attachment to experiences in his discussion of stories told by a witness to an accident. He points out that his interest is not that the story is "about an automobile accident," but rather that "stories are about – have to do with – the people who are telling them and hearing them" (Notes: April 24, 1968). Sacks suggests that the point of the witness's story about the accident was "the ways in which, in this case, she's making the automobile wreck into something in her life." Sacks focuses attention not on the experience as storyable or tellable,[19] but on the ways in which narrators assert tellability. In stories about actual occurrences, the assessment of tellability requires an assessment of the teller's accountability. The position of the narrator is crucial. As Sacks states regarding personal narratives:

> Stories are plainly ways of packaging experiences. And most characteristically stories report an experience in which the teller figures. And furthermore, in which the teller figures – for the story anyway –

as its hero. Which doesn't mean that he does something heroic, but that the story is organized around the teller's circumstances. (1971)

Stories organized around the teller's circumstances must somehow make those circumstances intelligible to the listeners. The circumstances of a story are one of the story's contexts. (Another context is the circumstances in which the story is told.) A story may describe several contexts, and the teller's circumstances may be deeply embedded in the complexities of the situation described. Further, the teller may use the extent to which his or her particular point of view is exposed as a narrative strategy. That is, the teller's circumstances may be strategically hidden. The relative exposure of the teller's point of view contributes to the intelligibility of the narrative for the listeners. However, it is not a simple matter of supplying unlimited contextual explanations; it is not true that more contextual explanation necessarily leads to greater intelligibility. Rather, intelligibility depends upon the prior understandings of the listeners, upon the teller's expectations concerning those prior understandings, and upon shared understandings of conventions for narrating incidents. Further, unlimited intelligibility is rarely the goal of storytelling; people share their experiences in order to promote certain understandings and to discourage others.

Sacks insists that the issue in stories about experiences (whether historical or personal) is not the facticity of the account but the assertion of personal, certified, and otherwise authoritative knowledge of purportedly actual incidents. In other words, the issue is tellability rather than factuality. Similarly, in his discussion of historical discourse, Roland Barthes writes:

> In our civilization there is permanent pressure to increase the meaningfulness of history; the historian assembles not so much facts as significants; and these he connects and organizes in such a way as to replace the vacuousness of the pure catalogue with positive meaning. (1970:153)

Barthes is critical of the notion of "fact" and cites Nietzsche's statement, "There are no facts in themselves. . . . For a fact to exist, we must first introduce meaning!" (1970:153).

The concepts of storyability and tellability provide an alternative to the fact–fiction categories for understanding the significant differences between oral and written narrative and especially for understanding narrative as a way of categorizing experience. We can then ask how oral and written communication might categorize experience differently, if the same experiences are storyable in writing and speaking, and if they are told and tellable in the same ways. I suggest that the answer lies in the differences between writing and speaking situations.

The most obvious potential difference between writing and speaking situations occurs when spoken narratives are performed so informally that the narration is not even recognized by the listeners as a performance and the stories themselves are part of an ongoing situation that is familiar to the listeners, and when written narratives are authored by a person unfamiliar to the readers and concern a world unlike their everyday world. These two dimensions of proximity and distance in performance are the crux of the distinction between writing and speaking. When the conventions for narration are closely bound to conventions for other social interactions, performance blends in with life. In contrast, distance invites attention to the form of experience, to the product or *the* performance as a completed whole.[20] Art and everyday do not distinguish between oral and written, but the object and the process is a distinction that *does* work – the written captures objects; the oral, processes. And perhaps this association between writing and art has contributed to the erroneous association between art and products. Of course, not all writings are performances, although many are treated as completed texts, distanced and distinct from other kinds of social interaction. For examples of writing that involve less performance, we must turn to the more ephemeral texts that do not become collected products, such as notes and other ongoing unfinished communications. Oral communication can be performed in a highly formal manner. I contend that there is little difference between the most formally performed oral and written communications. Thus I have turned to conversational narrative and diaries for my exploration of differences between writing and speaking.

In his understanding of performance as a frame of communication, Richard Bauman offers an alternative to criteria such as familiarity or first-person experience or personal experience for distinguishing between different uses of narrative. Bauman reviewed the ethnography of spoken literature and found that performance is best identified by emic categories, cultural categories for distinguishing between more and less performed genres. On the basis of a number of emic classification systems of speaking, Bauman states:

> Art is commonly conceived as an all-or-nothing phenomenon – something either is or is not art – but conceived as performance, in terms of an interpretive frame, verbal art may be culturally defined as varying in intensity as well as range. We are not speaking here of the relative quality of a performance – good performance versus bad performance – but the degree of intensity with which the performance frame operates in a particular range of culturally defined ways of speaking. (1975:297)

For the adolescents, writing was not a more performed mode of communication than speaking. For them, the great difference between speaking and writing was not in the kinds of thought demanded by either channel, but in the contexts of use. In the collaborative written complaints, the adolescents relied upon the combination of writing and speaking to produce their statements. In the solitary productions of diary entries, the adolescent girls often wrote as they spoke. The most significant contrast between written and spoken forms of communication among the adolescents was that although everyone had a story to tell, not everyone had something to write. When the adolescents did have something to write, as in their protests and complaints to the authorities, they wrote collaboratively. Those who had something to write wrote it in the name of the others. When asked to write as students, most of the adolescents produced the rudiments of the formula. Writing was a matter of sufficiency unless one had something to protest. However, when they did have something to protest, they chose writing as their channel of communication. Part of the protest involved the elaborate use of a written form.

The diaries allowed the girls to complain without accepting the consequences of oral complaints. Not all of the entries were complaints; some were listings of their activities, and in some diaries the entries followed the model of sufficiency familiar to other adolescent writings. However, the adolescents sometimes wrote beyond the demands of sufficiency, beyond the demands of the form. They sometimes wrote stories that were similar to those they told. And as in their oral tellings, where they talked as long as they could hold the floor, they extended their written complaints about offenses to say as much as they wanted to say. The diaries demonstrated the essence of the adolescents' writing. They depended not upon an ability to provide decontextualized descriptions but upon having something to write. The essence of adolescent communication, oral or written, was having something to say and knowing how to use the form in order to hold the floor and to take a stance. In speaking, the stance had to be guarded against potential challenges to entitlement, but writing was outside the system of offenses and challenges and belonged largely to the domain of adults and authorities. The adolescents appropriated writing for their own purposes, both to make their complaints in writing to adults and to carry on solitary communications not subject to adolescent challenges. Writing provided a means for the adolescents to speak as a group and to speak silently.

In terms of contextual reference, or familiarity and distance, the adolescents' uses of writing and speaking differed little. I have suggested that their uses of such contextual devices as referents, sequential ordering of events, and background orientations are better explained by constraints on entitlement than by the use of written or spoken channels of communication. In making this suggestion, I have shifted the direction of inquiry from the texts themselves to their contexts of use. I have found the distinction between contextualized and decontextualized texts as a means for distinguishing between qualities of speaking and writing inadequate, since it relies upon impossible ideals. (No text is either contextualized or decontextualized.) Rather than categorize the adolescents' written texts as contextualized, I have attempted to understand the ways in which the adolescents made their texts intelligible (and the corresponding ways in which they concealed information). The different storytelling rights, or constraints on entitlement, accorded written and oral narration depend not only on the distance available to absent authors or the familiarity of face-to-face communication, but also on factors less related to speaking and writing, especially the difference between resolved, mediate storytelling and ongoing, immediate storytelling. Personal narratives make the claim that "this happened to me," and whether or not the teller/writer is perceived as having made such a claim is more a matter of the consequences of the communication than of the channel used.

6.5   Literacy as an invention/the deinvention of literacy

In literacy discussions, the dimensions of the issues have been constantly subject to change. Investigations on one level of analysis have yielded to speculations on another level. Thus discussions of changes in the measured reading and writing abilities of school children have led to comparisons of different cultures' orientations toward literacy in general, or findings on the uses of reading and writing in specific situations have been explained by historical patterns of the development of civilization.[21] The benefit of such jumps in focus and mushrooming areas of inquiry has been the integration of many disciplines of study, including the psychological approach to education, linguistics, history, anthropology, communications, critical theory, and folklore. Scholars have recognized the need for an interdisciplinary study of literacy as the subject of literacy has come to encompass both situation-specific, culture-specific behaviors and a broad spectrum of theoretical inquiry. Scholars now recognize the impossibility of investigating one person's reading habits without considering cultural uses of literacy and cultural notions of texts. Literacy involves both artifacts representing communication and culture-specific ideas about communication. These ideas include both rules for the appropriate social uses of written texts and larger principles of language itself. The notion of literacy is exploding as scholars continually find premises of the past grounded in untenable notions of literacy. This is the nature of a bandwagon growth of a field. Fields of inquiry can be rewritten in terms of literacy. As Foucault has suggested, categories of thought are created by domains of investigation (1970:344). The humanities did not exist before being created by nineteenth-century works that demanded such a category. The great irony of the recent surge in literacy studies is that in exploring the basic principles of literacy, the assumptions about standard language and representation, the very principles claimed to be created by literacy, are totally undermined. In investigating the uses of literacy, we cannot help but discover that written and spoken texts cannot be definitively distinguished, that the fundamental requirements of writing do not necessarily preclude face-to-face communication, and that ultimately literacy involves not only the pursuit of universal intelligibility but also, through standardization, the creation of specialized languages involving both clarification and concealment. Literacy creates both texts that have no parallel in speech and texts that exist only by virtue of spoken parallels.

Literacy is a field based upon, dependent upon, and assuming a concept of texts. Ultimately, the exploration of textuality reveals that differences between writing and speaking are not located where scholars expected to find them. The distinction that placed either novelty or stability on the side of writing and either tradition or multiple versions on the side of speaking is better addressed as a difference between the appropriate use of rehearings in writing and speaking. What are the circumstances for repeatability? Among the adolescents, reported speech was repeatable; written statements were supposed to be original, rather than copied, and rereadings demanded revision (as in the same form with different answers). The distinction that placed decontextualization on the side of writing and contextualization on the side of speaking is better addressed as a matter of standardization for the purpose of conveying intelligible messages rather than for playful concealment. Here distinctions between formal and informal, public and private, can become more important than distinctions between writing and speaking. Distinctions between writing as intertextual and speaking as contextual are not meaningful unless they refer to different kinds of contextualization – for example, and especially, the difference between mediate (resolved) and immediate (ongoing) communication situations. Finally, distinctions between oral and written narrative, and especially the categorization of some written narratives as literature, can be recast as historically traceable conventions for classifying texts. To call authorship a question of entitlement, as I have done, is to extend conventions for oral narrative to the study of both oral and written narrative. The study of literacy invites us to examine the premises of writing and especially to understand writing within the larger context of writing and speaking as modes of communication. Each investigation of literacy seems to undermine rather than assert assumptions about writing. I do not suggest that writing and speaking have no significant differences, but rather that if we wish to understand the problem of contextualization, our best tools are those developed for the study of the relationship between text and context. The idea of literacy begins with texts, but in turning to the question of contexts, literacy undermines itself, and the privileged status of writing becomes a question of who is entitled to grant the privilege.

NOTES

Introduction

1. I use the term "conventions" without claiming that either writing or speaking is governed by a set of rules or that certain texts are representative or privileged.
2. As will be discussed in detail, the fight stories often refer to fights that have not yet occurred. The fight story is part of the fight, which consists of challenges and claimed offenses as well as actual battles, and talking about fighting often averts the physical fight.
3. Pseudonyms are used for the name of the school, as well as for the names of all people mentioned in this book. The students and their parents gave their permission for participation in the study, and the project was authorized by the school. I have decided to maintain anonymity for everyone to protect the students' privacy.
4. "Performances" here refer to observable events. "Texts" are not artifacts, but rather collections of words isolated either by me (through tape recording or physical collection of documents) or by the adolescents.
5. For clarity, I use the past-tense (rather than the ethnographic and textual present-tense) reports of my observations of the adolescent community and the present tense for discussions of concepts and for reference to scholarly texts.
6. "P.A.T.H." (or PATH) is a pseudonym for the acronym used at the school to refer to a special program for girls who needed special attention.
7. Shirley Brice Heath recommends an ethnographic method. She writes, "There are scarcely any data comparing the forms and functions of oral language with those of written language produced and used by members of social groups within a complex society" (1982:93).
8. Raymond Williams traces the term "literate" to its eighteenth-century use to describe a "man of letters." The man of letters was someone with sufficient education to understand the scriptures. Being "well read" referred to both the ability to read and the state of one's education. It was only later that the term "literature" was used to refer to fictional writings (1976:151).
9. See John Gumperz (1982) on miscommunication.
10. See James Phelan (1981).
11. Consider Ruth Finnegan's distinction between reciters and composers (1977:190).
12. See Foucault (1977).
13. See Mikhail Bakhtin (1981:3–40).
14. See Tannen (1982) and Bakhtin (1981).
15. See Foucault (1972:50).

1. Fight stories: what counts is the recounting

1. See Susan Sniader Lanser (1981:285).
2. See Robert A. Georges's discussion of the relationship between stories and events (1969).
3. The word "event" as used in folklore scholarship can be traced through Dell Hymes's notion of a speech event to Roman Jakobson (1957). Jakobson distinguishes between a

speech event and a narrated event. He uses the word "event" to refer to a single verb. In Hymes's work, the word "event" is used to indicate an entire conversation: A speech event may be a conversation within the larger unit of a party, the speech situation. The word "event" has been used to refer both to large categories of behavior and to single actions. Since it is possible to describe many activities as belonging to a single category of activity (such as a party), no a priori conditions for the extent of the application of the event are established. Thus, when it is claimed that narratives include two or more events, the boundaries of the events are not established; that is, such definitions do not prescribe a certain amount of activity as qualification for a narrative. Jakobson suggests that the term "event" refers to any verbal category, that is, any single use of a verb. Jakobson's model allows for the changing scope of an event within his framework of narrated event, speech event, and narrated speech event. That is, a narrator can report someone else's report of what happened.

Briefly, the problem is the twofold application of the word "event" both to what happened and to the telling of what happened. In Alan Dundes's structural model, "lack" and "lack liquidated," for example, cannot indicate what happened; the terms indicate only that something happened. The question is, what level of description is necessary to constitute an event qualifiable as a narrative?

Mikhail Bahktin has addressed a similar problem in his discussion of the double directedness of the word (1973:133).

4. The term "replay" is used by Goffman (1974:504–6). The term "recapitulations" is used by Labov in "The Transformation of Narrative Syntax" (1972:359).

5. Labov suggests that a "good" narrative (my term) recapitulates sequence, in contrast to a vicarious narrative, which confuses it (1972:367).

6. Garfinkel and Sacks suggest that the term "members" is preferable to the term "individuals" (1970:342). I agree with their reasons for rejecting the term "individual" as falsely assuming that individuals exist apart from social groups or society, and I use the term with that understanding.

7. See Lanser (1981:11–63).

8. Goffman writes: "Whenever an individual participates in an activity, he will be situated in regard to it, this entailing exposure over a given range to direct witness, and an opportunity, over much the same range, to acquire direct observations. These latter implications of 'situatedness,' in conjunction with his auditing capacities, generate a series of points beyond which he cannot obtain evidence as to what is going on. He will find barriers to his perception, a sort of *Evidential boundary*. Everything beyond this boundary will be concealed from him. Just as one can think of an activity as affording possibilities for disattending events and directional cues, so one can think of an activity as affording the possibility of concealment, this embracing the sum of matters that can occur beyond the evidential boundaries of its participants" (1974:215).

9. Goodwin notes that such stories are often directed to the offended person; that is, a teller tells a listener something that a third party said about the listener: "In building her stories, the speaker is oriented toward constructing them such that the target of the absent party's offense is a listener in the present. The structure of the immediate interaction is thus relevant to the organization of the description of the past being reported through these stories" (1978:518).

10. For an example, see the discussion of oral narrative 8.

11. I use the word "participant" to refer to people present in the storytelling situation or in other activities. I use the word "character" to refer to people mentioned in a story.

12. See Katharine Young's discussion of story realm and tale world (forthcoming).

13. For transcript notation, I have mostly used an abbreviated version of Gail Jefferson's "Transcript Notation" in Atkinson and Heritage (1984). *Studies in Conversation Analysis*, Cambridge: Cambridge University Press, 1984.

Brief pauses are indicated by line breaks. Pauses of more than three seconds are shown by ellipses.

Initials identify speakers. The abbreviations *Tchr* and *Std* are used to identify teachers and students when necessary.

Commas are used only for clarification – appositives, for example.

Ellipses in brackets [. . .] indicate unintelligible recorded speech.

Author interpolations appear in brackets – for example, [laughter], [interruption]. Question marks indicate rises in intonation.

Dashes indicate self-correction or -interruption by speaker.

Standard spelling is used except for "gonna" and the omission of "g" on "-ing" words.

The word [*sic*] is interpolated *only* in written texts where misspelling or incorrect usage has resulted in substitution of an intended word by another *recognizable word* – for example, "store" instead of "story."

A single closing bracket indicates two people speaking at the same time and is placed at the point where overlap begins.

Italics, where used in speech, indicate speaker's emphasis.

Oral narratives have been numbered in boldface for easy reference. When one is excerpted out of sequence, its "source" number is given parenthetically.

Quotation marks indicate reported speech.

14. See William Labov's discussion of the orientation section of narratives in "The Transformation of Narrative Experience" (1972).

15. Sacks points out the difficulties of this point when he states: "If it's a story in which you play some part, then what part is it that you play.[?] You could play any part. Of the characters A, B, C, and D, the prior storyteller is B. If you consider as a possibility that you can then be any of the four characters in your story, it turns out to generate real possibilities of disruption. If you tell a story about the time you saw an automobile accident and went over and looked at the people who were injured; then if the other guy tells you a story about the time he was in an automobile accident and all these idiots crowded around to look, then that's kind of embarrassing" (Notes, April 24, 1968:9).

16. On "Information States," see Goodwin (1978:573) and Sacks "Puns" (1973:139–41).

17. I am using "rumor" as a noun, to refer to a category of he-said–she-said narratives, in contrast to "gossip," which is the process, or one possible process, for spreading rumors. This contrasts to other uses of the terms in scholarship, such as that proposed by R. Rosnow and G. Fine, who suggest that gossip concerns personal affairs and rumor concerns more public events (1976:11).

   Roger Abrahams's discussions of gossip are relevant here, especially in terms of the relationship between he-said–she-said narratives and literacy. Abrahams states, in regard to the "talk about talk," that "Vincentian peasants retain an essentially oral culture in spite of the high degree of literacy in the community" (1970:292).

18. See also William Labov and David Fanshell's discussion of challenging propositions (1977:97–8).

19. Consider Derrida's remarks on the absence of the addressee (1971:171).

20. In contrast, Linda Degh and Andrew Vazsony state that legend tellers may deny a claim to authorship of the stories they tell ("Legend and Belief," Ben Amos, ed., 1976:101–2). This may imply a relevant distinction between personal narratives and legends in some cultures and/or a different use of entitlement among storytelling participants.

21. For example, Labov defines narrative as "one method of recapitulating past experience by matching a verbal sequence of clauses to the sequence of events which (it is inferred) actually occurred" (1972:359–60).

22.   See also Thomas Kochman (1972).
23.   Goodwin notes a similar situation in her study of black children: "The speaker, in that she has been affronted by having been talked about behind her back, and in that this is public knowledge, is *obliged* to construct the appearance of having taken action against the offense in order to maintain face. Failure to do so can itself be considered a form of offense, or a demonstration of lack of character, which can be commented upon by onlookers to a dsipute. A person who does not keep her commitment to confront another is said to 'mole out,' 'swag,' or back down from a fight by onlookers to a dispute (those neither accuser nor defendant). Consequently, an accuser may argue that the sole reason she is having a dispute with another is so that others will not be in the position to argue that she is backing down from her obligations" (1978:436).
24.   See Paul Ricoeur (1980).

2. Storyability and tellability

1.   Harvey Sacks discusses tellability in detail in his May 8, 1968 lecture. Marjorie Harness Goodwin says, with specific regard to he-said–she-said stories, "Within the immediate play cluster the he-said–she-said is highly tellable; but as it is told to individuals at the perimeters of the cluster, the story becomes a much less reportable object" (1978:559–60).
2.   Raymond Williams also discusses the terms "mediate" and "immediate." He criticizes the term "mediate," which, although intended as a needed replacement for the term "reflection," nevertheless dichotomizes "art" and "reality" (1977:97, 99). It is not my intention to further this dichotomy, and that is not my proposed use of the terms. Rather, I am interested in the relationship between mediacy and immediacy in terms of the distribution of knowledge. I could also use the terms "direct" and "indirect," but these do not imply differences in time and space, as do "mediate" and "immediate." See also Mosher (1980:178).
3.   Mediated storytelling relationships can involve unresolved stories, such as stories with ambiguous endings. I am grateful to Chava Weissler for pointing out "The Lady and the Tiger" as an example.
4.   See Simon Lichman's discussion of the relationship between metanarrative and mumming play (1981).
5.   *The Philadelphia Inquirer,* August 5, 1979.
6.   See Walter Benjamin (1976).
7.   This issue is discussed by Dan Schiller (1981).
8.   In his remarks on historical accounts of movements, Henry Glassie discusses how events can be differently shaped: "At its worst the account of a movement is a gossipy pastiche that titillates the reader's voyeuristic predilections. At its best the study of a movement describes how people, embedded in a particular environment, bring their own psyches, talents, and learning into engagements where they shape new ideas that lead to new arts, new actions, new nations" (1978:10).
9.   JoAnn Bromberg discusses the use of second storying and points out that second stories can be strategically used to make a statement about the relationship between participants in a storytelling occasion (1982).
10.   Susan Stewart writes: "In true stories, omniscience is taken for granted, 'played down.' The teller is concerned with putting himself in the audience's shoes and having the audience put themselves in his shoes, and so events are narrated as they would be experienced in everyday life, one after another. This is how narratives of fright like ghost stories work – the audience is never allowed to know more at any given time than the victim knows. Once we have moved to the horror film technique of showing

the monster or the murderer waiting behind the door, we have moved to irony and tragedy with their split voices, 'If only I had known' " (1979:149).

11. Labov and Fanshel do not make a distinction between news and art, and prefer the term "reportable" for tellable stories: "The proposition that many narratives represent is usually an affective one: the type of affect is governed by the events themselves: 'Let me tell you something funny/amazing/fascinating/fantastic/peculiar that happened . . . ' A central fact about all of these affective propositions is that they revolve about the social concept of 'reportability.' The justification for such narratives is that the event which is being reported at some length is different from ordinary experience, and in itself justifies holding the listener's attention" (1977:105).

12. As a case in point, consider Jane Edwards's observation: "In Mr. Williams' narrative his participation in the bringing down of the sheep constitutes a narrative in part because it was a unique experience: had he done this each year he would have given an account of what he called as the quintessential journey or else a series of noteworthy incidents from several journeys, but because for him there were no subsequent occasions to interfere, this particular journey can be recalled as a unique incident, in narrative form" (1978:23).

Dell Hymes makes a similar point: "If what persons can or will report is less than what they can interpret, what they can or will do is less than what they can report. In a recent class I had thought that a clear instance of something that everyone could interpret (recognize as culturally possible and structured), report (recognize as having occurred), and also do would be to recite the Pledge of Allegiance to the flag. I was mistaken. Eventually the class settled for recitation of the alphabet. . . . There is thus a polarity between voluntarily doing and performing on the dimension of REPEATABIL-ITY, taking performing in the sense of truly or seriously performing" (1975:16).

13. Michel Foucault discusses the transition from the everyday to the remarkable in "Tales of Murder," in his comments on Pierre Riviere's murders: "We should note carefully the words that were so often repeated in the titles of the broadsheets – "particulars," "circumstance," "explanation," "occurrence" – for they denote very plainly the function of this sort of discourse as compared with the importance given to the same facts in newspapers or books; their purpose was to alter the scale, to enlarge the proportions, to bring out the microscopic seed of the story, and make narrative accessible to the everyday. The first requisite in bringing about this change was to introduce into the narrative the elements, personages, deeds, dialogues, and subjects which normally had no place in them because they were undignified or lacking in social importance, and the second was to see that all these minor events, however commonplace and monotonous they may be, appeared "singular," "curious," "extraordinary," unique, or very nearly so, in the memory of man. In this way such narratives could make the transition from the familiar to the remarkable, the everyday to the historical" (1975:204).

14. In her study of the uses of speech in a Malagasy community, Elinor Keenan reported that Malagasy men do not provide complete information about incidents, but rather intentionally provide incomplete information. New information is a rare commodity and people are reluctant to part with it. Further, there is a fear of committing oneself explicitly to some particular claim. For example, if asked how to open a door, a person might say, "If one doesn't open the door from the inside, it won't open." The passive tense, as in "The dishes were washed with soap," or the circumstantial tense, as in "The soap was that with which the dishes were washed," is preferred in order to avoid naming an actor. Keenan notes that these characteristics primarily concern men's speech and that women do speak out and gain power by their frankness and gossip. However, men admonish their families not to convey news, and new information is often withheld until it gains importance in building anticipation (1974).

15. See Robin Lakoff (1975).
16. For examples of the varied ways in which information can be veiled, see Maurice Bloch (1975). See also Dell Hymes's discussion of stories not told simply because the occasions for telling them were few and his discussions of repeatability and performance (1975:16).
17. See Judith T. Irvine (1979).
18. See Emile Benveniste (1966, 1971).
19. Evaluation of victims and aggressors is discussed in Chapter 4.

3. Collaborative uses of literacy in the adolescent community

1. Some of this discussion is reported in Shuman (1982).
2. See John Szwed on the uses of literacy (1981).
3. See Edward B. Fiske (1978).
4. See Sue Fiering (1980).
5. Mrs. Hoober is the mother of a central character in Judy Blume's *And Then Again Maybe I Won't*, a book that was previously read by the entire class.
6. See Alan Dundes and Carl R. Pagter (1978:3–10).
7. The suggestion that the love letters were playful is part of a larger conception of writing as inherently fictional (see Smith 1978 and Fish 1980). Further, claims for decontextualization have used play for their illustrations. See Scollon and Scollon (1981).
8. On the relationship between reading aloud and discourse, see Scollon and Scollon (1981:57–98).
9. The relationship between disputes and writing is discussed further in Chapter 4. See also R. Barthes, who writes, "It is power or conflict which produces the purest types of writing" (1953:20).
10. Barthes writes about the use of the third person as "a typical novelistic convention; like the narrative tense, it signifies and carries through the action of the novel" (1953:35). Interestingly, the adolescents made the most use of the third person in oral narratives.
11. I have found this to be quite opposite in other junior high groups, where girls exchanged written notes daily.
12. On writing the unspeakable, Barbara Herrnstein Smith writes: "Fictive discourse allows us to speak the unspeakable – but only if we agree not to *say* it" (1978:110).
13. See John Szwed (1981).
14. It is important to note that this correspondence between written production and the learning experience involves the *imposition* of correspondence and does not support a dual temporal model. See Gerard Genette (1980).
15. See P. Pedraza et al. (1980).
16. See P. Van den Berghe (1973:959–78).
17. Jerome C. Harste and Robert F. Carey suggest that children may understand the difference between forms before they know how to write them. They cite M. W. Hill's work, in which she asked four-year-olds to write both a story and a letter. The "writings" (scribbles) looked similar, but the children "read" them differently. One girl read the letter as follows: "Once upon a time – there was – wait – uh huh. Dear Mary, I would like you to bring me . . . here everyday. The end. Megan." The story, in contrast, was read as follows: "Once upon a time there was a ghost. Three ghosts family. One day they went out for a walk. They honked on the horn cause they saw Mrs. Wood and said 'I' then they went back to Mrs. Corners and they honked the horn and sa-said 'hi.' The end." From M. W. Hill, "Look I Can Write: Children's Print

Awareness from a Socio-Psycholinguistic Perspective,'' cited in Jerome C. Harste and Robert Carey in ''Comprehension as Setting,'' in Harste and Carey (1979:4–22.)

18. The relationship between literacy abilities and other competencies has been discussed by other writers. For a review, see Michael Stubbs (1980:139–56).

    Basil Bernstein's writings on education and language also have bearing upon this research (1971).

19. A. L. Brown has made the point that knowing and knowing what one knows are quite different. The second involves evaluation, which, although a major part of the adolescent talk, was not part of the approach to writing. The belief that everyone knew how to write militated against evaluative differentiations (1975).

20. For a discussion of decontextualization, see Patricia M. Greenfield (1972).

21. See Elliot G. Mishler (1979).

22. Dell Hymes and Claire Woods Elliott discuss their preference for the term ''recontextualization'' in ''Issues in Literacy: Different Lenses'' (unpublished manuscript).

23. See Pierre Macherey (1978:44), who writes that literary language changes the nature of language, especially in terms of the relationship between ''the word and its meaning, between language and its object.''

24. See Stanley Fish (1980).

4. Retellings

1. See William Labov's dicusssion of the coda in ''The Transformation of Experience in Narrative Syntax'' (1972:354–96).

2. Their anger was similar to those expressed a few years later by the residents of the South Bronx, who felt that the film *Fort Apache: the Bronx* had wrongly depicted their neighborhood as the scene of nothing but street crimes, drugs, and prostitution. Some young people from the South Bronx who had participated in a neighborhood documentation project through an alternative school program were interviewed on television, radio, and for the *Village Voice*, and stated their complaints about the film: ''They say that the South Bronx is nothin' but pimps, pushers, and prostitutes; well, we live here. People wouldn't let those guys kill that cop; there's people in the streets all the time. Someone would of called the cops.'' The students from the alternative project did not deny that there were pushers, pimps, and prostitutes in the South Bronx; their complaints were directed at the fact that such people were used to represent all of the South Bronx. These students also complained about the lack of jobs and new housing (to replace derelict buildings). Their complaints about the film can be seen as a concern with who has the right to speak for the South Bronx. They did not think that the film was a fair statement, but fairness was judged in terms of not only the factuality of the film but also on the public nature of the film's statement. They saw no value in a film that portrayed the South Bronx at its worst, in an exaggerated form (in the eyes of residents), and ignored what they knew as daily life in the area. Their complaints also addressed another concern widely discussed in the media: the stereotyping of Puerto Ricans. The focus on the South Bronx and on Puerto Ricans made the film into one about Puerto Ricans in a particular place and depicted them as criminals. The distorted representation of an actual group of people in an actual place was the source of their anger. This particular representation gave the residents of the South Bronx the entitlement to respond, and, in responding, to deny entitlement to the filmmakers as spokespersons for the South Bronx. See Darlene Belton et al. (1981) and ''This Is Not Fort Apache, This Is Our Home: Students Document Their South Bronx'' (1981).

3. Heda Jason has demonstrated the importance of understanding different contexts for narrative in her discussion of Numbskull Tales. Jason points out that the numbskulls

of the tales are not equivalent to stupid people in everyday life. The numbskulls do things, such as dress a "naked" tree, that are not part of the "normal" world. In order to explain the logical properties of Numbskull Tales, Jason has introduced the concept of "the realm of the numbskull world," in which certain categories of experiences are familiar. She writes: "Each genre of oral literature has its own world. The world of the fairy tale, for instance, is populated by golden castles and glass mountains, talking animals and flying carpets. The world of the legend contains ghostly, dark ruins, hidden treasures and curiously formed stones which are in reality sinners who have been petrified for punishment" (1972:214).

4.   See Katharine Young (1983).

5.   Kenneth Leiter writes: "When two or more accounts arise, each claiming to be *the* version of 'what really happened,' the presupposition of mundane reason is brought into question. Since the presupposition of a factual and determinate world independent of perception predicts unanimity of accounts, conflicting accounts challenge that presupposition" (1980:101).

6.   See Gerard Genette's discussion of the narrator's presentation of information in "Mood" (1980:187–95).

7.   Stacie presented the same justification in a retelling two years later.

8.   Note Virginia Hymes's observation as reported by Dell Hymes: "Virginia pointed out that in going around with a friend from Warm Springs one often *saw* a bit of experience becoming an event to be told, being told and being retold until it took shape as a narrative, one that might become a narrative told by others." Courtney Cazden and Dell Hymes (1978:22).

9.   Dan Ben-Amos writes, "Unlike written literature, music, and fine art, folklore forms and texts are performed repeatedly by different peoples on various occasions" (1971:5). Also, Dell Hymes suggests "repeatability" as a major characteristic of folklore in "Breakthrough into Performance" (1975:11–74).

10.   See Dell Hymes's remarks on standard languages. He writes: "It has become clear that mutual understanding depends not only on common linguistic means, in the narrow sense, but also on common ways of using and interpreting speech" (Introduction, Cazden et al. 1972:xxxvii).

11.   The adolescents used the word "stories" to refer to television soap operas.

12.   Dell Hymes describes channels as a "choice of oral written, telegraphic, semaphore, or other medium of transmission of speech" and genres as "categories such as poem, myth, tale, proverb, riddle, curse, prayer, oration, lecture, commercial, form letter, editorial, etc." He discusses both categories as part of an ethnography of communication (1974:58–61).

13.   Consider Roland Barthes's interpretation of this approach to writing (1953:27–8).

5. Varieties of contextuality

1.   Most authors who address the uses of writing for distanced communication have been interested in written texts that make information intelligible to distant audiences. Both Walter Ong (1982) and Ron and Suzanne B. K. Scollon (1981) discuss the use of contextual detail and the concept of authorship for both writing and speaking.

2.   See Perry W. Thorndyke (1975) and J. M. Mandler et al. (1976).

3.   See M. L. Stein and C. G. Glenn (1977).

4.   William Labov, "The Transformation of Narrative Experience" (1972:364–6).

5.   Michel Butor writes: "It is easy to show that, in the novel, the simplest, most basic narrative form is the third person, and that each time an author uses another, he does so in a sense figuratively – inviting us not to take it literally but to superimpose it on the basic form which is always implied" (1965:60).

6. For a discussion of narrative and authorial voice, see Mikhail Bahktin (1973:158).
7. See Bahktin's discussion of persuasive discourse (1981:342).
8. For a discussion of reported and described speech, see Marie Laure Ryan (1981).
9. See William Labov (1972:380–93).
10. See Erving Goffman's discussion of ratified hearers (1976).
11. See Wayne Booth's discussion of reliable narrators (1961:169–209).
12. See H. P. Grice (1975:41–58).
13. Discussions of literacy and/or discourse by Ong (1982), Scribner and Cole (1981), Scollon and Scollon (1981), and Goody (1977) are all concerned with the idea that decontextualized texts provide intelligibility to readers.

6. Familiarity and distance: toward a theory of oral and written personal narration

1. Most of the discussions of the differences between literacy and orality by cognitive psychologists have relied not on examinations of texts, the products of reading and writing, but on the processes of reading and writing, which, some scholars insist, are cognitively different. However, the cognitive differences may not be necessary. Sylvia Scribner and Michael Cole spent seven years researching the relationship between literacy and cognition among the Vai, and their book, *The Psychology of Literacy: A Case Study Among the Vai*, suggests that neither their ethnographic research nor their psychological tests revealed evidence to support inherent cognitive differences.

2. J. T. Clanchy's historical study of literacy in England claims that writing preceded systems for retrieving records and that until archives and retrieval systems were established, writing could not be efficiently used for the purpose of record keeping. Clanchy suggests that writing documents, keeping them in archives, and using them for references were three distinct stages of development (1979:138).

3. From a sociolinguistic point of view, literacy consists of a "cluster of rather different skills" (Stubbs 1980:10). In particular, literacy implies forms of language usage ranging from functional literacy to "essayist literacy" (Scollon 1979). In general, literacy is regarded as the arena for standardizing grammar, spelling and usage, in contrast to the perpetuation of variety in oral forms.

4. See Whiteman (1980).

5. See Szwed (1981) and David R. Olson (1977) for discussions of perspectives on literacy.

6. Missing pieces may be perceived in terms of entire segments of a narrative, so that a narrative may be seen as "missing the orientation section," or in terms of specific missing referents. Memory scholars have been concerned with the former (Mandler and DeForest 1977). Literacy scholars have been concerned with the latter, which they have seen as evidence of contextualization (Olson 1977).

7. Pierre Macherey has elaborately discussed the problem of the finitude of the text. He has pointed out that this finitude is not a matter of an enigmatic meaning that needs to be discovered: "The work does not contain a meaning which it conceals by giving it its achieved form. The necessity of the work is founded on the multiplicity of its meanings; to explain the work is to recognize and *differentiate* the principle of this diversity. *The postulated unity of the work which, more or less, explicitly, has always haunted the enterprise of criticism, must now be denounced:* the work is not created by an intention (objective or subjective); it is produced under determinate conditions" (1978:78).

8. Ron and Suzanne B. K. Scollon have discussed essayist literacy (1981:47–53). See also Olson (1977:271–4).

9. Erving Goffman has also discussed ellipsis in terms of literal versus intended meaning

and in terms of conventionalized utterances (1976). Gérard Genette has addressed the alternatives of "giving less information than is necessary in principle, or of giving more than is authorized in principle." He distinguishes the alternatives as paralipsis and paralepsis, respectively (1980:195). Roland Barthes has also pointed out the complexity of conveying information. His structural model provides for information on both the syntagmatic and paradigmatic levels of narrative. This understanding is applicable to the adolescents' fight narratives, in which this understanding of the general category of fights informs their comprehension of specific stories (1974–5).

10. Dell Hymes and Claire Woods Elliott also discuss their preference for the term "recontextualization" (unpublished manuscript).

11. See R. Barthes on indices (1974–5).

12. Stanley Fish, for example, argues, "one cannot make a clean break between the literary and the nonliterary" (1976). In contrast, Umberto Eco has suggested that literature, or literary criticism, is the best source for understanding textuality: "Today one learns about textual machinery more from the researchers who dared to approach complex narrative texts than from those who limited themselves to analyzing short portions of everyday textuality" (1979:13). See also Finnegan (1977) and Ong (1979) for discussions of oral literature and literacy.

13. For example, see Steven J. Zeitlin's discussion of the category of "courtship stories" (1980).

14. Barbara Herrnstein Smith has discussed the problem of establishing taxonomies for versions and points out that any attempt to locate a plot summary or an original reveals just another version (1980).

15. Stanley Fish has discussed the fallacy of this distinction and states: "Literature is language . . . it is language around which we have drawn a frame, a frame that indicates a decision to regard with a particular self-consciousness the resources language has always possessed. What characterizes literature then is not formal properties, but an attitude – always within our power to assume – toward properties that belong by constitutive right to language. (This raises the intriguing possibility that literary language may be the norm, and message bearing language a device we carve out to perform the special, but certainly not normative, task of imparting information.) Literature is still a category, but it is an open category, not definable by fictionality, or by a disregard of propositional truth, or by a statistical predominance of tropes and figures, but simply by what we decide to put into it. The difference lies not in the language but in ourselves. Only such a view, I believe, can accommodate and reconcile the two intuitions that have for so long kept linguistic and literary theory apart – the intuition that there *is* a class of literary utterances, and the intuition that any piece of language can become a member of that class" (1980:108–9).

16. Gérard Genette writes, "Legrandin talks 'a little too much like a book' and reveals the 'too perfect mimesis of language, which finally annuls itself in circularity' " (1980:165).

17. See Mary Louise Pratt (1977:3–37).

18. Although some scholars might claim that storytelling or reading as an event is insignificant, others, such as reader-response critics, suggest that meaning is lodged in the relationship between text and reader rather than that between between author and text. See Robert Young's discussion of Michael Riffaterre's "Interpretation and Descriptive Poetry" (1981:103). Further, any attempt to identify a literary work within a historical or ideological frame implies that the meaning is situated, that the levels of text and storytelling situation are mutually implicated. See Etienne Balibar and Pierre Macherey, "On Literature as an Ideological Form" in Young (1981:84).

19. Harvey Sacks states, "The fact that a story is told does not establish that the events it reports were monitored for their tellability" (Notes, May 8, 1968).

20.   The issue of closure and the limits imposed on interpretation by the notion of a fixed text are discussed by Barbara Johnson, "The Cultural Difference: Balzac's 'Sarrasure" and Barthes' 'S/Z'," in Young (1981:165–74). The essays in Young's anthology provide a powerful contradiction to the idea of the fixed, closed, distanced text, an idea central to literacy discussion, and could be taken to suggest that the situated reading (or performance) provides a more workable model.

21.   See Jack Goody (1968).

BIBLIOGRAPHY

Abrahams, Roger. *Deep Down in the Jungle: Negro Narrative Folklore from the Streets of Philadelphia*. Chicago: Aldine, 1970.

"A Performance-Centered Approach to Gossip." *Man*, 5 (1970), 290–301.

and Geneva Gay. "Black Culture in the Classroom" and "Talking Black in the Classroom," in *Language and Cultural Diversity in American Education*. Roger Abrahams and Rudolph C. Troike, eds. Englewood Cliffs, N.J.: Prentice-Hall, 1972.

Altieri, Charles. "Presence and Reference in a Literary Text: The Example of Williams' 'This is Just to Say.'" *Critical Inquiry*, 6 (1979), 489–510.

Atkinson, J. Maxwell, and John Heritage. *Structures of Social Action: Studies in Conversational Analysis*. Cambridge: Cambridge University Press, 1984.

Ayoub, Millicent R., and Stephen A. Barnett. "Ritualized Verbal Insult in White High School Culture." *Journal of American Folklore*, 78 (1965), 337–44.

Babcock-Abrahams, Barbara. "The Story in the Story: Metanarration in Folk Narrative." *Studia Fennica*, 20, Special Issue on Folk Narrative Research (1976), 177–84.

Bahktin, Mikhail. *Problems of Dostoevsky's Poetics*. Ann-Arbor, Mich.: Ardis Press, 1973.

"Epic and Novel." In *The Dialogic Imagination*, trans. Caryl Emerson and Michael Holquist. Austin: University of Texas Press, 1981.

Baron, Naomi. *Speech, Writing, and Sign: A Functional View of Linguistic Representation*. Bloomington: Indiana University Press, 1981.

Barthes, Roland. *Writing Degree Zero*, trans. A. Lavers and C. Smith. New York: Hill and Wang, 1953.

"Historical Discourse," in *Introduction to Structuralism*. Michael Lane, ed. New York: Basic Books, 1970.

"Science Versus Literature." in M. Lane, Ed., *Introduction to Structuralism*. New York: Basic Books, 1970, pp. 410–16.

"Literature and Discontinuity." *Salamagundi*, 18–120 (1972), 82–93.

"An Introduction to the Structural Analysis of Narrative." *New Literary History*, 6 (1974–5), 237–72.

The Pleasures of the Text, trans. Richard Miller. New York: Hill and Wang, 1975.

Bartlett, F. C. *Remembering*. Cambridge: Cambridge University Press, 1932.

Basso, Keith. "The Ethnography of Writing," in *Explorations in the Ethnography of Speaking*. R. Bauman and J. Sherzer, eds., New York: Cambridge University Press, 1974.

Bateson, Gregory. *Steps to an Ecology of Mind*. New York: Ballantine, 1972.

Bauman, Richard. "Differential Identity and the Social Base of Folklore." *Journal of American Folklore,* 84 (1971), 31–41.

"Verbal Art as Performance." *American Anthropologist,* 77 (1975), 290–311.

Belton, Darlene, et al. "Growing Up in the South Bronx," *The Village Voice,* February 11, 1981, p. 12.

Ben-Amos, Dan. "Toward a Definition of Folklore in Context." *Journal of American Folklore,* 84 (1971), 5.

ed. *Folklore Genres.* Austin: University of Texas Press, 1976.

Benjamin, Walter. *Illuminations,* trans. Harry Zohn. New York: Schocken, 1969.

"The Storyteller and Artisan Cultures," in *Critical Sociology.* P. Connerton, ed. New York: Penguin, 1976.

Benveniste, Emile. *Problems de linguistique generale.* Paris: Gallimard, 1966. (*Problems in General Linguistics,* trans. Mary Elizabeth Meek. Coral Gables, Fla.: University of Miami Press, 1971.)

Bernstein, Basil B. *Class, Codes and Control,* Vol. 1. London: Paladin, 1971.

Bisseret, Noelle. *Education, Class Language and Ideology.* London: Routledge and Kegan Paul, 1979.

Bloch, Maurice, ed. *Political Language and Oratory in Traditional Society.* New York: Academic Press, 1975.

Bloomfield, Leonard. "Literate and Illiterate Speech," in *Language in Culture and Society.* Dell Hymes, ed. New York: Harper & Row, 1964.

Booth, Wayne. *The Rhetoric of Fiction.* Chicago: University of Chicago Press, 1961.

Borges, Jorge Luis. "Pierre Menard, Author of the Quixote," in *Labyrinths.* New York: New Directions, 1962.

Bouissac, Paul. "Circus Performances as Texts: A Matter of Poetic Competence." *Folklore Preprint Series,* 2 (1974).

Bovet, M. C. "Cognitive Processes Among Illiterate Children and Adults," in *Culture and Cognition: Readings in Cross-Cultural Psychology.* J. W. Berry and P. R. Dasen, eds. London: Methuen, 1974.

Brenneis, Donald, and Laura Lein. "'You Fruithead': A Sociolinguistic Approach to Children's Dispute Settlement," in *Child Discourse.* Susan Ervin-Tripp and Claudia Mitchell-Kernan, eds. New York: Academic Press, 1977.

Bromberg, Joann. "Storying and Changing: An Ethnography of Speaking in Consciousness Raising." Ph.D. diss., University of Pennsylvania, 1982.

Brown, A. L. "The Development of Memory: Knowing, Knowing about Knowing, and Knowing How to Know," in *Advances in Child Development and Behavior,* Vol. 10. H. W. Reese, ed. New York: Academic Press, 1975.

"Recognition, Reconstruction and Recall of Narrative Sequences by Pre-operational Children." *Child Development,* 46 (1975), 156–66.

"Semantic Integration in Children's Reconstruction of Narrative Sequences." *Cognitive Psychology,* (1976),

"Knowing When, Where, and How to Remember: A Problem of Metacognition," in *Advances in Instructional Psychology.* R. Glaser, ed. Hillsdale, N.J.: Erlbaum, 1977.

and S. S. Smiley. "Rating the Importance of Structural Units of Prose Passages: A Problem of Metacognitive Development." *Child Development,* 48 (1977), 1–9.

Brown, Roger. "The History of Writing and a Dispute about Reading," in *Words and Things*. New York: Free Press, 1958.

Bull, William. "The Use of Vernacular Languages in Fundamental Education," in *Language, Culture and Society*. Dell Hymes, ed., New York: Harper & Row, 1964.

Butor, Michel. "The Second Case," *New Left Review*, 34 (1965), pp. 60–8.

Carroll, John B., and Jeanne S. Chall. *Toward a Literate Society*. New York: McGraw-Hill, 1975.

Cazden, Courtney. "Peekaboo as an Instructional Model: Discourse Development at Home and at School." Child Language Research Forum. Keynote Lecture, Stanford University, 1980.

and Dell Hymes. "Narrative Thinking and Story-Telling Rights: A Folklorist's Clue to a Critique of Education," *Keystone Folklore*, 22 (1978), 21–36.

Vera P. John, and Dell Hymes, eds. *Functions of Language in the Classroom*. New York: Teachers College Press, 1972.

Chatman, Seymour. *Story and Discourse: Narrative Structure in Fiction and Film*. Ithaca, N.Y.: Cornell University Press, 1978.

Christie, D. J. "Memory for Prose: Development of Mnemonic Strategies and Use of High Order Relations." Paper presented at the meeting of the Society for Research in Child Development, New Orleans, 1977.

Cicourel, A. C. *Cognitive Sociology*. New York: Free Press, 1974.

et al. *Language Use and School Performance*. New York: Academic Press, 1976.

Clammer, J. R. *Literacy and Social Change*. Leiden: E. J. Brill, 1976.

Clanchy, J. T. *From Memory to Written Record*. London: Arnold, 1979.

Cohen, Albert. *Delinquent Boys: The Culture of the Gang*. New York: Free Press, 1955.

Cohen, Ann. *Poor Pearl, Poor Girl*. Austin: University of Texas Press, 1973.

Colby, B. N., and M. Cole. "Memory and Narrative," in Robin Horton and Ruth Finnegan, eds. *Modes of Thought: A Collection of Essays on Thinking in Western and Non-western Societies*. London: Faber and Faber.

Cole, M., and J. Gay. "Culture and Memory." *American Anthropologist*, 74 (1972), 1066–84.

and S. Scribner. *Culture and Thought*. New York: Wiley, 1974.

Culler, Jonathon. *Structuralist Poetics*. Ithaca, N.Y.: Cornell University Press, 1975.

"Fabula and Sjuzhet in the Analysis of Narrative." *Poetics Today*, 1 (1980), 27–38.

Davis, Natalie Z. "Printing and the People," in *Society and Culture in Early Modern France*. Stanford, Calif.: Stanford University Press, 1975.

Derrida, Jacques. "Signature, Event, Context," trans. Tzvetan Bogdanovich. Paper given at the Congrès International des Sociétés de Philosophie de Langue Française, Montréal, August 1971.

Of Grammatology, trans. B. Spivak. Baltimore: Johns Hopkins University Press, 1974.

Writing and Difference, trans. Alan Bass. Chicago: University of Chicago Press, 1976.

"The Law of Genre." *Critical Inquiry*, 7 (1980), 55–82.

Dolezel, Lubomir. Review of *The Role of the Reader* by Umberto Eco. *Poetics Today,* 1 (1980), 181–8.

"Truth and Authenticity in Narrative." *Poetics Today,* 1 (1980), 7–26.

Douglas, Jack. *Understanding Everyday Life.* Chicago: Aldine, 1970.

and John M. Johnson, eds. *Existential Sociology.* Cambridge: Cambridge University Press, 1977.

Dundes, Alan, and Carl R. Pagter. *Work Hard and You Shall Be Rewarded: Urban Folklore from the Paperwork Empire.* Bloomington: Indiana University Press, 1978.

Eco, Umberto. *The Role of the Reader: Explorations in the Semiotics of Texts.* Advances in Semiotics Series. Bloomington: Indiana University Press, 1979.

Edwards, Jane. "A Shared History." Ph.D. diss. University of Pennsylvania, 1978.

Fiering, Sue. "Unofficial Writing in the Classroom and Community." Unpublished in-house report, Center for Urban Ethnography, Graduate School of Education, University of Pennsylvania, 1980.

Finnegan, Ruth. *Oral Poetry: Its Nature, Significance, and Social Context.* Cambridge: Cambridge University Press, 1977.

Fish, Stanley. "How to Do Things with Austin and Searle: Speech Act Theory and Literary Criticism." *Modern Language Notes,* 91 (1976), 983–1025.

Is There a Text in This Class?: The Authority of Interpretive Communities. Cambridge, Mass.: Harvard University Press, 1980.

Fishman, Joshua A. "Ethnocultural Dimensions in the Acquisition and Retention of Biliteracy." Paper prepared for the Mina Shaughnessy Memorial Conference, City University of New York, 1980.

Fiske, Edward B. "Illiteracy in the U.S.: Why John Can't Cope," *The New York Times,* April 30, 1978, Section 12, p. 1.

Foucault, Michel. *The Order of Things: An Archaeology of the Human Sciences.* New York: Random House, 1970, Vintage edition 1973.

"What Is an Author?" trans. D. F. Bouchard, in *Language, Counter-Memory, Practice: Selected Essays and Interviews.* New York: Cornell University Press, 1977.

ed. *I, Pierre Riviere, Having Slaughtered My Mother, My Sister, and My Brother . . . A Case of Parricide in the 19th Century.* New York: Pantheon, 1975.

Gadamer, Hans-Georg. "The Historicity of Understanding," in *Critical Sociology.* P. Connerton, ed. New York: Penguin, 1976.

Garfinkel, Harold. "The Relevance of Common Understandings to the Fact That Models of Man in Society Portray Him as a Judgmental Dope," in *What We Say/What We Do.* Irwin Deutscher, ed. Glenview, Ill.: Scott Foresman, 1973.

and Harvey Sacks. "On Formal Structures of Practical Actions," in *Theoretical Sociology: Perspectives and Developments.* John C. McKinney and Edward A. Tiryakian, eds. New York: Appleton-Century-Crofts, 1970.

Garvin, Paul L. "The Standard Language Problem: Concepts and Methods," in *Language in Culture and Society.* Dell Hymes, ed. New York: Harper & Row, 1964.

Geertz, Clifford. *Local Knowledge: Further Essays in Interpretive Anthropology.* New York: Basic Books, 1983.

Genette, Gérard. *Narrative Discourse: An Essay in Method,* trans. Jane E. Lewin. Ithaca, N.Y.: Cornell University Press, 1980.

Georges, Robert A. "Toward an Understanding of a Storytelling Event." *Journal of American Folklore,* 82 (1969), 313–28.

Gilmore, Perry. "Ethnography and Education: A Description of Trends and Issues with Special Emphasis on the Ethnography of Communication." Unpublished paper, 1978.

Glassie, Henry. "Meaningful Things and Appropriate Myths: The Artifact's Place in American Studies." *Prospects,* 2 (1978), 1–61.

Gluckman, Max. "Gossip and Scandal." *Current Anthropology,* 4 (1963), 307.

Goffman, Erving. "Communication and Conduct in an Island Community." Ph.D. diss., University of Chicago, 1953.

    Interaction Ritual. Garden City, N.Y.: Doubleday, 1967.

    Relations in Public. New York: Harper & Row, 1971.

    Frame Analysis. New York: Harper & Row, 1974.

    "Replies and Responses." *Language and Society,* 5 (1976), 257–313. Reprinted in *Forms of Talk.* Philaldephia: University of Pennsylvania Press, 1983.

    "Footing." *Semiotica,* 1–2 (1979), 1–29.

Goodman, N. *Languages of Art.* Indianapolis: Bobbs-Merrill, 1968.

Goodwin, Marjorie, H. "Conversational Practices in a Peer Group of Urban Black Children." Ph.D. diss., University of Pennsylvania, 1978.

Goody, Jack. *The Domestication of the Savage Mind.* Cambridge: Cambridge University Press, 1977.

    "Literacy and Classification: On Turning the Tables," in *Text and Context: The Social Anthropology of Tradition.* Ravindra K. Jain, ed. Philadelphia: Institute for the Study of Human Issues, 1977.

    and Watt, Ian. "The Consequences of Literacy," in Goody, ed., *Literacy in Traditional Societies.* Cambridge: Cambridge University Press, 1968.

Graff, Harvey J. *The Literacy Myth: Literacy and Social Structure in the Nineteenth-Century City.* New York: Academic Press, 1979.

Greenfield, Patricia M. "Oral or Written Language: The Consequences for Cognitive Development in Africa and the United States." *Language and Speech,* 15 (1972), 169–77.

Grice, H. P. "Logic and Conversation," in *Syntax and Semantics, Vol. 3: Speech Acts.* P. Cole and J. L. Morgan, eds. New York: Academic Press, 1975.

Gumperz, Jenny C., and John J. Gumperz. "From Oral to Written Culture: The Transition to Literacy," in *Variations in Writing: Functional and Linguistic-Cultural Differences.* Marcia Farr Whiteman, ed. Hillsdale, N.J.: Erlbaum, 1977.

Gumperz, John J. *Discourse Strategies.* Cambridge: Cambridge University Press, 1982.

Hall, Edward T. *Beyond Culture.* Garden City, N.Y.: Anchor, 1977.

Harste, Jerome C., and Robert F. Carey, "Comprehension as Setting," *Monograph in Language and Reading Studies,* No. 3. (1979), 4–22.

Havelock, Eric A. "The Preliteracy of the Greeks." *New Literary History,* 8 (1977), 369–92.

Heath, Shirley Brice. "Research in Classroom Language: Bibliography." Unpublished manuscript, 1978.

"Teacher Talk: Language in the Classroom." *Language in Education: Theory and Practice,* 9 Washington, D.C.: Center for Applied Linguistics, (1978),

"'What No Bedtime Story Means.' Narrative Skills at Home and School." Paper prepared for the Terman Conference, Stanford University, November 20–22, 1980.

"Toward an Ethnohistory of Writing in American Education," in *Variations in Writing,* Functional and Linguistic-Cultural Differences. Marcia Farr Whiteman, ed., Hillsdale, N.J.: Erlbaum, 1981.

"Protean Shapes in Literacy Events. In *Spoken and Written Language: Exploring Orality and Literacy.* Deborah Tannen, ed. Norwood, N.J., Ablex, 1982.

Ways with Words: Language, Life and Work in Communities and Classrooms. Cambridge: Cambridge University Press, 1983.

Herzog, George. "Drum Signaling in a West African Tribe," in *Language in Culture and Society.* Dell Hymes, ed. New York: Harper & Row, 1964, pp. 312–29.

Henige, D. P. *The Chronology of Oral Tradition: Quest for a Chimera.* Cambridge: Clarenden, 1974.

Hockett, C. F. "Speech and Writing." *Report of the Third Annual Round Table Meeting on Linguistics and Language Teaching.* Washington, D.C.: Georgetown University Press, 1952.

Honko, Lauri. "Memorates and the Study of Folk Beliefs." *Journal of the Folklore Institute,* 1 (1964), 5–19.

Horton, Robin, and Ruth Finnegan, eds. *Modes of Thought: Essays on Thinking in Western and Non-Western Societies.* London: Faber and Faber, 1973.

Hymes, Dell. "The Ethnography of Communication." *American Anthropologist,* 66 (1964), 6–56.

"Models of the Interaction of Language and Social Life," in *Directions in Sociolinguistics.* J. J. Gumperz and D. Hymes, eds. New York: Holt, Rinehart & Winston, 1972.

Foundations in Sociolinguistics: An Ethnographic Approach. Philadelphia: University of Pennsylvania Press, 1974.

"Breakthrough into Performance." In *Folklore: Performance and Communication.* Dan Ben-Amos and Kenneth Goldstein, eds. The Hague: Mouton, 1975.

"Folklore's Nature and the Sun's Myth." *Journal of American Folklore,* 88 (1975), 345–69.

"Discovering Oral Performance and Measured Verse in American Indian Narrative." *New Literary History,* 8 (1977), 431–58.

and Claire Woods Elliott. "Issues in Literacy: Different Lenses." Unpublished manuscript.

Irvine, Judith T. "Formality and Informality in Communicative Events." *American Anthropologist,* 81 (1979), 773–90.

Iser, Wolfgang. *The Act of Reading.* Baltimore: Johns Hopkins University Press, 1978.

Jacob, Evelyn, and Jo Ann Crandall. "Job-Related Literacy: A Look at Current and Needed Research." *Proceedings of the Functional Literacy Conference.* Bloomington: Indiana University Press, June 1979.

Jakobson, Roman. "Concluding Statement: Linguistics and Poetics," in *Style in Language.* Thomas A. Sebeok, ed. Cambridge, Mass.: MIT Press, 1960.

　Shifters, Verbal Categories and the Russian Verb. Cambridge, Mass.: Harvard University Russian Language Project, 1957.

　and Petr Bogatyrev. "On the Boundary Between Studies of Folklore and Literature," in *Readings in Russian Poetics: Formalist and Structuralist Views.* Ladislav Matejka and Krystyna Pomorska, eds. Ann Arbor: University of Michigan Press, 1978.

Jameson, Fredric. *Marxism and Form: Twentieth-Century Dialectical Theories of Literature.* Princeton, N.J.: Princeton University Press, 1971.

　"The Ideology of the Text." *Salamagundi,* 31–4 (1975–6), 204–46.

Jason, Heda. "Jewish Near-Eastern Numbskull Tales: An Attempt at Interpretation." *Asian Folklore Studies,* 31 (1972), 1.

Jones, Sidney R. "Arabic Instruction and Literacy in Javanese Muslim Schools." Paper presented at the meeting of the American Anthropological Society, Washington, D.C., 1980.

Keenan, Elinor O. "Norm-Makers, Norm-Breakers: Uses of Speech by Men and Women in a Malagasy Community," in *Explorations in the Ethnography of Speaking.* Richard Bauman and Joel Sherzer, eds. New York: Cambridge University Press, 1974.

Kellogg, Robert. "Literature, Nonliterature and Oral Tradition." *New Literary History,* 8 (1977), 532–4.

Kirshenblatt-Gimblett, Barbara. "The Concept and Varieties of Narrative Performance in East European Jewish Culture," in Richard Bauman and Joel Sherzer, eds. *Explorations in the Ethnography of Speaking.* Richard Bauman and Joel Sherzer, eds. New York: Cambridge University Press, 1974.

　"A Parable in Context: A Social Interactional Analysis of Storytelling Performance," in *Folklore: Performance and Communication.* Dan Ben-Amos and Kenneth S. Goldstein, eds. The Hague: Mouton, 1975.

　ed. *Speech Play: Research and Resources for Studying Linguistic Creativity.* Philadelphia: University of Pennsylvania Press, 1976.

Kochman, Thomas, ed. *Rappin' and Stylin' Out.* Chicago: University of Illinois Press, 1972.

Labov, William. "The Logic of Non-standard English" and "The Transformation of Experience in Narrative Syntax," in *Language in the Inner City.* Philadelphia: University of Pennsylvania Press, 1972.

　and David Fanshell. *Therapeutic Discourse.* New York: Academic Press, 1977.

Lakoff, Robin. "Forms of Politeness," in *Language and Women's Place.* New York: Harper & Row, 1975.

Lanser, Susan Sniader. *The Narrative Act: Point of View in Prose Fiction.* Princeton, N.J.: Princeton University Press, 1981.

Layne, Linda. "Social and Cultural Ramifications of Popular Literacy in Jordan." Unpublished manuscript, Princeton University, 1980.

Leiter, Kenneth. *A Primer on Ethnomethodology.* New York: Oxford University Press, 1980.

Levi-Strauss, Claude. *The Savage Mind.* Chicago: University of Chicago Press, 1960.

Lichman, Simon. "The Gardener's Story and What Came Next: A Contextual Analysis of the Marshfield Paper Boys' Mumming Tradition." Ph.D. diss., University of Pennsylvania, 1981.

Lipking, Lawrence. "The Marginal Gloss." *Critical Inquiry,* 4 (1977), 609–55.

Lipski, John M. "From Text to Narrative: Spanning the Gap." *Poetics,* 5 (1976), 191–206.

Lomax, Alan. "A Stylistic Analysis of Speaking." *Language in Society,* 6 (1977), 15–36.

Lord, Albert. *The Singer of Tales.* New York: Atheneum, 1973.

McDermott, R. "Achieving School Failure: An Anthropological Approach to Illiteracy and Social Stratification," in *Education and Cultural Process.* G. Spindler, ed. New York: Holt, Rinehart & Winston, 1974.

Macherey, Pierre. *A Theory of Literary Production.* London: Routledge & Kegan Paul, 1978.

McHugh, Peter. *Defining the Situation.* Indianapolis: Bobbs-Merrill, 1968.

McLuhan, Marshall. *The Mechanical Bride: Folklore of Industrial Man.* Boston: Beacon, 1951.

The Gutenberg Galaxy. Toronto, 1962.

Mandler, J. M., and M. DeForest. "The Code in the Node: Developmental Differences in the Use of a Story Schema." Paper presented to the Society for Research in Child Development, 1977.

"Remembrance of Things Parsed: Story Structure and Recall." *Cognitive Psychology,* 9 (1977), 111–51.

and N. S. Johnson. "A Structural Analysis of Stories and Their Recall from 'Once Upon a Time' to 'Happily Ever After.'" Center for Human Information Processing, University of California, San Diego, 1976.

Mehan, Hugh B., and H. Lawrence Wood. *The Reality of Ethnomethodology.* New York: Wiley, 1975.

Menig-Peterson, C. L. "Structure of Children's Narrative." Paper presented at the Meeting of the Society for Research in Child Development, New Orleans, 1977.

Michaels, Sarah. "Sharing Time." Paper presented at the Ethnography in Education Research Forum, University of Pennsylvania, 1980.

Mishler, Elliot G. "Meaning in Context: Is There Any Other Kind?" *Harvard Educational Review,* 49 (1979), 1–19.

Mosher, Harold F. "A New Synthesis of Narratology." Review of *Story and Discourse* by Seymour Chatman. *Poetics Today,* 1 (1980), 171–86.

Mountford, John. "Some Psycholinguistic Components of Initial Standard Literacy." *Journal of Typographic Research,* 4 (1970), 295–306.

Murphy, Robert F. *The Dialectics of Social Life: Alarms and Excursions in Anthropological Theory.* New York: Basic Books, 1971.

Myerhoff, Barbara. *Number Our Days.* New York: E. P. Dutton, 1978.

Natanson, Maurice. *Literature, Philosophy and the Social Sciences.* The Hague: Martinus Nijhoff, 1962.

220   *Bibliography*

Olson, David R. "From Utterance to Text: The Bias of Language in Speech and Writing." *Harvard Educational Review,* 47 (1977), 257–81.
Ong, Walter J. "Literacy and Orality in Our Times." *Profession* (M.L.A.), (1979), 1–7.
    Orality and Literacy: The Technologizing of the Word. London: Methuen, 1982.
Otto, W., T. C. Baret, and K. Koenke. "Assessment of Children's Statements of the Main Idea in Reading." *Proceedings of the International Reading Association,* 13 (1969), 692–97.
Pedraza, P., et al. "Rethinking Diglossia." *Centro Working Papers,* 9 (1980), 1–45.
Pentikainen, Juha. *Oral Repertoire and World View: An Anthropological Study of Marina Takalo's Life History.* Helsinki: Suomalaine Tiedeakatemia Academia Scientiarum Fennica, 1978.
Phelan, James. *Worlds from Words.* Chicago: University of Chicago Press, 1981.
Phillips, Susan U. "Participant Structures and Communicative Competence: Warm Springs Children in Community and Classroom," in *Functions of Language in the Classroom.* Courtney B. Cazden, Vera P. John, and Dell Hymes, eds. New York: Teachers College Press, 1972, pp. 370–94.
Pratt, Mary Louise. *Toward a Speech Act Theory of Literary Discourse.* Bloomington: Indiana University Press, 1977.
Quasha, George. "Dialogos: Between the Written and the Oral in Contemporary Poetry." *New Literary History,* 8 (1977), 485–506.
Reisman, David. *The Oral Tradition, the Written Word and the Screen Image.* Yellow Springs, Ohio: Antioch Press, 1956.
Ricoeur, Paul. "The Model of the Text: Meaningful Action Considered as Text." *New Literary History,* 5 (1973), 91–117.
    "Narrative Time." *Critical Inquiry,* 7 (1980), 169–90.
Robinson, John A. "Personal Narratives Reconsidered." *Journal of American Folklore,* 81 (1981), 58–85.
Rosenberg, Neil V. "'It Was a Kind of a Hobby': A Manuscript Song Book and Its Place in Tradition," in *Folklore Studies in Honour of Herbert Halpert: A Festschrift.* Kenneth Goldstein and Neil V. Rosenberg, eds. St. Johns: Memorial University of Newfoundland, 1980.
Rosnow, R., and G. Fine. *Rumor and Gossip.* New York: Elsevier, 1976.
Rothkopf, E. Z. "Structural Text Features and the Control of Processes in Learning from Written Materials," in *Language Comprehension and the Acquisition of Knowledge.* J. B. Carroll and R. O. Freedle, eds. Washington, D.C.: Winston, 1972.
Rumelhart, D. E. "Notes on a Schema for Stories," in *Representation and Understanding.* D. G. Bobrow and A. Collins, eds. New York: Academic Press, 1975.
    "Understanding and Summarizing Brief Stories," in *Basic Processes in Reading: Perception and Comprehension.* D. LaBerge and S. J. Samuels, eds. Hillsdale, N.J.: Erlbaum, 1977.
Ryan, Marie Laure. "When 'Je' is 'Un Autro': Fiction, Quotation, and the Performative Analysis." *Poetics Today,* 2:2 (1981), 127–155.
    "Puns," in *Georgetown 23rd Linguistic Round Table,* 23, R. Shuy, ed. (1973), 139–41.

Sacks, Harvey. Unpublished lecture notes, U.C.L.A. 1967, 1968; Univ. of Calif. Irvine 1970, 1971, 1972.

Emmanual Schegloff, and Gail Jefferson. "A Simple Systematics for the Analysis of Turn Taking in Conversations." *Language*, 50 (1974), 696–735.

Schegloff, M., and Harvey Sacks. "Opening Up Closings." *Semiotica*, 8 (1973), 289–327.

Schenkein, Jim, ed. *Studies in the Organization of Conversational Interaction*. New York: Academic Press, 1978.

Schiller, Dan. *Objectivity in the News: The Public and the Rise of Commerical Journalism*. Philadelphia: University of Pennsylvania Press, 1981.

Scollon, Ron, and Suzanne B. K. Scollon. "Literacy as Interethnic Communication: An Athabaskan Case." Unpublished manuscript, 1979.

"The Literate Two Year Old: The Fictionalization of Self," in *Narrative, Literacy and Face in Interethnic Communication*. Norwood, N.J.: Ablex, 1981.

Schutz, Alfred. *The Phenomenology of the Social World*. Evanston, Ill.: Northwestern University Press, 1967.

On Phenomenology and Social Relations. Chicago: University of Chicago Press, 1970.

Structures of the Life World. Evanston, Ill.: Northwestern University Press, 1973.

Scribner, Sylvia, and Michael Cole. "Unpackaging Literacy." *Social Science Information*, 17 (1978), 19–40.

The Psychology of Literacy: A Case Study Among the Vai. Cambridge, Mass.: Harvard University Press, 1981.

Shuman, Amy. "Adolescent Personal Narratives: Blow by Blow Accounts of Fights That Never Came to Blows." *Papers in Comparative Studies*, 2 (1982–3), 137–58.

"Collaborative Literacy in an Urban Multiethnic Neighborhood." *International Journal of the Sociology of Language*, 42 (1983), 69–81.

"Playful Uses of Literacy." *Practicing Anthropology*, 1/2 (1985), 12–13.

Smith, Barbara Herrnstein. *On the Margins of Discourse*. Chicago: University of Chicago Press, 1978.

"Narrative Versions, Narrative Theories." *Critical Inquiry*, 7 (1980), 213–36.

Smitherman, Geneva. "A Comparison of the Oral and Written Styles of a Group of Inner City Black Students." Ph.D. diss., University of Michigan, 1969.

Talkin and Testifyin: The Language of Black America. Boston: Houghton Mifflin, 1977.

Sparks, Colin. "The Abuses of Literacy." *Cultural Studies*, 6 (1974),

Stahl, Sandra. "Style in Written and Oral Narrative." *Folklore Preprint Series*, 3 (1974), 1–24.

"The Oral Personal Narrative in its Generic Context." *Fabula*, 18 (1977), 18–39.

Stein, M. L., and C. G. Glenn. "The Role of Structural Variation in Children's Recall of Simple Stories." Paper presented to the Society for Research in Child Development, New Orleans, 1977.

Steiner, George. "Humane Literacy," in *Language and Silence: Essays on Language, Literature, and the Inhuman*. New York: Atheneum, 1967.

"After the Book?" *Visible Language*, 6 (1972), 197–210.

"*After Babel: Aspects of Language and Translation*. London: Oxford University Press, 1975.

Stewart, Susan. *Nonsense: Aspects of Intertextuality in Folklore and Literature*. Baltimore: Johns Hopkins University Press, 1979.

Stock, Brian. "Literary Discourse and the Social Historian." *New Literary History*, 8 (1977), 183–94.

Stockton, Frank R. "The Lady or the Tiger," in *The Bedside Book of Famous American Stories*. Angus Burrell and Bennett A. Cerf, eds. New York: Random House, 1936.

Stubbs, Michael. "Initial Literacy and Explanation of Educational Failure," in *Language and Literacy: The Sociolinguistics of Reading and Writing*. London: Routledge & Kegan Paul, 1980.

Sullivan, Helen. "Literacy and Illiteracy." *Encyclopedia of the Social Sciences*. New York: Macmillan Co., 1933.

Sutton-Smith, Brian, M. Botvin, and D. Mahony. "Developmental Structures in Fantasy Narratives." *Human Development*, 19 (1976), 1–13.

Szwed, John F. "An American Anthropological Dilemma: The Politics of Afro-American Culture," in *Reinventing Anthropology*. Dell Hymes, ed. New York: Vintage, 1974.

"The Ethnography of Literacy, in *Variations in Writing: Functional and Linguistic-Cultural Differences*. Marcia Farr Whiteman and Carl H. Frederikson, eds. Hillsdale, N.J.: Erlbaum, 1981.

Tannen, Deborah, ed. *Spoken and Written Language: Exploring Orality and Literacy*. Norwood, N.J.: Ablex, 1982.

"This Is Not Fort Apache, This Is Our Home: Students Document Their South Bronx." Herb Mack, director, Conference on the Folk Culture of the Bronx, May 15–17, 1981.

Thorndyke, P. W. "Cognitive Structures in Human Story Comprehension and Memory." Ph.D. diss., Stanford University, 1975.

Tomashevsky, Boris. "Thematics," in *Russian Formalist Criticism*. Lee T. Lemon and Marion J. Reis, eds. Lincoln: University of Nebraska Press, 1965.

Tynjanov, Juri, and Roman Jakobson. "Problems in the Study of Literature and Language," in *Readings in Russian Poetics: Formalist and Structuralist Views*. Ladislav Matejka and Krystyna Pomorska, eds. Ann Arbor: University of Michigan Press, 1978.

Uldall, Hans. "Speech and Writing." *Acta Linguistica*, 4 (1944), 11–16.

Van den Berghe, P. "Pluralism," in *Handbook of Social and Cultural Anthropology*. J. J. Honigman, ed. Chicago: Rand-McNally, 1973.

Van Dijk, Teun A. "Cognitive Processing of Literary Discourse." *Poetics Today*, 1 (1979), 143–60.

Vansina, Jan. *Oral Tradition*. Chicago: Aldine, 1965.

"Once Upon a Time: Oral Traditions as History in Africa." *Daedalus*, 100 (1971), 442–68.

Varenne, Herve. "Culture as Rhetoric: Patterning in the Verbal Interpretation of Interaction between Teachers and Administrators in an American High School." *American Ethnologist*, 5 (1978), 635–49.

Volosinov, V. N. "Reported Speech," in *Readings in Russian Poetics: Formalist and Structuralist Views.* Ladislav Matejka and Krystyna Pomorska, eds. Ann Arbor: University of Michigan Press, 1978.

Wagner, Daniel. "The Effects of Formal Schooling on Cognitive Style." *The Journal of Social Psychology,* 108 (1978), 145–51.

"Memories of Morocco: The Influence of Age, Schooling and Environment on Memory." *Cognitive Psychology,* 10 (1978), 1–28.

Ward, Barbara E. "Readers and Audiences: An Exploration of the Spread of Traditional Chinese Culture," in *Text and Context: The Social Anthropology of Tradition.* Ravindra Jain, ed. Philadelphia: Institute for the Study of Human Issues, 1977.

Watson-Gegeo, Karen Ann, and Stephen T. Boggs. "From Verbal Play to Talk Story: The Role of Routines in Speech Events Among Hawaiian Children," in *Child Discourse,* Susan Ervin-Tripp and Claudia Mitchell-Kernan, eds. New York: Academic Press, 1977.

Wesker, Arnold. *Words as Definitions of Experience.* London: Writers and Readers Publishing Cooperative, 1976.

White, Hayden. "The Value of Narrativity in the Representation of Reality." *Critical Inquiry,* 7 (1980), 5–28.

Whiteman, Marcia Farr. "What We Can Learn from Writing Research: A Review of Current Work." *Theory into Practice,* 19 (1980), 150–6.

ed. *Writing: The Nature, Development and Teaching of Written Communication.* Vol. 1: *Variation in Writing: Functional and Linguistic-Cultural Differences.* Hillsdale, N.J.: Erlbaum, 1981.

Williams, Raymond. *Keywords.* Oxford: Oxford University Press, 1976.

Marxism and Literature. Oxford: Oxford University Press, 1977.

Wolfson, Nessa. "The Conversational Historical Present in American English." Ph.D. diss., University of Pennsylvania, 1976.

Young, Katharine. "Indirection in Storytelling." *Western Folklore,* 37 (1978), 46–55.

Tale Worlds and Story Realms: The Phenomenology of Narrative. The Hague: Martinus Nijhoff, forthcoming.

Young, Robert, ed. *Untying the Text: A Post-Structuralist Reader.* Boston: Routledge & Kegan Paul, 1981.

Zeitlin, Steven J. "'An Alchemy of Mind': The Family Courtship Story." *Western Folklore,* 39 (1980), 17–33.

INDEX

Printed in the United Kingdom
by Lightning Source UK Ltd.
99363UKS00001B/81